D0923577

RENEWALS: 691-4574

DATE DUE

FEB 10			
FEB 24			

Demco, Inc. 38-293

GOETHE: CONVERSATIONS AND ENCOUNTERS

GOETHE IN 1832

GOETHE
CONVERSATIONS
AND ENCOUNTERS

edited and translated by

DAVID LUKE and ROBERT PICK

OSWALD WOLFF
LONDON, W.1
1966

First published 1966

© OSWALD WOLFF (PUBLISHERS) LTD.

MADE AND PRINTED IN GREAT BRITAIN BY
THE GARDEN CITY PRESS LIMITED
LETCHWORTH, HERTFORDSHIRE

TO W. H. AUDEN

LIBRARY
The University of Texas
At San Antonio

LIBRARY
The University of Texas
At San Antonio

INTRODUCTION

"What is more splendid than gold?—Light.
—What is more refreshing than light?—
Conversation."

(GOETHE[1])

IN 1813, when Goethe was about sixty-three, a visitor to his house in Weimar, hearing conversation in the next room, asked the servant whether the poet had company, and was told: "The Herr Geheimrat is talking to himself".[2] It would be pleasant to think that on this occasion Goethe was indulging in the "peculiar habit" mentioned in the third book of his autobiography, which he was writing at this time, "of converting even his soliloquies into dialogues.—As it was my custom and pleasure" (he goes on to explain) "to spend most of my time with other people, I would even transform my solitary thinking into social intercourse, and I did so in the following manner. When I was alone I would, in imagination, summon some person of my acquaintance into my presence. I would request him to be seated, walk up and down or stand still in front of him, and discuss with him the subject that I happened to have in mind. He would then occasionally reply or express his agreement or disagreement by the usual gestures.... I would proceed to develop further those parts of my discourse that appeared to please my guest, and those parts of which he disapproved I would qualify or define more closely, or even end by politely abandoning my thesis. The strange thing was that the persons whom I selected for this purpose were never those of my closer acquaintance, but others whom I hardly ever saw, indeed some who lived in an entirely different part of the world and with whom I had had only fleeting contact. But usually they were persons of a receptive rather than productive nature, who were prepared to listen quietly, with interest, and with a mind free of prejudice, to things which lay within their scope; although occasionally, for these dialectical exercises, I would summon natures more given to contradiction."[3]

This passage, written by the elderly Goethe but referring to his youth, casts an interesting light on his conviction (expressed elsewhere in his works) of the supreme importance of the spoken word, the irreplaceability of conversation as a creative medium. It suggests that his whole intellectual life was an inner dialogue, and all his works, so to speak, fragments of a great conversation. In one of his aphorisms he wrote : "The deepest concerns of the mind and heart, our most important observations and reflections, should be discussed only by word of mouth".[4] His appetite for verbal discussion and discourse, whether with his more intimate associates or in wider social circles, was certainly enormous, even in the busiest periods of his life; he evidently found that talking was an aid to production and indeed a form of production. His habit, too, in his middle and later years, of dictating many of his works and nearly all his letters, perhaps served not only a practical purpose but also this deep need for speech, the need to address real or imaginary hearers who would elicit his thoughts from him, at the same time imparting to their expression the peculiar charm of living utterance. This is confirmed by the extraordinary description by his secretary Schuchardt[5] of how he dictated the latter part of *Wilhelm Meister's Travels*, walking round and round the room and occasionally stopping to gaze at a group of invisible figures. It is evident that many of Goethe's works were alive and finished in his head, like Mozart's compositions, before ever being written down; according to Schuchardt he would never lose the thread of his dictation despite constant interruptions, and Goethe's friend Meyer recalls how the poet once recited the whole of the *Elective Affinities* to him during a drive in the country, as fluently as if he had been reading it aloud, although no manuscript of the novel yet existed.[6] It has been said that his adoption of the practice of dictating to secretaries rather than writing was one of the most characteristic signs of Goethe's transition from his youthful "Storm and Stress" phase to the "Weimar classicism" of his maturity. The young Goethe is to be imagined (according to his own account[7]) waking and leaping out of bed to scribble down some nocturnal inspiration before he forgets it, not bothering first even to put the paper straight; or penning long passionate intimate quaintly spelt letters to almost complete strangers. But the characteristic attitude of the middle-aged and elderly Goethe was not that of a writer bowed crabbedly over his desk and papers : we must think of him as upright, looking straight before him and delivering period after well-turned period in his deep sonorous voice.

The young poet's transformation into the more sedate figure reflected by most of his "conversations and encounters" began when he moved at the age of twenty-six from his native Frank-furt-am-Main to the then culturally as well as politically insigni-ficant provincial court of Weimar in Thuringia. In 1775, hun-dreds of separate sovereign territories, with the Holy Roman Emperor as their merely titular head, still made up the chaotic confederation loosely known as Germany; only a very few of these, such as Austria and Prussia, were of European impor-tance, and most were mere splinter principalities, of which the Duchy of Saxe-Weimar-Eisenach was one of the smallest—a straggling, discontinuous complex of inherited lands, the whole of it no larger than a medium-sized English county, buried in the central area of the Empire. It was in the first instance due to the good sense and initiative of the Duchess Anna Amalia and afterwards of her son, the young reigning Duke Karl August (1757–1828) that within a few decades Weimar, their capital, a town of about five thousand inhabitants, became a focal point of European cultural life and the place of literary pilgrim-age which it has remained to this day. Three years before Goethe's arrival Anna Amalia, who was then still Regent, had appointed the famous novelist and poet Wieland as tutor to her son. After the Duke's coming of age Wieland continued to live in Weimar until his death in 1813, as the highly esteemed *doyen* of the literary circle—the so-called "court of the Muses" —of which Anna Amalia had become the centre. The Duchess had, as W. H. Bruford has said, "by appointing Wieland... brought a literary man of middle-class origin into the closest association with her family and thus unwittingly started a pro-cess which was to result in that partial fusion of two culture-groups, an aristocratic and a middle-class one, that finds its literary expression in Weimar classicism".[8]

Johann Wolfgang Goethe, born in 1749, was the key figure in this process of fusion. His youthful play *Götz von Berlichingen* had made him the acclaimed leader of the "Storm and Stress movement" which was so vital a feature of the whole German middle-class intellectual and literary revival in the later eigh-teenth century; and after the publication of his passionate and tragic novel *The Sorrows of Werther* in 1774 he became a European celebrity at the age of twenty-five. The eighteen-year-old Karl August, who made his acquaintance the following year while engaged on the conventional educational tour of a young ruler, knew little of literary matters, but liked Goethe's personality and invited him to come to Weimar. This was the normal act of a young prince extending patronage to men of talent from outside his own territory, and Goethe's acceptance of it was only to be expected. He had little taste or qualification for the legal profession into which he had drifted, and one could not in those days, in Germany at least, make a living solely as a writer, however famous. He arrived in Weimar not yet committed, simply as the guest and favourite of the young Duke, whom he genuinely liked; but an instinct which turned out to be a fortunate one decided him in the end to settle there for the rest of his life. Other men of outstanding importance followed Wieland and Goethe. One of the first things the latter had done was to persuade Karl August to appoint his friend Herder, the chief critical theorist, philosopher and theologian of the literary revival, to the highest ecclesiastical post in the duchy; Herder too was to remain in Weimar until his death in 1803. Later, in 1789, the dramatist Friedrich Schiller became Professor of History at the neighbouring university of Jena, of which Karl August was a patron; gradually, and especially after his establishment of closer friendly relations with Goethe in 1794, Schiller came more and more into contact with the society of the little capital, to which he moved altogether in 1799; this period, ending with his premature death in 1805, was also that of his greatest literary achievements. Lesser writers, thinkers, scholars and artists were soon also attracted to Jena and to Weimar; the great classical age of German culture, the "age of Goethe", had begun.

Goethe's activities in Weimar, however, were very far from being exclusively literary, and this fact is of particular significance for his whole development and personality. Karl August's new friend had only been in the principality for a matter of months before he was persuaded, middle-class outsider though he was, to play a leading part in the government, to the scandal, at first, of the established ministers and civil servants. Goethe assumed responsibility for a number of miscellaneous matters, including mines, roads, waterways, recruiting and finally finance. He was raised to the nobility, acquiring the particle "von", the title "Geheimrat" (roughly equivalent to Privy Councillor) and the style of "Excellency". He was also closely

concerned with the administration of the university of Jena. He
found these public activities both stimulating and oppressive.
His famous "flight" in 1786 to Italy, where he stayed for nearly
two years, was an act of intellectual and personal self-liberation.
After his return he contracted out of most of his official duties,
and the second half of his life was devoted almost exclusively
to literary and scientific work. The most important public office
that he retained was his management of the Weimar court
theatre, a position which he held for twenty-seven years altogether. But he had become, and remained throughout his life,
something more than a pure artist and intellectual: he was also
a public figure and man of the world.

A few weeks after his return from Rome in 1788 Goethe took
Christiane Vulpius, an attractive young woman of scant education, into his house to live with him as his mistress. Neither she
nor their only surviving child August were ever really accepted
by Weimar society, even after Goethe had married Christiane
in 1806. She died in 1816. The unhappy August, in the following year, married an intellectual and rather hysterical girl,
Ottilie von Pogwisch; they lived on the upper floor of Goethe's
large town house, and it was Ottilie who acted as hostess ("Frau
von Goethe") to her father-in-law's guests during the period in
which most of the conversations in the present selection took
place. Goethe also lived from time to time in a small villa in
the park by the river Ilm to the east of the town. An important
feature of the elderly Goethe's social life was that on the advice
of his doctors he spent part of nearly every summer, between
1806 and 1823, at the fashionable watering-places in Bohemia
such as Carlsbad or Marienbad. Here he could meet the high
Austrian nobility, the Empress Maria Ludovica, the patrons of
Beethoven; he also met Beethoven himself, though the acquaintance never deepened. It was at Marienbad in 1823 that his
much-discussed passion for the young Ulrike von Levetzow
inspired one of his greatest poems, the *Elegy*, which he discusses with Eckermann in November of that year. After 1823
he never left Thuringia again. He died in March 1832, nearly
eighty-three years old.

Even the briefest selective survey of Goethe's most important
writings gives some idea of the versatility of his genius—of what
T. S. Eliot called the "numberless aspects"[9] of this man who
not only led a literary revolution in his youth but was also as
creative in old age as Verdi or Titian. His lyric poetry alone

has a uniquely wide range. It includes, besides his well-known
youthful lyrics and ballads, which gave a completely new direction to German and indeed to European poetry, such notable
later collections as the *Roman Elegies* (a cycle of erotic poems in
a style based on that of Propertius, published in 1795) and the
mysterious *West-Eastern Divan* (a sequence inspired by Persian
models, published in 1819), in both of which tradition and
originality are most subtly blended. Goethe had, as W. H.
Auden has remarked, an "amazing command of every style of
poetry, from the coarse to the witty to the lyrical to the sublime",[10] and he wrote in all the main literary genres. Of his epic
poems, *Hermann and Dorothea* (1797), an idyll in nine cantos
written in hexameters, at once became justly famous. His best-
known dramatic works, apart from *Götz von Berlichingen*
(1773), are *Iphigenia in Tauris* (1787), *Egmont* (1788), *Torquato Tasso* (1790), and, of course, the vast poetic drama *Faust*.
"Part One" of the latter was first published as a whole in 1808,
and the complete "Part Two" did not appear until after the
poet's death in 1832; each part had taken thirty years or more
to gestate and write. It is probably in *Faust* Part One that
Goethe is most accessible to most readers, and even to English
readers, despite the insuperable difficulties of translation. The
novel that made his reputation in his lifetime, as already mentioned, was *Werther* (1774); his others were *Wilhelm Meister's
Apprenticeship* (1795); *The Elective Affinities* (*Die Wahlver-
wandtschaften*, 1809), one of the subtlest novels about marriage
and adultery ever written; and *Wilhelm Meister's Travels* (Book
I 1821, remainder 1829). His main autobiographical work was
Dichtung und Wahrheit (a title which can be translated "Poetry
and Truth" or "Fiction and Fact"); in this Goethe tells the story
of his youth until 1775, though most of it was written and published between 1811 and 1814, the last book appearing posthumously in 1833. An important and eminently readable supplement to it was the *Italian Journey* (1816–17, 1829). In addition,
Goethe's complete works include numerous miscellaneous essays
on literature and art, some important translations and adapta-
tions, and his various scientific writings. The latter include essays
and treatises on anatomy (in which field his observations led him
to an independent discovery of the human intermaxillary bone),
on botany (*The Metamorphosis of Plants*, 1790), on morphology
(a branch of science which he founded and to which he gave its
name), as well as on geology, mineralogy, meteorology, and optics

in general; of his *Theory of Colours* (1810) he was particularly proud. The scientific value of many of these works is disputed, but they reflect the extraordinary extension of Goethe's interests into almost every branch of knowledge that was open to investigation in his lifetime, and his ceaseless curiosity about all natural phenomena. When we consider this together with his literary output, his passionate lifelong interest in the arts generally (more especially in the visual arts), his vast correspondence and his various practical activities, we can understand why it has so often been said that Goethe was the last great all-embracing mind, the last *"uomo universale"* of European civilisation.

In the present volume we are chiefly concerned with one aspect of Goethe : the Goethe of the spoken word, as represented in the countless records of his conversations and sayings which were made by his contemporaries. We have already seen that there is good reason for regarding these records not as a mere biographical supplement to his complete works, but as an essential element of his own output. To those at least who knew him, as some of them have attested, the charm of his talk could seem infinitely superior to that of his writings.[11] He himself once remarked : "During my best years I was often told by my friends, who presumably knew me well enough to judge, that what I lived was better than what I said, and the latter better than what I write, and what I have written better than what has been printed".[12] Goethe's long life is one of the best documented lives in history, and in upwards of a century since his death more and more of what he said, or is alleged to have said, has found its way into print. His views were reported, his *obiter dicta* noted down, his conversation recorded or reconstructed or recalled, in innumerable letters, diaries, memoirs and reminiscences, and above all in books by certain of his closer associates, such as Riemer, Müller, and Eckermann. Needless to say, even the best of these sources cannot be relied upon to give us more than an approximation to Goethe's actual words. Often they are at second or third hand, and even the first-hand reports were never written down during the conversation, but at best soon after it and often long after it. Even the most conscientious and diligent listeners were faced with great difficulties. It is evident that Goethe's talk was unusually copious, fluent and fascinating; and it is tantalising to find how often his visitors and interlocutors admit to having been so carried away by his manner of speaking or the sheer impressiveness of his personality that they have almost entirely forgotten what the conversation was about, or that the flow of his persuasive eloquence was so rapid that by the time they had heard and taken in one idea it had been swallowed up by two or three more, so that in the end they could remember little or nothing. Again and again the extant records tell us that on this or that occasion the poet's remarks had been exceptionally brilliant, profound and original, but we are not told what he said. And when we are, we must make allowance not only for the limits of the witness's memory and intelligence, but also for his or her attitude to Goethe, preconceptions about Goethe, and general prejudices. All "Goethe's conversations" are more or less coloured in style and content by transmission through a non-Goethean medium. Inevitably there has been much editing, rounding off, filling in of gaps, simplification and trivialisation. The author of the report may have wished to represent himself in a favourable light or to ascribe his own views to Goethe; at worst, the whole conversation may be pure invention. Apart from these factors of error or inauthenticity on the listener's side, we must also bear in mind that these varied and often conflicting accounts reflect Goethe at different times and in different moods. He himself never claimed to be absolutely consistent in his views, as he once remarked to Müller.[13] He also showed different aspects of his personality, perhaps deliberately promoting different images of himself, to different interlocutors. Nevertheless, with all these allowances made, the sum of the evidence yields a well-balanced total impression of Goethe as he was known by his contemporaries, and perhaps enables us to see him more objectively than they could. In assessing the historical value of this chorus of voices all centring on this unique and fascinating figure, we may do well to ponder his own remark after reading Ségur's account of Napoleon's Russian campaign, "that a large number of details, not all of which are quite correct, may nevertheless together compose a picture which is true when taken as a whole".[14]

By far the greater number of the "conversations" that have been preserved for posterity took place during the last fifteen or twenty years of Goethe's life. That the gatherers and gleaners of his talk should become more numerous as he grew older was a natural consequence of his increasing fame. The most important of them did their work during his sixties and seventies. There is unfortunately no equivalent of Eckermann for Goethe

in his youth or even in his prime. Most of the intimate friends
he had made during those years (Karl August, Knebel, Wieland,
Schiller, the painter Meyer, the composer Zelter) are for various
reasons disappointing as sources of conversational records. Our
chief informants for the years immediately following the turn
of the century are Riemer and Falk; later they are joined by
Müller, and finally, in the 1820s, by Soret and Eckermann.

Friedrich Wilhelm Riemer (1774–1845) lived from 1803 to
1812 in Goethe's house as tutor in Latin and Greek to the poet's
son August. A quarrel with his pupil estranged him from the
household for several years, during which he worked as a school-
master in Weimar; he and Goethe were not reconciled until
1819. He was a fat pompous man with protruding eyes, a very
sound scholar, a pedant and a bore. Goethe found him useful as
a literary assistant and walking dictionary of classical erudition;
he eventually appointed him as one of his literary executors. In
1841 Riemer published his *Memoirs of Goethe*,[15] partly compiled, as he claims, from verbal sources. It is a ponderous and
sanctimonious work, with its materials systematically classified
in subdivided sections; but the second volume in particular contains a large number of valuable notations of the poet's views—
not in the form of living dialogues and conversational exchanges,
which Riemer had no gift for recording, but mostly couched in
direct speech as separate short pronouncements or aphorisms on
a variety of intellectual subjects. These make, however, a strong
impression of authenticity, and Riemer has preserved much
that is undoubtedly interesting and profound; his devotion to
Goethe had been both sincere and intelligent.

The memoirs of Johann Daniel Falk (1768–1826) are more
lively and discursive. This man was a frequent visitor to Goethe's
house during these middle years, though it is doubtful if he can
be counted as one of the poet's intimate friends. He was a
journalistic writer and philanthropist who settled in Weimar in
1798. During the Wars of Liberation he founded a home for
destitute children which still exists today. His reports, which go
back to the 1790s, are collected in his book *Goethe: a record
from personal knowledge*,[16] which was published in 1832 several
years after Falk's death; he had stipulated that it should not
appear during Goethe's lifetime. Falk claims that it is based on
authentic extracts from a diary which he had kept regularly.
Goethe's friend Wilhelm von Humboldt, the distinguished
Prussian statesman and philosopher, thought highly of the book

and wrote of it that this was exactly how Goethe had talked.[17] Riemer, on the other hand, regarded Falk as "an insufferable windbag" and his records as untrustworthy,[18] and their reliability has been disputed ever since. Another contemporary witness wrote that Falk in his reports "adds so much from his imagination and intermingles so many of his own extravagant rhetorical expressions with the poet's simple words that the resulting picture of Goethe is quite unrecognisable".[19] It is certain that Falk embellished and expanded his materials; nevertheless, modern critics are largely agreed that despite his inflated and over-garrulous presentation there is a kernel of authenticity in his transmission of Goethe's thought. It has been shown that the poet's astonishing discourse on the evening after Wieland's funeral, as Falk reproduces it, is in no way at variance with Goethe's metaphysical views as elsewhere attested; there is the ring of truth also in his reported remarks about the unfortunate genius Heinrich von Kleist, even to the very phrases used.

Of all the main collections, perhaps the most realistic and humanly interesting account of Goethe and his moods and ideas is given by Friedrich von Müller, whose records cover the period from 1808 to 1832. Müller (1779–1849) was himself a highly gifted and interesting man. He began his career as a lawyer and civil servant in Weimar in 1801, was ennobled in 1807 and appointed Chancellor (the equivalent of a Minister of Justice) in 1815. He became one of the innermost circle of Goethe's associates during his latter years, meeting him frequently, almost daily, both on business and privately, and Goethe made him his legal executor. Müller kept a diary during the whole period of his association with the poet, but it was not until long after his death that the material compiled from this diary was published (*Goethe's Conversations with Chancellor von Müller*, edited by C. A. H. Burckhardt, 1870).[20] Goethe and Müller treated each other as social equals and colleagues; unlike Eckermann and even Riemer, Müller was not His Excellency's humble famulus and *protégé*. He shared something of the poet's frequently Mephistophelean turn of mind; Goethe thought highly of his intelligence, and Müller was one of the few people to whom the poet confided his moods of dissatisfaction and boredom, bordering on despair. They sometimes found each other very irritating; but it was partly the existence of some disharmonious elements in Müller's own nature that enabled him to appreciate the less Olympian side of Goethe, and his reports are thus a happy complement to those of the guileless worshipper Eckermann. Müller is clear-sighted and critical, his records are fresh, spontaneous, day-to-day notations. Müller's Goethe is not surrounded by a heroic aura; he sits in his shirt-sleeves drinking and making cynical remarks, or embarrasses the company by relapsing into prolonged moody silence punctuated by monosyllabic grunts. Yet for all his realism Müller is no irreverent denigrator : he too felt a deep and lasting affection and admiration for the poet, which shows itself at certain great moments, such as the almost lyrical closing lines of his description of his meeting with Goethe at Dornburg in 1818.[21]

Eckermann arrived in Weimar in 1823, but he was preceded in the previous year by a lesser-known recorder of Goethe's conversations, who although only minimally represented in the present selection nevertheless deserves some mention here, since without him it is doubtful if the supplementary volume (Book III) of Eckermann's famous work would ever have been written. Frédéric Soret (1795–1865) was a French-speaking Swiss from Geneva, born in St. Petersburg. His father had made a fortune there as a portrait painter for the Russian court; it happened that one of the Tsar's daughters, Maria Pavlovna, married Karl August's heir, and in 1822 she engaged the young Soret as tutor to her four-year-old son Prince Karl Alexander. As a simple rationalist and republican, Soret occupied a somewhat paradoxical position in the service of a German prince, but his charm and integrity made him a welcome member of the Weimar court circle. He was a trained mineralogist, and he translated Goethe's treatise on the metamorphosis of plants into French; he was in fact the only real scientist among Goethe's closer associates, and there is a further note of irony in his accounts of the poet's scientific views and activities. He had come to Weimar thinking of Goethe as "the German Voltaire", and there were limits to their understanding of each other; at first, too, Soret spoke hardly any German. He was an adherent of the enlightened utilitarianism of Jeremy Bentham, whom Goethe described as "that radical idiot".[22] For ten years, however, Soret was a frequent visitor at Goethe's house, and he kept records of their conversational and argumentative exchanges; these show him to have been, like Müller, a casual and spontaneous, realistic and occasionally critical observer of Goethe, though in the end a note of personal warmth may be discerned in them. Soret never published his diaries himself, but he had also become

personally attached to Eckermann, and in the 1840s he gener-
ously put his manuscript at the latter's disposal to help him
with the compilation of a sequel to his already very successful
Conversations. Eckermann used this additional material with
grateful acknowledgements, but adapting and rewriting it in
his own way.

The story of the author of the best known of the Goethe con-
versation-books is full of pathos. Johann Peter Eckermann
(1792–1854) was born of humble working-class parents in a
desolate province near Hamburg, and had had to struggle
hard against poverty to acquire a scant education. He had
hardly any schooling until he was fourteen. Later, working for
sixteen or seventeen hours a day, he tried to combine atten-
dance at school with earning his living in an office, but had to
give this up after a few months. He eventually scraped into
Göttingen, but his university career too was cut short by lack of
means. In the course of his voracious reading he had discovered
the works of Goethe, and the resulting enthusiasm was to shape
his entire destiny. In the winter of 1822–3, after withdrawing
from Göttingen, he wrote the book on which he pinned all his
hopes: his *Essays on Poetry, with special reference to Goethe*—
a work of criticism which, like some of Eckermann's own poetry,
is still readable today. When it was finished, he sent the manuscript to Goethe, who decided to recommend it to his own publisher. Early in the hot June of 1823 Eckermann himself
arrived in Weimar, having travelled on foot from Hamburg.
Goethe was at this time preparing the final edition of his works,
and he more than ever needed further assistance to relieve him
of some of the drudgery which this involved. Here was a timid,
utterly devoted, penniless student of thirty, apparently willing
to be engaged, or indeed eager to be accepted, as a kind of un-
official secretary and general editorial factotum. Goethe found
him a lodging near his house and set him to work, though he
neither promised him a salary nor arranged for Karl August to
pay him one, nor indeed ever gave him anything more than
occasional pocket-money. Eckermann accepted this situation,
and eked out a meagre living by teaching German to the young
Englishmen attracted to Weimar by Goethe's fame. He would
have liked to get married, having left a faithful fiancée behind
him at home, who in the event had to wait for him for eleven
years and even help to support him from her savings. His own
position as a close associate of the poet became known outside

Weimar, and he was offered advantageous work by editors and publishers, but Goethe, who wanted to have him entirely at his own disposal, discouraged him from accepting it. Eckermann eventually married in 1831, but his wife died three years later.

Unlike Müller and Soret, Eckermann never moved in the court circle at Weimar, and unlike Riemer he never lived in Goethe's house. Visitors noticed his unbounded devotion to the poet and spoke of him rather patronisingly as "Goethe's faithful little subordinate, a quite talented fellow",[23] or "Goethe's adjutant and blind admirer".[24] It cannot be denied that Goethe exploited Eckermann's devotion, but in a certain sense he was justified by the final results : the whole relationship was a curious creative experiment, a kind of vicarious self-expression. Eckermann was eminently trainable and malleable, full of enthusiasm which could be canalised; he had come to Weimar with no plans, certainly not expecting to remain there permanently and become the Boswell to a greater man than Johnson. The items dated 1823 in Book I of his *Conversations* are later reconstructions, based on letters written at the time. The idea of compiling a book of conversations with Goethe did not form itself until a year or two later; it no doubt originated from Eckermann but was evidently encouraged by the poet. The book was conceived as a supplementary volume to the definitive edition of Goethe's works, in the preparation of which Eckermann now played an increasingly important part. It is clear that Goethe saw him as a potential mediator capable of transmitting at least a particular image of him to posterity. At the same time, his own diaries indicate that he came to take Eckermann himself more and more seriously; he was probably touched by his singleminded adoration, and needed him as a younger confidant. At all events, Eckermann somehow had the gift of making Goethe talk and of eliciting his views on subjects of importance. During the last nine years of the poet's life he was in almost daily contact with him. He was in the end formally appointed as his literary co-executor along with Riemer; but in 1828 Goethe paid him an even higher compliment by entrusting to him the manuscript of the continuation of *Wilhelm Meister's Travels* with a request for his advice on how the book should be arranged and finished. And two years later Goethe stated that without Eckermann's stimulus and interest, *Faust* Part Two would never have been completed : "Eckermann", he said to Müller, "knows better than anyone else how to extract literary work from me, by his intelligent interest in what I have already done and begun. He is in fact the main reason why I am going on with *Faust*."[25]

Faust Part Two was published posthumously in 1832 under Eckermann's supervision, with Riemer's assistance. Books I and II of Eckermann's *Conversations with Goethe during the last years of his life* appeared in 1836. Its success encouraged him to prepare a sequel in the hope of augmenting his meagre pension; Book III, incorporating Soret's material, was published in 1848, but owing to the disturbances of that time little notice was taken of it. Eckermann died six years later.

It must be admitted that these *Conversations*, which have been ironically described as the poet's most widely read work, were largely responsible for the establishment of the nineteenth-century legend of the "Olympian" Goethe, the tranquil sage looking down at human affairs from a sublime and untouchable height. It was perhaps a psychological necessity for Eckermann to deify this man to whom he had devoted his life and sacrificed his personal happiness. But his book should not be judged as a scientifically realistic, unvarnished biographical record, which it was not intended to be. Eckermann "idealises" in the best sense of the word, the sense understood by Goethe and Schiller when in their aesthetic writings they distinguished between "truth" (*das Wahre*) and mere "reality" (*das Wirkliche*). Eckermann stylises Goethe : he selects and omits, refines and transfigures. In other words, his book is a consciously shaped work of art, and as such it differs from the compilations of Riemer and Müller, which are straightforward raw material. In Eckermann there is something of Goethe's own "classical" method : the attempt to create a harmonious image, to resolve dissonances, to separate the permanent from the fortuitous, to liberate the inner characteristic essence. His balanced, elevated style, modelled on Goethe's own written work, lays a patina of nobility over the poet's whole manner of speech : he excludes vivid colloquialisms and coarse expressions, such as Goethe certainly used and is recorded by others as using. Eckermann simply does not wish to present the untidy mixture of the significant and the insignificant which is "real" everyday life, and which we find in Müller. Müller's Goethe is visibly subject to time; he shows signs of age, is tired, hard of hearing, moody. But the years pass over Eckermann's Goethe leaving scarcely a trace. His account of how he gazed at the poet's naked body on the day after his death has been censured by some critics as tasteless, but it is a fitting symbolic conclusion to his work. The flesh and limbs are perfect in their "divine magnificence", and he cannot believe that Goethe is dead. He has left a curious record of a dream which he claims to have had in November 1836, in which he sees Goethe and his son August suddenly walk into their house in Weimar looking hale and hearty and bronzed. "Dead?" exclaims the poet, who had himself never really been able to believe in the possibility of death, "what nonsense! I have been travelling." He congratulates Eckermann on the *Conversations*, in which, as he says, he appears advantageously "in a south light". He encourages him to write Book III and then mysteriously disappears with August in a boat, towards "a land not inhabited by men".[26] Eckermann himself knew quite well that he was presenting Goethe to posterity "in a south light". In a letter written in 1844 he stated that he had not intended his book as a record of "the common day", but to serve "a higher purpose; and although I have invented nothing in it and it is all perfectly true, it is nevertheless selected".[27] And in the preface to the book itself he specifically disclaimed that it was "a portrayal of the whole of Goethe's mind... He was different in different situations and to different people, and so for myself I can only say with all due modesty: this is my Goethe".[28] Ernst Beutler, writing of Goethe's capacity both for faith and for scepticism, remarks: "He sometimes pessimistically, almost nihilistically, calls in question the value of life and of the world, and at other times he reverently and gratefully affirms them. In the last resort this affirmation was and remains the dominant note, perpetually reasserted after a great struggle. Eckermann saw this vindication of faith as Goethe's highest achievement. He wanted to proclaim it to posterity. This is the meaning of his book."[29] Goethe's life and Eckermann's were both, in their different ways, tragic, but neither of them wanted to present life as being so. It is small wonder that Nietzsche, with his own desire to construct affirmation on a basis of tragedy, his own profound appreciation of Goethe, and his declared belief in the aesthetic, monumentalising approach to the history of great men, should in a hyperbolic moment have described Eckermann's *Conversations with Goethe* as "the best German book ever written".[30] Eckermann's book is one-sided; it is marred by a certain naïvety and pomposity; modern research has revealed its factual inaccuracies in dating and similar matters; despite all this it possesses an undeniably impressive coherence and inner verisimilitude. It is significant that when it was published both Müller and Soret applauded it unreservedly, as did Goethe's daughter-in-law and his other friends and associates, and the great majority of the critics. It was and remains the crowning achievement of the diarists of Goethe's circle.

Apart from these four or five main sources, there are of course the memoirs and reminiscences of many other friends and acquaintances of the poet, and the recorded impressions of innumerable casual visitors. More and more of the latter, from further and further afield, were drawn to Weimar as it increased in importance as a cultural centre and as Goethe became more and more of an international institution. Many Germans and foreigners, who had never even read his works, came out of mere curiosity or intellectual snobbery: the aged "author of *Werther*" was what would nowadays be called a tourist attraction. One had to be able to say that one had called on the man who since writing that rather immoral book had made good as a Minister of the local State and was now a distinguished-looking old gentleman living in a large house full of pictures and classical busts. English visitors were especially frequent: the old man's daughter-in-law Ottilie was known to have a predilection for them, and they would usually be a great social success in Weimar. It was inevitable that to the inquisitive and usually ignorant public Goethe should present a defensive official mask. One pattern constantly repeats itself in the reports: new acquaintances are treated with chilling ceremony, like a monarch's subjects being received in audience. They are embarrassed; Goethe's reputation of heartless arrogance appears to be only too well justified; they do not yet realise that his embarrassment and nervousness are often no less than theirs. Later, in the case of unpretentious and deserving visitors with whom some kind of *rapport* can be established, visitors who interest Goethe by their talent or promise or personality or from whom he can learn something, the Minister thaws and unbends, and everything is transformed. They are invited to call again, to come to lunch, to join the family circle, even to spend hours with Goethe *tête-à-tête*. Some callers never succeed in penetrating beyond the ministerial mask and are left with an unfavourable impression; others again are treated kindly and charmingly at first sight. Some who come to see him are themselves men of original genius, and with some of these he makes real intellectual contact (Mendelssohn, or the great Polish poet Mickiewicz) while with others he makes none or disappointingly little (Hegel, Schopenhauer, Grillparzer). But for the variety of Goethe's visitors, and for the variety of conversation and social behaviour attributed to him, the reports must be allowed to speak for themselves. The long description by Stephan Schütze of his behaviour in Johanna Schopenhauer's salon is particularly revealing.[31] Two points may here be mentioned. One is that Goethe was evidently not a brilliant debater or conversationalist in the stricter sense, like the great French or English wits. Lightning repartee and epigrammatic coruscation were not his style, and he responded badly to interrogation. He preferred to retain the initiative and develop his ideas at leisure, without interruption. Falk[32] compared the even, unflamboyant, often gently ironic flow of his talk to Mozart's music—deceptively simple, seemingly commonplace, then suddenly revealing its radiant superiority. The other point is that Goethe, this urbane and abundant talker, whom Schiller had called "the most communicative of men",[33] was in fact deeply reserved, not given to exposing his most intimate feelings even to those nearest to him. Only occasionally is a hint dropped of his essential loneliness.[34] When stricken by some immediate personal anguish (the death of Schiller, of his wife, of his son) he makes no attempt to put it into words, and allows no one else to do so. When August von Goethe's friend Preller returned from Rome and called on the bereaved father, Goethe afterwards fell ill with delayed shock, but at the time he talked calmly to Preller about art.[35] The rest was silence—a silence more eloquent than speech.

The first attempt at a comprehensive collection of Goethe's "conversations", based not only on the Eckermann–Soret book (which amounts only to less than one-third of the total relevant material) but also on Riemer, Falk, Müller, and innumerable other sources, was made by Baron Woldemar von Biedermann, a rich gifted amateur; his monumental but faulty and untidy edition appeared in ten volumes between 1889 and 1896. After his death a somewhat improved and much enlarged version of it (though concentrated into five volumes) was issued, with the assistance of expert Goethe scholars, by his son Flodoard von Biedermann, in 1909–11. Since then, research has proceeded apace; Eckermann and Soret have been carefully disentangled, and the latter's contributions reassembled and re-edited.[36] The whole mass of available relevant material has been sifted and increased still further; a critical edition of it in fifteen volumes, on new and extended lines, is at present being prepared by Ernst Grumach, though only the first volume has so far been published.[37] The present brief selection in English is based almost entirely on the relevant volumes of the Artemis Verlag centenary edition (*Gedenkausgabe der Werke, Briefe und Gespräche*, 26 vols., 1948–64, general editor Ernst Beutler) which is still the most complete edition of Goethe to have appeared since the war. Vol. 24 is the Eckermann–Soret book in its traditional form; vols. 22 and 23 are a comprehensive selection of the remaining material, arranged chronologically to cover Goethe's life from the age of three until his death. These two volumes are themselves based mainly on the second edition of Biedermann. Yet another revised collection of the *Gespräche* is now also being prepared for the Artemis Verlag by Wolfgang Herwig, in four volumes; the first of these has appeared but could not be consulted before the present selection went to press. In the Artemis editions and in Grumach's the principle is adopted of including numerous documents which are not strictly "conversations" with Goethe or pronouncements by him at all, but merely contemporary descriptions of him or reminiscences of his personality and views by people who knew him or had met him. To some extent we have followed this more liberal editorial practice even in the present selection, since there are a number of items of great interest which it would be pedantic to exclude on the grounds that they contain no alleged *ipsissima verba* of the poet. We have also adopted the chronological principle in preference to attempting an arrangement under classified headings. (The dating refers in all cases to the date, so far as it is known, of the alleged conversation or encounter.) About one-third of our selection consists of extracts from Eckermann, chronologically inserted among the rest. These have here been newly translated. (The 1850 version by John Oxenford—abridged and minimally revised by J. K. Moorhead for the Everyman's Library edition, last reprinted in 1951—is not only full of inaccuracies and misunderstandings of the German and occasionally even bowdlerised, but also stylistically so clumsy and tasteless that it can have done little service to Eckermann's reputation or to Goethe's.) None of the other material (Müller, Riemer, etc.) has appeared in English before.

In making the selection we have had the general reader in mind and have tried to present a varied range of texts which a

non-specialist would find interesting and intelligible. Our aim
has been to emphasise the human reality of Goethe, while at the
same time offering some representative documentation of his
views on literature and art generally, his own works, and other
matters. There are many passages which for reasons of space
we have excluded or abbreviated with regret; in addition, those
selected have been pruned of redundant or ephemeral or over-
specialised matter and superfluous proper names. Occasionally,
in the interests of these abridgements or of clarification, the
text has been slightly adapted, and one or two items are com-
pounded from more than one entry in the Artemis edition. A
list of page-references to the latter (which itself contains an
apparatus referring to its sources) has been provided (Index,
part III) for the assistance of any reader who might wish to con-
sult the corresponding German texts. Part I of the Index is a
list of persons who appear in the selected texts as authors of the
reports or who are mentioned in them; part II lists the passages
in which works by Goethe are discussed or alluded to. In the
translation we have attempted to be accurate in all essentials
while remaining sufficiently free to be readable. We have sometimes had to resort to paraphrase or expansion in the case of
such technical terms as *Idee*, *Vernunft*, or *Verstand*, which
would require an explanatory treatise in themselves. The original
archaic text of reports by contemporary English-speaking visitors
is distinguished by italics. In a few cases (e.g. the reports by
Soret) the original texts are in French.[38]

NOTES TO INTRODUCTION

(References by volume and page are to the Artemis edition unless
otherwise stated; those by numbers are to the present selection.)

(1) *Das Märchen*, 1795 (9, 374f.).
(2) No. 104.
(3) *Dichtung und Wahrheit*, Book 13 (10, 630).
(4) *Maximen und Reflexionen* (9, 616).
(5) No. 184.
(6) No. 184.
(7) No. 272.
(8) *Culture and Society in Classical Weimar, 1775–1806* (1962),
p. 22.
(9) In his essay "Goethe as the Sage" (in *Poetry and Poets*, 1957).

(10) Introduction to the translation of Goethe's *Italian Journey* by W. H. Auden and Elizabeth Mayer (1962).

(11) Cf. Nos. 85 and 133.

(12) 12, 605f.

(13) No. 284.

(14) 23, 393.

(15) *Mitteilungen über Goethe*, 2 vols. (critical edn. by A. Pollmer, 1921).

(16) *Goethe aus näherem persönlichem Umgang dargestellt* (crit. edn. by K. G. Wendriner, 1911).

(17) Letter to Rennenkamp 17.8.1832.

(18) Riemer, op. cit., I 21.

(19) 22, 741 (Schütze).

(20) Cf. the more recent crit. edn. by E. Grumach (F. von Müller, *Unterhaltungen mit Goethe*, 1956).

(21) No. 124.

(22) No. 275.

(23) 23, 435 (Boisserée).

(24) 23, 473 (Bähr).

(25) 23, 709f.

(26) 24, 774–8.

(27) Letter to H. Laube 3.3.1844.

(28) 24, 12.

(29) 24, 790f.

(30) *Menschliches Allzumenschliches* II 2, aphorism 109.

(31) No. 110.

(32) 22, 885f.

(33) 22, 744f.

(34) No. 279.

(35) No. 292.

(36) F. Soret, *Conversations avec Goethe*, ed. A. Robinet de Cléry, 1932; cf. the German crit. edn. by H. H. Houben (F. Soret, *Zehn Jahre bei Goethe*, 1929); cf. also Houben's edn. of Eckermann's *Gespräche mit Goethe* (1948).

(37) *Goethe: Begegnungen und Gespräche*, ed. E. Grumach and R. Grumach, vol. I (1749–76), 1965.

(38) Nos. 20, 49, 71, 75, 121, 146, 212, 213, 272, 273, 289, 293, 318.

ACKNOWLEDGMENTS AND BIBLIOGRAPHICAL NOTE

Acknowledgments are due to the Artemis Verlag, Zürich, as publishers of the *Gedenkausgabe*, on vols. 22, 23 and 24 of which the present edition is based; we are indebted also to the Introductions to these volumes (by W. Pfeiffer-Belli and the late Ernst Beutler) and to Ernst Grumach's Introduction to his recent selection of the Conversations (*Goethe im Gespräch*, Fischer-Bücherei, 1960). For assistance in connection with the illustrations we wish to thank the Nationale Forschungs- und Gedenkstätten der klassischen deutschen Literatur in Weimar, and Mrs. L. Newman, Librarian at the University of London Institute of Germanic Studies, to whom we are also grateful for bibliographical information.

The following publications may be of interest to the general English reader of Goethe :

TRANSLATIONS : *Faust*, Parts I and II, in the trans. by Sir Theodore Martin (1816–1910), revised by W. H. Bruford, with introd. and notes (Everyman's Library No. 335, 1954). *Faust*, Parts I and II, trans. with introd. and notes by C. E. Passage (Ungar, 1965). (These two editions, particularly the first, are in our opinion superior to the other currently available versions of *Faust*.) *Götz von Berlichingen*, trans. by C. E. Passage (Ungar, 1965). *Ironhand*, a free adaptation of *Götz von Berlichingen* by John Arden (Methuen, 1965). *Egmont*, trans. by W. Trask (Barron, 1960). *Iphigenia in Tauris*, trans. by C. E. Passage (Ungar, 1963). *Torquato Tasso*, trans. by C. E. Passage (Ungar, in preparation). *Selected Verse*, bilingual edn. with prose translations and introd. by David Luke (Penguin, 1964). *Hermann and Dorothea*, trans. by D. Coogan, bilingual edn. (Ungar, in preparation). *The Sufferings of Young Werther*, trans. by B. Q. Morgan (Calder, 1957). *The Sorrows of Young Werther*, trans. by V. Lange (Holt, Rinehart and Winston, 1962; this volume also contains translations of the stories *Die neue Melusine* and *Novelle*). *Wilhelm Meister's Apprenticeship*, trans. by Thomas Carlyle (reprinted by Collier, 1962). *Kindred by Choice* (= *The Elective Affinities*), trans. by H. M. Waidson (Calder, 1960). *Poetry and Truth from my own life*, trans. by R. O. Moon (Public Affairs Press, 1949). *Italian Journey*, trans. by W. H. Auden and Elizabeth Mayer (Collins, 1962). *Letters from Goethe*, selected and trans. by Marianne von Herzfeld and C. M. Sym, with introd. by W. H. Bruford (Edinburgh U.P., 1957). *Conversations with Eckermann*, abridged edn., trans. by G. C. O'Brien (Ungar, 1965). *Great Writings of Goethe* (a selection containing a number of poems in verse translation, the version of *Faust* Part I by Louis MacNeice, and miscellaneous other writings and extracts), edited by Stephen Spender (Mentor Books, 1958). *Wisdom and Experience*, a selection by L. Curtius, trans. and introd. by H. J. Weigand (Ungar, 1964).

BIOGRAPHICAL AND CRITICAL STUDIES IN ENGLISH : G. H. Lewes, *Life and Works of Goethe* (1855, reprinted in Everyman's Library, No. 269. This very readable book was one of the first biographies of Goethe in any language, and is still of value). R. Friedenthal,

Goethe: his life and times (Weidenfeld and Nicolson, 1965). W. H. Bruford, *Theatre, Drama and Audience in Goethe's Germany* (Routledge, 1950). W. H. Bruford, *Culture and Society in Classical Weimar, 1775–1806* (Cambridge U.P., 1962). H. Hatfield, *Goethe: a critical introduction* (New Directions, 1963, and Harvard U.P., 1964). B. Fairley, *A Study of Goethe* (Oxford U.P., 1947). B. Fairley, *Goethe's 'Faust', six essays* (Oxford U.P., 1953). E. M. Butler, *The Fortunes of Faust* (Cambridge U.P., 1952). E. M. Wilkinson and L. A. Willoughby, *Goethe: Poet and Thinker* (Arnold, 1962). R. Peacock, *Goethe's Major Plays* (Manchester U.P., 1959). See also the annual publications of the English Goethe Society (1886–1912, new series 1924ff.).

D. L.
R. P.

LIST OF ILLUSTRATIONS

Conversations and Encounters

1. Elisabeth Goethe (*reported by Bettina Brentano*) 1752

He did not like playing with small children unless they were very good-looking. At a party he suddenly began to cry. When asked the reason, he screamed: "I don't like the black child, they're to take it away!" And he did not stop crying until he got home, where his mother questioned him about his naughtiness: he was quite inconsolable that the child should be so ugly. He was three years old at the time.

He already had the tenderest affection for his little sister Cornelia when she was still in her cradle: he would conceal pieces of bread in his pocket and stuff them into the child's mouth when it screamed. If any attempt was made to remove it he would become wild with rage: he would climb on to people's shoulders and tear out their hair. In general it was much easier to anger him than to make him cry.

2. Elisabeth Goethe (*reported by Bettina Brentano*) 1754

I, for my part, never tired of telling him stories, just as he never tired of listening. There I would sit, and he would almost devour me with his great black eyes, and when the lot of one of his favourite characters did not fall out quite according to his fancy, then I would see the angry vein swelling on his forehead and he would choke back his tears. Often he would interrupt, and while I was still searching for a phrase he would say: "Mother, the princess doesn't marry the damned tailor, does she? even though he *has* killed the giant". If I then stopped and postponed the dénouement until the following evening, I could be sure that by then he would have rearranged the whole course of events: and thus my imagination, when it proved no longer adequate, was frequently replaced by his. The next evening I would then spin the thread of destiny further in the direction he had indicated, and say: "You guessed quite rightly; that is how it happened". At this he would take fire with excitement, and one could see his little heart beating under his ruff. To his grandmother, who lived at the back of the house and whose favourite he was, he would now confide every day his views on how the story would probably fall out, and from her I learnt how my text was to continue in accordance with his wishes; thus there developed between us a diplomatic interchange of which neither of us betrayed the secret to the other. In this way I had the satisfaction of delivering my tales to the delight and astonishment of all listeners, and Wolfgang, without ever admitting himself to be the author of all these marvels, would sit with eyes aglow, awaiting the fulfilment of his boldly conceived plans, and would greet their detailed execution with enthusiastic applause.

3.   *Elisabeth Goethe (reported by Bettina Brentano)*   *1759*

It struck his mother as odd that he shed no tears at the death of his younger brother Jacob, who had been his playmate; on the contrary, the lamentations of his parents and sisters seemed somehow to annoy him. So after a week his mother asked the sulky creature whether he had not loved his brother, whereupon he ran to his room and fetched out a whole lot of paper from under the bed, with lessons and little stories written all over it; and he had done all this, he told her, in order to teach it to his brother.

4.   *J. A. Horn*   *(Leipzig) August 1766*

And now let me tell you about our friend Goethe! He is still the same proud quixotic madcap as he was when I came here. If you could only see him, you would either go wild with rage or burst with laughing. It is beyond me how a man can change in so short a time. All his habits and his entire present behaviour are totally different from his former manner. He is a fop as well as proud, and all his clothes, fine as they are, are in an eccentric taste which makes him conspicuous in the whole university. But for all this he cares not in the least, however much one may point out his folly to him.

> *One may be Amphion and charm the trees and grass—*
> *One thing's impossible: make Goethe not an ass.*

His entire doings and dreamings are designed merely to please himself and his lady-love. On all social occasions he makes himself ridiculous rather than agreeable.

He now habitually affects (merely because her ladyship likes it) such gestures and porte-mains that it is impossible not to laugh at him. His gait has become quite preposterous. If only you could see it!

> *Il marche à pas comptés*
> *Comme un recteur suivi des quatres facultés.*

I find his company increasingly intolerable, and he too tries as far as possible to avoid mine. He does not consider me good enough to cross the street with him. Do write to him again soon and give him a piece of your mind. Otherwise he will go on being an eccentric, he and his chère amie. He is not the first to make a fool of himself for a Dulcinea. I only wish you could see her, she's the dreariest creature in the world. A mine coquette and an air hautain are all she has needed to enchant Goethe. My dear fellow! I'd be twice as happy here if only Goethe were still as he was in Frankfurt. We were such good friends before, but now we can scarcely bear to be together for a quarter of an hour. And yet I still have hopes of curing him in time, hard though it is to teach a fool sense. But I will try my utmost.

> *Ah, were such triumph granted me!*
> *And could my efforts but bear fruit!*
> *Some great Reformer I should be:*
> *Not Luther or Calvin should outdo't.*

By all means, when you write to him, repeat everything I have told you. I shall be glad if you do so. I care neither for his anger nor for her ladyship's. In any case, he does not get angry with me all that easily. Even when we have quarrelled, he sends next day and invites me round.

I am to give you his compliments and say that he would like to write to you, but is afraid he might appear at her ladyship's tomorrow with inkstained hands. What fools we are when we are in love!

5. *J. A. Horn*   *Autumn 1766*

You will be delighted to hear that we have not lost a friend in our Goethe, as we mistakenly thought. He had been playing a part, which deceived not only me but several other people as well, and he would never have disclosed the true state of affairs to me if your letters had not first warned him that he was about to lose a friend. He is in love, but not with the lady I suspected. He loves a girl* who is beneath him socially, but a girl whom—I

* Kätchen Schönkopf.

2—G

think I am not exaggerating—you yourself would love if you saw her. He loves her very tenderly, with the perfectly honourable intentions of a virtuous man, although he knows that she can never be his wife. Whether she returns his love I do not know. But observe how cunning he has been! To prevent any-one suspecting him of such a love, he undertook to persuade the world of the exact contrary, and in this he has hitherto been remarkably successful. He put on the fine gentleman, and ap-peared to be paying court to Fräulein—well, why should I tell you her name—and is even teased in society on her account. Perhaps she herself thinks he loves her, but the good lady is mis-taken. Since that time he has honoured me with his closer con-fidence. He is more of a philosopher and moralist than ever, and innocent though his love is, he nevertheless deprecates it. We argue a great deal about it, but whatever side he takes, he wins; for you know what authority he can lend to the most specious reasons. I pity him and his warm heart, which must really be in a very uncomfortable condition, since he loves the most virtuous and perfect of girls without hope. And if we assume that she returns his love, must he not be all the more miserable?

6. *Marie Körner*   *(Leipzig) 1765–8*

Father spent most of his working time doing little vignettes for Breitkopf, the bookseller and publisher; he also earned some money by teaching his art. His keenest pupil, and at the same time the one most given to playing all kinds of high-spirited pranks, was Goethe, who later became so famous; at that time he was a law student of sixteen. This acquaintanceship caused our dear mother a lot of worry and vexation. When Father was still sitting busily at his work in the late afternoon, his young friend would urge him to take an early evening off, and when Mother protested, he would soothe her by arguing that to work with the fine engraving-needle in the fading light was bad for the eyes, especially when it meant looking through a glass. And when Mother then retorted that looking through a glass was not so bad for the eyes as looking into a glass, and sometimes looking a good deal too deeply, the high-spirited student would still not give way, and would carry Father off to visit the Schönkopfs or to Auerbach's Tavern. This association cost our dear mother many a tear. But when Monsieur Goethe—for young gentlemen of good family were addressed as Monsieur—reappeared next morning, and Mother scolded him thoroughly for taking Father into such wild student company, quite unsuitable for a married man with a wife and children to look after, he would manage with all sorts of jokes and tricks to put her in a good humour again. Then she would call him "the Frankfurt Struwelpeter" and force him to let her comb out his hair, which she said was as full of feathers as if sparrows had been nesting in it. Only at Mother's repeated bidding would we sisters bring our combs, and it was a long time before his hair was tidy again. Goethe had beautiful brown hair; he wore it unpowdered, and fastened behind his neck, though not in a stiff pigtail like old King Fritz, but letting the thick wavy locks hang down freely. When I reminded Goethe of all this in later years, he would never admit it, but assured me that my mother had taken a particular delight in combing him, and so it had been she who would untidy his coiffure and then tease him most unkindly.*

What chiefly made our merry student friend unpopular with us children was the fact that he much preferred playing with Father's greyhound to playing with us. It was a nice little beast called Joli, and he spoiled it and let it do all sorts of naughty things, while behaving like a strict tutor to us. He would always arrive with some tit-bit for Joli, but when we looked in vexation at this we were informed that sweetmeats spoil the teeth and roasted almonds and nuts spoil the voice. Goethe and Father even carried their whim to the length of setting up a Christmas tree for Joli on Christmas Eve, with sweet things hanging all over it; they dressed him in a red woollen waistcoat and walked him on two legs to the small table on which a feast was laid out for him, while we had to content ourselves with a little packet of brown gingerbread-cakes which my godfather had sent from Nürnberg. Joli was so unintelligent, indeed I may say so unchristian a creature, that he showed not the slightest respect for the Manger which we had so attractively arranged under our table; he sniffed it all over, snatched the sugar Christ-child out of his manger and gobbled him up at one gulp, at which Herr Goethe and Father roared with laughter, while we burst into tears. It was lucky that the Virgin Mary, St. Joseph and the oxen and donkeys were made of wood and were therefore spared.

Our education was restricted to a very small range of sub-

* Cf. No. 311.

jects. At eleven in the morning a dessicated Leipzig dominie, whom Breitkopf employed at his press as a proof-reader, would arrive at our house; he wore black clothes and a white ruff to make himself look like a theologian. He taught us reading, writing and arithmetic and turned a solid penny for the hour. What put literally the crowning touch to his costume was his wig, which was woven of extremely fine wire and fell down in thick curls. As soon as he entered he would call out to us from the threshold : "Children, your prayers!" And we would recite in unison a verse from a hymn, after which there would be an hour's reading from the Bible. There was only the one room for the whole lot of us, and so it often happened that Goethe came in during our lesson and sat down at Father's work-table. One day it so chanced that we were having to read aloud from a chapter in the Book of Esther which struck Goethe as unsuitable for young girls. For a while he had listened in silence; then suddenly he leapt up from Father's table, snatched the Bible out of my hand, and exclaimed in tones of extreme wrath to our teacher : "Sir, how dare you make young girls read such bawdy stuff!" Our dominie trembled and quaked; for Goethe continued his invective with increasing vehemence until Mother intervened and tried to calm him down. The dominie stuttered out something about it all being the Word of God, whereupon Goethe enjoined him to "prove all things, and hold fast that which is good and virtuous!" Then he opened the New Testament and thumbed about in it for a little until he found what he was looking for. "Here you are, Dolly!" he said to my sister. "Read this out to us : it's the Sermon on the Mount, and we'll all listen together." Then, as Dolly faltered and could not read for nervousness, Goethe took the Bible from her and read the whole chapter aloud, adding very edifying comments such as we had never heard from our teacher. The latter now took heart again and enquired humbly : "No doubt, Sir, you are a theological student? With God's help you will become a worthy labourer in the Lord's vineyard and a faithful shepherd of his flock". "You may be sure", added Father jestingly, "that he will have a well-pressed vineyard and a well-fleeced flock, and plenty of docile penitents." And thus our lessons ended on a merry note; everyone laughed at Father's joke, and we girls laughed too, without really knowing why.

7. F. Lerse (reported)   *6.8.1771*

Goethe had to take his doctorate in Law at Strasbourg, and for this purpose he wrote a dissertation in which he proved that the Ten Commandments were not really the laws of the Israelite covenant, but that according to Deuteronomy there had never really been ten commandments, merely ten ceremonies. This was censored by the Dean of the Faculty, and so Goethe wrote an even more heretical thesis instead. Lerse conducted his viva voce examination, and pretended to be taking up a position of extreme orthodoxy. He so effectively cornered Goethe that the latter broke into German and exclaimed: "I think, my dear fellow, that you are trying to be Hector to my Achilles!" When Lerse noticed that the Dean thought the joke had gone a little too far, he ended with a finely turned compliment, and this concluded the matter. At that time Goethe and Lerse were inseparable. They would often go to the Minster and sit for hours up on the roof. It was there that Goethe composed his essay *On German Architecture*, the first of his printed works. They would often take a boat up the Rhine, read Ossian and Homer by lamplight in Rupprechtsau, and share the same bed, though without sleeping. Goethe would then often get into a state of high exaltation and speak words of prophecy, making Lerse apprehensive that he would take leave of his wits. He had an unbounded confidence in Lerse, who could lead him any way he pleased. Six months after he had left Strasbourg, he sent him his *Götz von Berlichingen*, completely finished, though he had certainly not been working on it before leaving. Lerse criticised certain rather too ribald passages, and these were duly omitted.

8. Elisabeth Goethe (rep. by H. C. Robinson) Sept.–Oct. 1771

Goethe came home one evening in high spirits, Oh, mother, he said, I have found such a book in the public library, and I will make a play of it! What great eyes the Philistines will make at the Knight with the Iron-hand! That's glorious—the Iron-hand!

9. Caroline Flachsland to Herder   *March 1772*

A few days ago I made the acquaintance of your friend Goethe. He is such a warm-hearted, high-spirited man, with no pedantic frills. He was very attentive to the children, and is rather like you in his manner of speech or somehow, with the result that I followed him everywhere. He and my sister and I sat together just for a moment in the evening sun, which was very beautiful, and we talked about you. He lived for six months with you in Strasbourg and speaks of you with great enthusiasm. We spent the second afternoon going for a very delightful walk and sitting round a bowl of punch in our house. We were not sentimental, but in very high spirits, and Goethe and I danced minuets to the piano; and then he recited to us a wonderful ballad of yours* which I had never heard : *Why does your brand sae drop wi' blude, Edward, Edward?*

10.   J. Ch. Kestner   May–June 1772

Dr. Goethe has many talents, is a true genius, and a man of character; he possesses an extraordinarily lively imagination, and accordingly expresses himself for the most part in images and similes. Indeed he himself often says that he always expresses himself metaphorically, and never can speak literally : but that he hopes that when he is older he will be able to think his thoughts as they really are and to speak them directly.

He is intense in all his emotions, but can often exercise considerable control over himself. His outlook is generous and quite free of prejudice, so that he acts as his impulse prompts him, without stopping to consider whether what he does will please other people or conform to fashion or to the received code of behaviour. He detests all constraint.

He loves children and can spend a great deal of time in their company. He is bizarre and there are various features in his conduct and external appearance that could make him disagreeable. But he stands high in favour with children, women and many others. He has the very greatest respect for the fair sex.

11.   L. J. F. Höpfner (reported)   17.8.1772

One day a young man with rather shabby clothes and an awkward demeanour called at Höpfner's house in Giessen and sent in word that he would like to speak to the professor on an urgent matter. Höpfner, although he was busy preparing a lecture, admitted the young man. The latter's whole manner as he entered and took a seat gave Höpfner the impression that this

* Herder had translated the traditional Scottish ballad here referred to.

was a student in circumstances of financial embarrassment. He was confirmed in this view by the fact that the young man began the conversation with a highly detailed description of his family and domestic situation, in the course of which he hinted occasionally that this situation was not all that it might be. Pressed for time by his approaching lecture, the professor very soon decided to administer pecuniary assistance to the young man without further ado, and thereby also to put an end to so embarrassing a conversation. But no sooner had he indicated this intention by feeling in his pocket for his purse, than the supposed mendicant student began talking of learned matters, and very quickly allayed the suspicion that he had come to demand a gift of money. As soon as the young man noticed, however, that the professor had changed his view of him, the conversation took the former turn, and the student hinted more and more broadly that to request assistance was indeed his purpose after all. After Höpfner had in this way been brought two or three times to the point of offering the young man money and then again feeling that he must refrain from doing so, the student suddenly departed and left the professor pondering in complete perplexity on this mysterious visit.

That evening when Höpfner, rather later than usual, entered the tavern at which the university professors habitually foregathered, he found the place in complete chaos. The company, quite unusually numerous, was grouped round a single table, some sitting, some on their feet, and indeed some of these learned gentlemen were standing on chairs gazing over the heads of their colleagues into the assembled circle, from the centre of which the voice of one man rang out loud and clear, enchanting his hearers with inspired eloquence. When Höpfner asked what was happening, he was told that Goethe from Wetzlar had been here for an hour already, and that the conversation had gradually become little more than a monologue by Goethe, with everyone listening to him with admiration and enthusiasm. Höpfner, full of curiosity to see the poet, climbed on to a chair, looked into the circle, and beheld his mendicant student transformed into a young Apollo.

12. *Baron von Schönborn to H. W. von Gerstenberg 11.10.1773*

On the very evening of my arrival in Frankfurt I also spoke to Herr Goethe, the author of *Götz von Berlichingen*. We were at once introduced and at once became friends. He is a slight young man of about my height. He has a pale complexion, a large, rather curved nose, a longish face and fairly dark eyes and black hair. His expression is serious and sad, but a comical, hilarious and satiric vein shows through as well. He is very eloquent and overflows with witty ideas. He indeed possesses, as I know him, an exceptionally visual poetic gift, and the power of feeling his way right into things, so that everything becomes localised and individualised in his mind. Everything with him at once takes on dramatic form. He was delighted when I told him that you had thought highly of his play.

13.   J. H. Jung-Stilling   July 1774

Early one morning Stilling was summoned to an inn at Elberfeld; he was told there was a sick traveller there who would like to see him. So he got dressed and went to the place, and was taken to the stranger's bedroom. And here he found the patient with a thick towel round his neck and his head all wrapped up. The stranger held out his hand from the bed and said in a weak and hollow voice: "Doctor! just feel my pulse; I'm very ill and weak". Stilling felt, and found the pulse perfectly regular and healthy; so he gave his opinion accordingly and replied: "I can find no symptom here; the pulse is in very good order". No sooner had he spoken than Goethe's arms were thrown round his neck.

14.   J. K. Lavater (reported)   July 1774

Rektor Hasenkamp from Duisburg happened one day in Elberfeld to be sitting at table not far from Goethe, who was there with Lavater and a lot of other people. There was a general mood of joviality, and both Goethe and Lavater were delighting everyone with their high-spirited and lively talk. Suddenly Hasenkamp, a devout man but one who through lack of tact sometimes forgot the right time and place for things, addressed Goethe and enquired in a solemn voice: "Are you Herr Goethe?" "Yes!" "And are you the author of that infamous book *The Sorrows of Werther*?" "Yes." "Then I feel bound by my conscience to express to you my abomination of that impious work. May God lead your perverse heart to repentance! For woe, woe to him by whom the offence cometh!" and so forth. Everyone was filled with acute embarrassment, and waited anxiously for what would happen to the honest but pedantic and academic Hasenkamp. But Goethe entertained the whole company by replying : "I quite see that from your point of view that is how you must judge me, and I respect your frankness in rebuking me. Pray for me!"—There was general satisfaction at Goethe's well-bred behaviour; the Rektor was disarmed in a quite unexpected manner, and the conversation resumed its former light-hearted course.

15. J. G. Jacobi   24.7.1774

I hastened to Düsseldorf, where Herr Goethe was waiting for me. Herr Goethe has written deeply insulting things about me in the public press, but he has also written the tragedy *Götz von Berlichingen*. We shook hands. I had met one of the most outstanding of men, full of high genius, glowing imagination, deep feeling, and rapidly changing moods, whose powerful, occasionally gigantic intellect walks ways which are quite its own. I wish I could have written down his table-talk.

On Sunday we took a carriage at five o'clock in the morning to visit Schloss Bensberg. I enjoyed travelling with our visitor, widely as we differed in our manner of seeing, hearing and feeling. Just as I live among the ancient Greeks, so he lives among the ancient Scots, Celts and Teutons. When we returned to our inn, Goethe recited old Scottish ballads to us in the twilight : they were full of a true, deep sense of nature, mingled with ghostly apparitions, and he spoke them so inimitably, and the last of them was so completely authentic and artless, that we were as genuinely startled, as seriously disturbed, as we had once been in our childhood, when our nurses had told us adventure stories and we had listened with all our hearts, believing every word.

We ate our evening meal in high spirits. Not far from us we saw the Rhine : the moon turned it to silver, and there was something solemn about the murmur of its waters in the quiet of the night.

16. Elisabeth Goethe (reported by Bettina Brentano) 14.11.1774

One bright winter's day, when your mother had company, you suggested to her that you should both drive out to the Main with

the visitors : "But, Mother, you haven't seen me skating yet, and
the weather's so fine today", etc. "I put on my scarlet fur coat",
your mother told me; "it had a long train and was fastened down
the front with golden clasps. And so out we drove; and there
went my son, gliding in and out among the others like an arrow.
The air had reddened his cheeks and the powder had all blown
out of his brown hair. So when he saw my red fur, he came
right up to the coach and smiled very nicely at me. 'Well, what
do you want?' said I. 'Oh, come, Mother, you're not cold in the
carriage : give me your fur coat!' 'But surely you're not going to
put it on!' 'Of course I'm going to put it on!' Well, so I took
off my fine warm coat, he put it on, flung the train over one
arm, and off he went over the ice, like a son of the gods."

17.   K. L. von Knebel   December 1774

I have made the acquaintance of Goethe, and I take a somewhat enthusiastic view of him. It has been and will remain for
me one of the most extraordinary experiences of my life.

I have in my possession a number of fragments of his writings, for example the fragments of a *Dr. Faustus*, in which there
are quite exceptionally splendid scenes. He fetches out manuscripts from every corner of his room. He worked for two months
on the *Sorrows of Werther*, and he assures me that he did not
cross out so much as one whole line of it. *Götz von Berlichingen*
took him six weeks.

18.   G. M. Kraus   Feb.–March 1775

Goethe is the life and soul of parties now, going to balls and
dancing like mad! But he still has his old whimsicality. In the
middle of the liveliest conversation he may suddenly take it into
his head to get up and leave, and not come back. He is wholly a
law unto himself, conforms to no usages, and at times and places
at which everyone appears very formally dressed, he arrives in
the most casual attire, and vice versa.

19.   From the records of the André family   Spring 1775

On one misty moonlit night he wrapped himself up in white
sheets, stalked in this fashion round the little town [Offenbach-

am-Main] on tall stilts—for Goethe in his youth was a very practised stiltwalker—and peered in at many people's first-floor windows, striking them into panic terror at the sight of this tall white ghostly figure. On another occasion, when Anton André was christened, the whole company was sitting at the christening feast; and in came Goethe, after absenting himself briefly, with a covered dish, which he silently placed on the table. And when, presently, the napkin was removed, there on the platter, carefully swaddled, lay the tiny baptismal infant.

20. *J. G. von Zimmermann (reported)*   *September 1775*

Faust had been announced well in advance, and we were expecting at that time to see it published before long. Zimmermann asked his friend how this composition was getting on. Goethe fetched a sack full of little scraps of paper, emptied it on to the table and said : "This is my Faust!"

21. *Charlotte von Stein*   *(Weimar) March 1776*

Goethe is both loved and hated here; you will realise that there are a number of clever people who fail to understand him. A few hours ago he called on me. I confessed that I myself wished he would moderate his wild behaviour which exposes him to so much criticism, although indeed it really amounts to nothing more than hunting and hard riding and cracking his great whip, all in the Duke's company. I am sure these are not his natural inclinations, but he must behave like this for a time in order to win the Duke's favour and then be in a position to do good, or so I interpret it. He did not tell me the reason, but defended himself with extraordinary arguments, and I still felt he was wrong. He was very affectionate to me, and in his trusting open way called me *du*; I admonished him in the gentlest possible tone not to get into the habit of doing so, because after all no one will understand it the way I do, and in any case he is too apt to ignore certain social realities. At this he leapt up from the sofa in a frenzy saying "I must go", ran to and fro several times trying to find his stick, failed to find it, and rushed out of the room without saying goodbye or good night. So that, you see, was our friend's mood today.

22. *C. M. Wieland (reported)*   *1776*

Twenty years later Wieland recalled that it had been really astonishing how Goethe's genius at that period revealed itself on any and every occasion. He had improvised not only the most beautiful poems but even whole dramas. Wieland remembered in particular how one day they had been talking about what a splendid subject Caesar would be for a play. Goethe had at once begun to describe the characters and to recite the whole drama scene by scene from beginning to end. If one could have written down the plays he improvised in this manner, the world would be the richer by several even more remarkable than those by which he is well known.

23. *Karl von Stein*   *1776*

Goethe was standing in front of the dining-room fire, and to warm himself better he had lifted his coat-tails. I was standing to one side just behind him, and I quietly picked up the bellows, surreptitiously inserted the nozzle into the usual gap just above the seat of his trousers, under the fastening, and greeted him with an unexpected blast of wind. This interrupted what he was saying and made him very angry; he not only roared at me but even threatened to beat me if anything of the kind happened again.

24. *J. W. L. Gleim*   *June 1777*

Shortly after Goethe had written his *Sorrows of Werther*, I arrived in Weimar wishing to make his acquaintance. In the evening I was invited by the Duchess Anna Amalia to a party at which I understood Goethe would also appear later on. As a literary novelty I had brought with me the latest number of the *Göttinger Musenalmanach* and was regaling the company with a few pieces from it. And while I was still reading, a young man whom I had scarcely noticed had mingled with the rest of my audience; he wore boots and spurs and a short green huntsman's coat. He sat opposite me and listened very attentively. He had a pair of black beaming eyes like an Italian, but I think there was nothing else about him that I found particularly striking. It had been ordained, however, that I was to become more closely acquainted with him. For during a short pause, while certain gentlemen and ladies were giving their opinions of this or that

piece, praising the one and criticising the other, this same elegant
huntsman—which was what I had first taken him for—rose
from his chair to speak, bowed to me very politely, and at the
same time offered, subject to my approval, to take turns with me
now and then in reading aloud, so that I should not tire myself
out. I of course could not decline this courteous offer, and at
once handed him the book. But what in the name of Apollo and
the nine Muses, not to mention the three Graces, was it then
my lot to listen to! At first indeed, things went very nicely:

'Mid hearkening zephyrs,
O'er murmuring streams,
The joyous sun scattered
Its rapturous beams.

Likewise the rather stronger meat of Bürger and others was
proffered in a manner to which no one could take exception.
But suddenly some boisterous devil seemed to take hold of the
reader, and I thought I must be watching the Wild Huntsman
in person. He read out poems which were not in the almanack
at all, straying into every conceivable key and melody. Hexameters, iambics, doggerel and all, just as it came. All pell-mell
and higgledy-piggledy, as if he were just shaking it out of a bag.

Heaven knows what a wealth of stuff his humorous fancy
produced that evening! From time to time he threw off such
marvellous ideas that, fleeting and disconnected as they were,
the authors to whom he attributed them would have fallen on
their knees to thank God if they had thought of them at their
desks. As soon as the guests realised what game he was up to, a
general hilarity spread through the room. He made fun in one
way or another of everyone who was present, not excepting
myself.

"This is either Goethe or the Devil!" I exclaimed to Wieland,
who was sitting opposite me at table. "Both", replied the latter.
"The devil is in him again today; it makes him kick out front
and back like an unruly colt, and one is well advised to keep
one's distance."

25. *J. F. Blumenbach*   *April 1783*

I have seen Goethe many times and in various company: at
court, among his colleagues, among the ladies, in conversation
with Wieland, and on several occasions in quite lengthy tête-à-

tête with myself, when he took me into his garden or out walking, etc.; and he has quite surpassed all the expectations I had formed of him from other people's reports. He was not at all ministerial and reserved; on the contrary I found him a mature and serious man but quite unaffected and extremely accessible; surprisingly frank, clear and yet deeply penetrating in his judgments, while at the same time absolutely fair and never dogmatic. Wieland and Goethe call each other *du*, of course, and are very good friends, but one feels Goethe's superiority.

26.   *C. M. Wieland (reported by B. R. Abeken)*   *1775–86*

As to the final ending of the tragedy (*Faust*), Goethe rather seems to have had different intentions at different times, at least if Wieland's memory serves him aright; he once told me in 1809 that Goethe had never talked about his plans for *Faust*, except that on one convivial occasion he had said: "You think the devil will fetch Faust. On the contrary: Faust fetches the devil." —This remark probably dates from the earliest Weimar period.

27.   *Caroline Herder to her husband*   *7.8.1788*

Goethe called again today, too, and said he was sure your journey to Italy would be a great success. Among other things he told me that for a fortnight before leaving Rome he had wept every day like a child.

28.   *F. Schiller*   *7.9.1778*

At last I can tell you my impressions of Goethe; I know you are very eager to hear about him. I spent almost the whole of last Sunday in his company. He is of medium height, stiff in his posture and walks stiffly as well; his features give nothing away but his eyes are very expressive and lively and it is a pleasure to watch them. His face is serious but there is much kindness and good will in it too. He is dark and seemed to me to look older than he can be by my reckoning. His voice is extremely pleasant and he is a fluent, witty and animated raconteur; it is a delight to listen to him; and when he is in a good humour, as he seemed to be on this occasion, he talks with interest and relish. We soon made each other's acquaintance, without the least constraint, though of course there were so many people there, all jealously competing for his attention, that it was impossible for us to be alone together for long or have any but the most general conversation. He enjoys talking about Italy and is full of enthusiastic memories of it; everything he told me gave me the most vivid and accurate picture of that country and its people. His accounts bring it home to one particularly clearly how the Italians, more than any other European nation, live in the enjoyment of present pleasures, since owing to their mild and fertile climate their needs are simpler and they can earn their living more easily. All their vices and virtues are the natural consequences of their fiery sensuality. He hotly disputes the assertion that so many of the inhabitants of Naples do not work. A child must start earning there, he says, at the age of five; but of course it is neither necessary nor possible for them to spend the whole of each day working, as we do. In Rome there is no debauchery with unmarried women but it is all the more customary with the married ones. In Naples it is the other way round. In general there is, he says, something very noticeably Oriental about the way they behave to the opposite sex there. Rome, he thinks, is not a town that commends itself to foreigners unless one stays there for some time. The cost of living in Italy is no higher and perhaps a little lower than in Switzerland. The filth, for foreigners, is very nearly unendurable.

I should like to tell you further details from his account, but I shall have to wait until I happen to remember them. On the whole my considerable admiration for him has not been diminished by this personal meeting; but I doubt if we shall ever get very close to each other. His whole nature is from the start very different from mine, his world is not my world, our ways of thinking seem essentially dissimilar. However, one cannot draw firm and well-founded conclusions from an encounter of this kind. Time will give the answer.

29. *Caroline Herder to her husband*   *March 1789*

Goethe told me in confidence the real meaning of *Tasso*. It is the disproportion between talent and living.

30. *L. Ch. Althof*   *June 1789*

Bürger and Goethe had never met, but they had at one time exchanged a number of letters. Goethe had initiated this correspondence, and being carried away with love and admiration for his brother in Apollo, had soon ceased to address the latter as *Sie* and begun writing *Du*. Bürger reciprocated this familiar approach. Goethe kept up the tone he had taken, and thus the pair of them became official intimates by letter. When Goethe subsequently rose to a position of higher worldly dignity, the style of his letters to Bürger likewise became more ceremonious; the *Du* changed back to *Sie*, and soon the correspondence came to an end altogether. In 1789, Bürger sent Herr von Goethe a copy of the second edition of his poems with a polite note, and soon after this made a journey which took him through Weimar. He debated with himself whether he should presume to visit Herr von Goethe, for he was gauche by nature and what he had heard from other people had not made him particularly confident of a warm welcome from his sometime crony. However, his friends encouragingly assured him that Herr von Goethe had become more affable since his journey to Italy; moreover on this particular occasion he was expecting some small word of thanks from Goethe for the gift of his poems and perhaps even some instructive criticism of these latest products; and so he screwed up his courage and betook himself one afternoon to the Minister's residence. Here he was informed by the manservant that his Excellency was, indeed, at home, but that Herr Reichardt, the conductor, was with him and they were just about to try out a new composition by the latter. "Oh, good!" thinks Bürger, "I have come at a very opportune moment after all; I shall not be interrupting his Excellency in State business, and perhaps I shall even be able to give my opinion on the music." So he asks the servant to announce to his Excellency that Bürger from Göttingen desires to pay his respects. The servant announced him, returned, and led him, not into the room in which the music was being played, but into an empty reception-room. And here, after a few minutes, Herr von Goethe appeared, responded to Bürger's greeting with a condescending bow, motioned him to take a seat on a sofa, and amid the increasing embarrassment of Bürger, who had expected a very different sort of welcome, enquired—how many students were at present attending the University of Göttingen? Bürger answered as best he could in his discomfiture and very soon stood up again to take his leave. Goethe remained standing in the middle of the room and dismissed Bürger with a gracious bow.

31.   Baron F. von Schuckmann   *17.8.1790*

The reason why it is hard to get to know Goethe more closely
is not any lack of good will on his part, but his very individual
nature; it lies in the difficulty of language which he encounters
when he tries to express his feelings and ideas just as they are; in
their underlying intention and in the emotional significance which
this necessarily gives to them. Until he knows that one divines
and senses his meaning and is looking in through every opening
he offers, he cannot talk. There are some men, and he is among
them, who would certainly be better and more fluent speakers
if they had coarser natures; for glib formulae will only accommodate trite thoughts.

32.   Baron F. von Schuckmann   *Aug.–Sept. 1790*

I have got to know Goethe very closely and intimately, and
have discovered what an excellent man he is. The difficulties of
expression about which I wrote to you were entirely dispelled as
soon as his warmth increased and he had set aside convention
in his dealings with me. It is not really natural to him to talk
coldly, and he tries to force himself to do so with strangers, for
which I dare say he has very good reasons. When on more
intimate terms with someone he follows his nature and casts up
ideas wholesale from his rich store. I am inclined to say that he
speaks as an algebraist reckons, not with figures but with quan-
tities; and his vivid expositions are never mere whimsical fancies,
on the contrary his images are always the true equivalent given
by nature to the object, and they lead the listener to it and not
away from it. This is now, a week after his departure from
Breslau, my unbiased opinion of his personality, uninfluenced by
the affection I have begun to feel for him. Needless to say, everyone else here thinks that he expresses himself oddly, that he is
unintelligible, and that he is intolerably pretentious.

33.   F. Schiller   *31.10.1790*

Goethe was with us yesterday, and the conversation soon
turned to Kant. It is interesting to see how he gives his own
personal colouring to everything he has read and how surprising
his reproductions of it are; nevertheless I should not care to
argue with him about matters which I have very much at heart.

He quite lacks the capacity to commit himself warmly to anything. To him the whole of philosophy is a matter of subjective
taste, and this of course makes both conviction and argument
impossible. I also do not altogether like his philosophy: it relies
too much on the world of sense-perceptions, whereas I rely on
the mind. In general I find his way of thinking too sensuous, it is
as if he were touching too many things with his hands. But his
mind is actively inquiring in all directions and striving to build
up a total view—and for me that is what makes him a great
man.

34. A Prussian artillery-officer   August 1792

During the French campaign I had already heard it said that
this Goethe was a very famous writer. When I was first told that
I must now be a good deal in this man's company and share the
same quarters, since I too was attached by my orders to the suite
of the Duke of Saxe-Weimar, I began by feeling some aversion
to the prospect. I had always supposed that these gentlemen
who wrote poetry were merely some kind of physical and moral
degenerates. But how surprised I was when I first met this Herr
Goethe in person! He was an uncommonly handsome, dignified,
most elegantly dressed man in the prime of life, with such a
gentlemanly bearing that one might really have taken him for a
prince rather than a middle-class official. There was great self-
confidence in his whole bearing, and the words flowed so finely
and readily from his lips that his listeners constantly had the
impression of hearing someone read aloud from a printed book.
And to be sure, he was also over-fond of hearing himself talk,
and sometimes made speeches, very fine-sounding but in fact
devoid of any real content, about matters which he could not
possibly understand. I still remember how on one occasion, at
the Duke of Weimar's dinner-table, he delivered a long lecture
on the science of artillery and in particular on the most effective
positioning of batteries, even trying to give advice to us artillery-
officers on this matter. I really did feel some justified annoyance
at this, and I said: "My dear Herr Legationsrat!" (for that was
his title at the time) "with all due respect, may I take the liberty
of replying to you with Pomeranian frankness? In our country
there is an old proverb: Cobbler, stick to your last! When you
talk about the theatre and literature and many other learned or
artistic matters, we are all delighted to listen to you; for you

understand these things thoroughly and can teach us a great deal about them. But it is quite another matter when you begin talking about gunnery and even trying to instruct us officers in it; for if you will excuse my saying so, this is something about which you know absolutely nothing. Your views on how guns should be used were completely mistaken, and if an officer were to follow your advice in setting up a battery, it would be totally ineffective and he would certainly make a fool of himself." Such was my frank and audacious speech; it at first struck most of those present into a kind of startled silence, and several of them even stared at me aghast that I should have spoken my mind so bluntly to so famous a man as Goethe then already was. Goethe himself at first turned quite red in the face at my words, whether with anger or with embarrassment I do not know, and his fine glittering eyes stared fixedly at me; but he soon regained his full presence of mind and said with a laugh : "Well, you gentlemen from Pomerania certainly believe in frankness, one might almost say in rudeness, as I have just heard for myself all too clearly. But let's not quarrel about it, my dear Lieutenant! You have just taught me a very downright lesson, and I shall take good care not to talk about gunnery in your presence again or try to teach officers their own business." So saying, he shook me very cordially by the hand, and we remained the best of friends; indeed, it even seemed to me that Goethe now sought my company still more than he had previously done.

35.   F. Schiller   24.7.1794

Goethe is now at last admitting me to his confidence. Six weeks ago we had a lengthy discussion about art and the theory of art, and told each other our main ideas, at which we had arrived by quite different paths. It turned out that in these ideas we were unexpectedly in agreement with each other, and this agreement was all the more interesting for having really developed out of a total difference of viewpoint. Each of us was able to give the other something he lacked, and to get something in return. Since then, these scattered ideas have taken root in Goethe, and he now feels a need to ally himself with me and to pursue in my company the path he has hitherto trodden alone and without any encouragement.

36. F. Hölderlin   November 1794

I have visited Schiller several times too. The first occasion was
not a very lucky one. I entered and was kindly greeted; in the
background was a stranger whom I hardly noticed; nothing in
his expression, and for a long time nothing that he said, gave
any hint of anything out of the ordinary about him. Schiller
introduced me to him, and also introduced him to me, but I did
not catch his name. Coldly, with scarcely a glance, I greeted
him, and remained inwardly and outwardly preoccupied with
no one but Schiller. For a long time the stranger was silent.
Schiller brought the *Thalia*, in which a fragment of my novel
and my *Ode to Destiny* are printed, and gave it to me. As
Schiller moved away from me a moment later, the stranger,
remaining beside me, took the periodical from the table by
which I was standing, and turned over the pages of my
Hyperion-fragment without uttering a word. I felt myself turning scarlet. Had I known what I know now, I should have turned
as pale as death. He then turned to me, asked after Frau von
Kalb and where our village was and what sort of neighbours we
had, and I answered all this in monosyllables, which I dare say
is quite unusual for me. But to be sure, this was my unlucky
hour! Schiller came back and we talked about the Weimar
theatre; the stranger let fall a few words which were significant
enough to give me some inkling of the truth—but I had none.
The painter Meyer from Weimar came up too, and the stranger
discussed various things with him; but I suspected nothing! I
left, and on the very same day, what do you think? I was told
that Goethe had been at Schiller's house that afternoon.

37. K. A. Böttiger   28.5.1795

We discussed dreams. Goethe agrees that dreamless sleep is
the most refreshing kind. Goethe told us a very subtle, philosophical dream which he had had the previous night.

38. Jean Paul (Friedrich Richter)   17.6.1796

I visited Goethe with trepidation. Charlotte Ostheim and
everyone else described him as completely lacking in warmth towards anyone or anything on earth. Charlotte said: "He no
longer admires anything, not even himself". According to her
every word he speaks is as cold as ice, especially to strangers,

whom he seldom admits; and he is as stiff and proud as one of our Imperial Free Cities—only works of art still warm the cockles of his heart. I accordingly requested Knebel to dip me first in a mineral well, so that I should be petrified and incrusted, and appear before him in a perhaps more advantageous light as a statue. I went along quite devoid of feeling, merely from curiosity. His house is striking : the only one in Weimar in the Italian style, with stairs to match, and a whole pantheon of pictures and statues. A chill of apprehension constricts the heart —and at last the god approaches : cold, monosyllabic, speaking without emphasis. Knebel for example remarks : "The French are marching into Rome". "Hm !" says the god. His figure is stalwart and energetic, his eyes luminous (but unattractive in colour). Finally, however, he was fired both by the champagne and by all the talk about art, the public and so forth, and—our host became Goethe. His speech is not so efflorescent and fluent as Herder's, but clear and incisive and calm. In the end he read us, or rather performed for us, a magnificent unpublished poem, and here his heart burned its way through the ice. His reading aloud is like a rather deep-rolling thunder, mingled with a light whisper of rain; there is nothing quite like it.

39. *Caroline von Wolzogen*   *September 1796*

It moves me to remember how Goethe read aloud to us, just after he had written it, the canto of *Hermann und Dorothea* which contains Herman's conversation with his mother by the pear-tree : he was in a state of deep emotion, and tears ran down his cheeks. "You see how one can be melted by one's own fire", he said, drying his eyes.

40. *J. D. Falk*   *December 1796*

Recently, in the club, Wieland worked himself up into a charmingly comical, half serious state of indignation about the quantity of tea which young people drink, despite (as he said) its obviously debilitating effects.

GOETHE (rocking to and fro in front of the stove, with his coat-tails lifted and his chest puffed out) : "You are wrong there, my old friend; tea fortifies."

WIELAND : "Another paradox !"

GOETHE : "Oh, I have proofs for it enough and to spare."

WIELAND: "To begin even with my weakest argument—"

GOETHE: "Don't do that, my old friend; don't do that, for God's sake! Always the strongest ones first! I'm armed to the teeth."

WIELAND: "Well, to begin with, for all your sophistry you cannot deny the deleterious nature of herbal infusions, or that warm water—"

GOETHE: "So tea, you say, is a debilitating drink?"

WIELAND: "Yes, but I—"

GOETHE: "Well, I say it is a fortifying drink."

WIELAND: "Not debilitating?"

GOETHE: "Fortifying and debilitating."

WIELAND: "Fortifying and debilitating?"

GOETHE: "Like all stimulants if taken too often; too fortifying."

WIELAND: "But the poison it contains."

GOETHE: "There's no such thing as poison."

WIELAND: "A new paradox?"

GOETHE: "It all depends on the dose. Even champagne can become a poison."

WIELAND: "I suppose the sophist will even end by asserting that there is no such thing as death."

GOETHE: "Well, well, let's not go into that."

WIELAND (making for the door): "This is too crazy!"

GOETHE (calling after him): "Run along, my dear fellow! or I'll challenge you on our immortality, and you will have lost."

41. L. Tieck (reported)   December 1799

Tieck told Goethe how he was studying Shakespeare and his contemporaries. This led him to mention Ben Jonson, and to describe how consistently he differed from Shakespeare. He ended by asking Goethe if he would not like to give this curious writer a trial. When Goethe readily consented, he suggested *Volpone* and brought him the folio edition. When he called on him some time later, Goethe had just finished perusing the recommended drama. He had the volume still in front of him and was in excellent humour. "Let me tell you, my dear friend", he exclaimed, smacking the cover of the book with his hand, "this fellow is a genius, by God, devil take me if he isn't!" Tieck said how glad he was to find that his advice had been sound. "Yes, damn it, what a fellow!" Goethe went on, repeating the same gesture, "what confoundedly clever ideas he has!" On being asked whether he would like to read a few more of Jonson's works to get to know him properly, he dismissed the suggestion with the words: "No, my dear friend, I've had enough! No more! I know him now, and that will suffice!"

42. *F. Schlegel* *September 1800*

Goethe behaved to the sickly, often moody Schiller like a tender lover, deferred to him in everything, indulged him, and had his tragedies produced. But occasionally Goethe's robust nature asserted itself, and once, when they had just been discussing *Maria Stuart* at Schiller's house, Goethe exclaimed on the way home: "I just wonder how the audience will react when* those two whores meet and start casting their amorous adventures in each other's teeth".

43. *Riemer* *1803*

"It becomes increasingly clear to me that every man ought simply to ply his trade conscientiously and take nothing else seriously at all. A few lines of poetry that I have to write interest me far more than many more important things over which I have no control; and if everyone does likewise we shall be living in a well-ordered community."

44. *Amalie von Helvig* *December 1803*

Goethe was just as eager to make Madame de Staël's acquaintance as she was to make his. After the meeting Goethe reported to his friends: "It was an interesting hour. I was unable to get a word in; she talks well, but at length, at great length."— Meanwhile a circle of ladies demanded to know what impression our Apollo had made on his visitor. She too confessed that she had failed to get in a word. "But" (she is said to have remarked with a sigh) "when anyone talks so well, it is a pleasure to listen to him." Who talked? Who listened?

45. *H. Voss* *26.1.1804*

Goethe rejected the distinction, of which everyone talks nowadays, between "romantic" and "classical", declaring that any

* Act III Sc. 4 (the meeting between the two queens, Mary and Elizabeth).

outstanding work of literature, of any genre, is eo ipso classical.
He would be more inclined, he said, to recognise a distinction
between "romantic" and "plastic" : a plastic work is one which
presents itself to the imagination of the beholder in a sharply
defined and finished form, whereas a romantic work hints vaguely
at many things and leaves the reader's own fancy room for free
play. The former kind is for the disciplined imagination, the
latter appeals to ungoverned and often chaotic fantasy.

46. Riemer   February 1804

Madame de Staël had put herself in the wrong with him from
the start by assuring him with extreme naïvety that she would
have every word he spoke to her printed once she had got hold
of it. Thus I still remember to this day that on one occasion,
when the lady was visiting Goethe, I heard the two of them
talking, in a room immediately beneath mine, at the tops of their
voices, vehemently, almost passionately : she in particular uttering such shrill and outraged cries that I feared she was about
to burst straight up through the thin ceiling and sail away
through the roof like an offended fairy. And indeed Goethe
assured me afterwards that he had argued her into such straits
that this did seem to be just what she was going to do. They did,
however, have some pleasant and friendly interviews as well.

47. K. A. Böttiger   Jan.–Feb. 1804

In her metrical translation of Goethe's ballad Der Fischer,
Madame de Staël had rendered the last word of the passage Was
lockst du meine Brut hinauf in Todesglut?* by "air brûlant";
but when she read her translation to Goethe he corrected her
and said that this meant the glowing coals in the kitchen where
the fish were fried. Madame de Staël thought it exceedingly
maussade and in bad taste that she should thus be suddenly sent
to the kitchen in the midst of her fine frenzy; she remarked that
this is precisely what our best writers lack—the τὸ πρῶτον, a
refined sense of propriety. In this she showed herself to be a true
Frenchwoman.

* Literally: "Why do you lure my young ones up into the glow of
death?"

48. H. Voss

On another occasion our table-talk took a philistine turn, and we discussed beef, potatoes, marzipan and celery; even Christiane Vulpius joined in. Goethe angrily attacked the Weimar butchers, these put him in mind of the tailors, whom he accused of equalling the butchers in incompetence (imitatorum servum pecus), and from the tailors he passed to the bookbinders. "One of these days", he said, "I shall have all these damned miserable wretches up before me and haul them over the coals; I'll put some spirit of ambition into them..." and so forth.

49. B. Constant

Very interesting supper with Goethe. He is very clever, full of sallies, profundities, and new ideas. But he is the least good-natured man I have ever met. Speaking of *Werther*, he said to me: "What makes that work dangerous is that it portrayed weakness as if it were strength. However, when I make something the way it suits me, the consequences are not my affair. If there are fools who take harm from reading it, then, damn it, so much the worse for them!"

50. H. Voss

There is no subject that escapes Goethe's attention; he infuses intelligence and life into everything, and even when he is talking of remote matters he still has recourse to the changing objects around him and clothes his thoughts in them. He never uses any metaphor that is not taken directly from what he happens to see in front of him, and one is often amazed at his ability to turn such poor material into something so splendid and exalting. Then, as his imagination takes fire, his step will quicken; or when he fixes his attention on something in order to grasp its very essence, he will even stand quite still, thrusting one foot in front of the other and leaning backwards. To sit right opposite him at table and look into his deep glowing eyes is a real joy. His features, for all their majesty, are full of such kindness and benevolence. But he is never more delightful and charming than in the evening in his room, when he has changed out of his formal clothes and is either standing with his back to the stove or sitting on the sofa. Then indeed it is impossible not to surrender to him entirely. Perhaps it is the stillness, the quiet of evening, the sense of relaxation after often laborious work: but whatever it is, that is when he is at his happiest and most talkative, that is when he really opens his heart. Yes, indeed, Goethe can be friendliness itself. And at such times his often terrifying gaze loses all its awe-inspiring quality.

51. *H. Voss*   1804

I must tell you another anecdote about Goethe which has again infinitely endeared him to me. During my second visit to his house it so happened that the diploma for my doctorate was issued in Jena and sent to Goethe to be handed over to me. He kept it a secret from me, and sent August out to Belvedere to fetch a garland of laurel and lemon twigs. At table I still knew nothing about it. At the end of the meal, Goethe said to Christiane Vulpius: "My dear! I think Voss is still looking rather hungry; we really should not be so inhospitable as not to give our friends enough to eat". I excused myself in the same light-hearted tone, assuring him that my appetite was completely satisfied. It was no good; August had to go out and fetch the dessert. He returned with an enormous dish which he placed on my head; I then had to promise to eat a little more at least, and the dish was set down before me. Imagine my astonishment! I stared at Goethe and could find no words. Then he and August and Christiane all congratulated me very warmly on my new dignity; Goethe embraced me and called me, for the first time, his "dear son", a flattering form of address which he has often repeated since. His spirits then rose immediately, and he said to Christiane: "It's our duty to drink the new Doctor's health in champagne". She had to go down to the cellar and fetch the exquisite stuff; we had drunk a bottle and a half already, but now we must needs down this divine nectar on top of it. We emptied the bottles to the last drop. During this operation they kept calling me Doctor, despite my protests. The champagne took effect, and I became not merely happy, I became ecstatic. I have never been able to express my thanks to Goethe as I would have wished—hitherto I had never even tried; but now I succeeded. When we rose, my head was rather heavier than usual, and perhaps Goethe's was too; for he was in a very good mood indeed. We went for a walk together for another two hours, and in the park Goethe gave me a lecture on natural history.

52. H. Voss   *May 1805*

When Schiller had died, there was general concern about how the news should be broken to Goethe. No one had the courage to tell him. Meyer was with him when the news reached the house that Schiller was dead. They called Meyer out of the room, and he did not have the courage to go back, but left without saying goodbye. Goethe found himself isolated, he sensed confusion all round him, he could not help noticing that everyone was trying to avoid him—and all this was scarcely calculated to raise his hopes. In the end he said: "I see. Schiller must be very ill". And he withdrew into himself for the rest of the evening. He had an inkling of what had happened; he was heard weeping in the night. Next morning he said to Christiane: "I believe Schiller was *very* ill yesterday?" The way he emphasised the "very" so upset her that she could contain herself no longer and burst into loud sobs instead of answering. "He's dead?" asked Goethe in a steady voice. She replied: "You know it yourself now". "He's dead!" repeated Goethe again; and he put his hands over his eyes and wept without uttering a syllable. At ten o'clock I saw him walking in the park, but could not face meeting him. He spent the day in gentle abandonment to his sorrow, and I was told that by the evening he had already regained his composure. I avoided him for three days; on the fourth I watched for a time when he had gone to the library. I followed him, wished him good morning and began enquiring about a dozen or so library matters; as I spoke, my thoughts were as far from what I was saying as Goethe's were from his answers, which he delivered with visible absence of mind but an air of great conscientiousness. Later, as I heard, he remarked that he had been grateful to me for not saying a word about Schiller, for he would scarcely have been capable of replying without distress. Goethe now very rarely mentions Schiller, and when he does so, it is to allude to the happier aspects of their great companionship.

58. H. Meyer   *21.3.1806*

Goethe declared that he had never given any prolonged and serious thought to literary theory, and that none of his poetical works had ever been the product of a clear understanding of what should and must be done, but merely of a feeling, an intuition not susceptible of further rational analysis, that such and such would be right. In the sphere of the visual arts on the other hand, although he had produced little, he had thought a great deal about the theory of them : they had, he believed, served him as a kind of symbolic substitute for literature, and reflection in the field of visual art had been extremely useful to him in his own field of literary creation.

54. H. Luden   10.8.1806

I can still remember more than one anecdote that Goethe told at Frau von Knebel's house; but I dare not try to repeat them. I should at least have to leave out what gave them their greatest charm and piquancy, namely Goethe's eyes, his voice, and his gestures; for they were not mere narratives, they were mimic performances. He would revert with particular frequency to the subject of two old countesses whom he had recently met while staying at Carlsbad. They were, he said, ladies of enormous girth, and had accordingly, when once seated, displayed a remarkable reluctance to move. For all that, they had retained great nimbleness of tongue and were capable of infinite discourse. Their voices were girlish and pure, but at times of animation or when they judged it necessary to stand on their dignity, these dulcet tones would be transformed into an engaging screech or an alluring twitter. "I myself", said Goethe, "found the strange spherical shapes of these ladies the most notable thing about them. It passed my comprehension how any human being, whether man or woman, could succeed in growing to so massive a size; nor should I have supposed that the human skin possessed such limitless extensibility. No sooner, however, did I have the honour of taking a meal with these noble ladies, than all became clear. I rather think it may be said that the rest of us also have some talent for eating and drinking, and that we are giving positive proof of it to our excellent hostess; but I confess that such eating as theirs—to say nothing of the way they drank—transcended all that I could have imagined to be possible. For example, each of the two ladies ate six hard-boiled eggs with her spinach : she cut each egg through the middle and tossed the half egg down with the ease of an ostrich swallowing half a horseshoe." In addition, Goethe retailed for our benefit a number of remarks by these noble ladies about their experiences of the physiological effects of the Carlsbad waters, or about

current affairs and local society, and some occasional observations on literature and the arts which were magnificent in their
naïve quaintness and baroque absurdity. But he then added in
all seriousness that there was much truth in these remarks and
observations and that the two ladies had taught him a great deal.

I can report one other anecdote which we found particularly
delightful in the way he told it. I shall give it in Goethe's own
words; the style of their delivery must of course be left to the
reader's imagination.

"While walking to and fro as is my custom, I had for the last
few days frequently passed an old gentleman of about seventy-
eight or eighty who walked up and down the same street as
myself, leaning on a gold-mounted walking-stick. I was told that
he was a retired, highly distinguished Austrian general who belonged to an ancient and very noble family. I had several times
noticed the old man giving me a sharp glance, even stopping to
stare round at me when I had passed. This, however, did not
strike me particularly, as it is the kind of thing that has happened to me before. But on one occasion I paused in the course
of my walk to look more closely at something or other, and now
the old man approached me in a friendly manner, raised his hat
slightly, a greeting which I of course returned, and addressed me
as follows : 'Your name's Goethe, isn't it?' 'It is.' 'From Weimar?' 'Quite so.' 'Written some books, haven't you?' 'Oh,
indeed.' 'Poetry too?' 'Poetry too.' 'They tell me it's good stuff.'
'Hm !' 'You written a lot, then?' 'Hm ! A certain amount.' 'Is
writin' poetry a difficult job?' 'Oh, so so.' 'Depends on the mood
you're in, I fancy; better after a good dinner and a good few
drinks, what?' 'I'm almost inclined to think so, certainly—'
'Well now, look here ! You ought not to stick in a hole like
Weimar, you ought to come to Vienna.' 'Indeed, that has sometimes occurred to me.' 'Well then ! it's a good life in Vienna,
you know; good food, excellent wine.' 'Hm !' 'And we think
well there of you chaps who can write poetry.' 'Hm !' 'Yes, it
can even happen that chaps like you—so long as they're gentlemen, of course, and know how to behave—can get into society,
meet the very best people and all that.' 'Hm !' 'You just come
along; send your name in to me; I've got family connections,
influence, friends at court; just write "Goethe from Weimar.
Acquaintance made at Carlsbad." You must add that second
bit, because I can never remember where I met people—got so
much to think about, y'know.' 'I shall make a point of it.' 'But

now tell me, sir : what sort of things have you written?' 'Oh, all sorts; every subject from Adam to Napoleon, Ararat to the Blocksberg, cedars of Lebanon to bramble bushes.' 'They tell me your stuff's pretty well known.' 'Hm! Moderately well.' 'Pity I haven't read a word of it. Never heard of you before the other day, I'm afraid. I suppose you've already brought out new revised editions of your works?' 'Oh, yes, indeed.' 'And I dare say there'll be further editions to come?' 'Let us hope so.' 'In that case, sir, I shan't buy your works. Fact is, I only buy final editions; otherwise one has a book which is all wrong, and that's damned annoying, or else one has to buy the same book twice. So to be on the safe side I always wait till authors are dead before I buy 'em. I make this a matter of principle. Can't depart from my principles even in your case, you know.' 'Hm!'"

55. H. Luden   19.8.1806

"A poet must not be his own interpreter, he should not analyse his poetry neatly into everyday prose: in so doing he would cease to be a poet. The poet puts his work out into the world: it is the business of the reader or aesthetic theorist or critic to enquire what his intentions were in creating it.

"In poetry there are no contradictions. These exist only in the real world, not in the world of literature. What the poet creates must be accepted as he created it. His world is as he made it and not otherwise. And what the mind of a poet has produced must be received by a poetic spirit. Cold analysis destroys poetry, and cannot give us reality. It leaves us with mere broken fragments, which serve no purpose and are merely an embarrassment."

56. A. Oehlenschläger   October 1806

During the battle of Jena Goethe married Fräulein Vulpius, and this made not the slightest difference to anything, except that her name was now Frau Geheimrat von Goethe. She had absolutely no appreciation of poetry, and Goethe himself once said jokingly : "How odd it is, the poor little thing can never understand a single word of a poem". The newly-wedded wife was always most respectful to her husband and invariably called him "Herr Geheimrat". We did so too. When I began by calling him "Excellency" he said good-humouredly: "'Geheimrat' will do". And in Germany this title sounds very bourgeois. Frau

Goethe had a quick and lively nature, and did not think much of the quiet life her husband led. "The Herr Geheimrat and I", she is said to have remarked on one occasion, "do nothing but sit and look at each other. It gets boring in the end."

57. *J. A. Ludecus* 20.10.1806

The friends and colleagues who visited his house daily were rather surprised when soon after his marriage to Christiane Vulpius he introduced her to them with the words: "She has always been my wife".

58. *Caroline von Wolzogen* *November 1806*

Goethe confided to me that it embarrassed him that we so seldom visited his house, since after all we were his oldest and dearest friends. It was plain that he wished to introduce his wife into good society; I told him that we should certainly receive her with kindness as his wife if she visited us. "She is a foolish little thing", he said. "She can't write, and can scarcely read; but, as you may suppose, having associated with her for so long one is bound to have influenced her a little."

59. *Riemer* 7.11.1806

"Nowadays books are not written to be read, to impart information and instruction; they are written to be reviewed, and can then be talked about and have opinions delivered on them ad infinitum.

"Since books began to be reviewed, they are no longer read by anyone except the reviewer, and he only half reads them. But on the other hand hardly any writer these days ever has anything to say and to communicate that is a new and personal and original contribution to knowledge, thought out and worked out by himself with love and care; so books now get the treatment they deserve."

60. *Riemer* *(?) November 1806*

"A man's good resolutions, his principles which nature overthrows again and again, are like cleaning and sweeping and dusting for Sundays and feast-days and special occasions. One keeps on getting dirty again, of course, but it is still a good thing that these partial cleansing operations should make it possible to be clean at all."

61. *Johanna Schopenhauer*   27.11.1806

Goethe feels very much at ease in my house and often visits me. I have put a special table with drawing materials for him in a corner: so when he feels like it he sits down and makes little ink drawings of landscapes out of his head, quite spontaneous, mere sketches, but full of life and truth, like himself and everything he does. What an extraordinary being this Goethe is! How great and how good! As I never know whether he is coming, I am startled every time he steps into the room; it is as if he were of a higher nature than everyone else; for I see plainly that he makes the same impression on all the others, who after all have known him much longer and many of them much more intimately than I do. He himself, when he arrives, is always a little tongue-tied and somehow embarrassed, until he has had a good look at the company to see who is there. Then he always sits down close beside me, a little behind me so that he can lean on the back of my chair; I start a conversation, and then he comes to life and is indescribably charming. He is the most perfect being I know, in outward appearance as well: a fine tall figure holding himself very straight, most carefully dressed, always in black or very dark blue, with his hair most tastefully dressed and powdered, as befits his age; and a really magnificent face with two clear brown eyes which are both gentle and penetrating. When he talks he becomes unbelievably more handsome, and I simply cannot look my fill at him. He takes part in every sort of conversation, constantly putting in little anecdotes, and never oppressing anyone by his greatness. He is as unaffected as a child; he inspires complete trust as soon as he speaks to anyone, and yet he impresses everyone without wishing to do so. Recently, as the custom is in Hamburg, I took his cup over to him so that it should not get cold, and he kissed my hand. Everyone standing nearby was astonished. And indeed, he looks so royal that the commonest courtesy appears in him as a condescension, and he himself seems quite unaware of this, but simply moves on his way in silent glory like the sun.

62. *K. L. von Knebel* 1776/1806

Goethe condemns smoking and snuff-taking. "Smoking stulti-fies", he says. "It makes a man incapable of thinking or writing. Moreover it is only a pastime for lazy, bored people who sleep through one-third of their life, fritter away the next with eating and drinking and other necessary or superfluous activities, and then have no idea what to do with the remaining third, although they are always talking about life being too short. These idle Turks love the company of their pipes and the comfortable spec-tacle of the clouds of smoke they puff into the air; this is the intellectual entertainment that gets them through the hours. And hand in hand with smoking goes beer-drinking, to cool the heated palate down again. Beer thickens the blood and simul-taneously increases the stupefying effect of the tobacco smoke. Thus the nerves are dulled and the blood grows so sluggish that it practically stops circulating. If things continue as they look like doing, it will only be two or three generations before we see what these beer-bellies and weedy willies have made of Ger-many. It will show itself first in the stunted poverty-stricken philistinism of our literature, and yet it will be these very gentle-men who will praise this babbling vacuity to the skies. And just think what the atrocious stuff costs! Even now, in Germany, twenty-five million talers go up in tobacco smoke, and this total may rise to forty or fifty or sixty million. And not one of the hungry fed nor one of the naked clothed. To think what one could do with that money! But what is more, smoking is the most appalling bad manners, an anti-social impertinence. Smokers contaminate the air and asphyxiate every decent man who can't smoke in self-defence. How can anyone enter the room of a smoker and not feel sick? How can anyone stay there without dropping dead?" Goethe is quite right in all these complaints, but he is wrong about snuff-taking. What is more, he is unable to produce any reasoned case against snuff-taking. "It is a piece of piggishness", he says.

63. *Riemer* 24.12.1806

Goethe said he would like one day to devise a plot dealing with the problem of whether a useful error, a useful lie, is pre-ferable to a harmful truth. I am to remind him of this, not-withstanding that he has already treated this subject in his

Iphigenio. Whereas Orestes and Pylades try to gain their end by
lies and deceit, Iphigenia seeks to achieve it in her own way, by
telling the truth.

64. *Riemer* *January 1807*

"Above all, one must not turn any activity into a trade. That
I loathe. Everything I can do I want to do as a game, just what
and when I like and for so long as it still gives me pleasure. I
played this game unwittingly in my youth; and now I intend to
go on doing so consciously for the rest of my life. To what purpose? For whose benefit? That is your business. You make use
of me; but I cannot think of myself in terms of sale or demand.
You will use my abilities and knowledge as soon as you want to
and need to. I refuse to be turned into an instrument; and every
trade is an instrument."

65. *Baron von Czettritz-Neuhaus*

At a small supper to which I had been invited, Goethe arrived
late, and the Duke called out to him: "Why so late?—But
something unusual must have happened to you today, I can see
it in your face..." Whereupon Goethe told the following story.

A rich bourgeoise from Berlin, who was an enthusiastic admirer of Goethe, decided to undertake the journey to Weimar,
which at that time was lengthy and by bad roads, in order to see
the great man and poet face to face. Arriving at last at her
destination, she sent in her name to Goethe and asked for an
audience, which was refused. Disconsolate and grief-stricken, she
hastened to Goethe's intimate friend Geheimrat von Müller—
how she had become acquainted with him Goethe's narrative
did not mention—and begged him to intercede for her. To this
he consented, and eventually talked the poet round to the point
of saying: "Tell your client that I will receive her tomorrow
morning at eleven". Late that evening the supplicant was given
this joyful news, which caused her a sleepless night, and early
next morning she put on her full finery and impatiently watched
the snail-like crawling of the hands of the town clock. At last
they pointed to a quarter to eleven, and she sped to the great
man's residence, where a servant received her and conducted
her to the reception room. In extreme excitement the good lady
paced up and down the salon, until at last the object of her

passion appeared, whereupon she rushed up to him, fell on her knees, and dramatically declaimed:

> *"Firm its walls with earth surrounded*
> *Stands the house of well-fired clay!"**

Goethe replied: "I am glad to see that you respect my friend Schiller!"—and left the room.

66. *Riemer* 3.2.1807

"Extraordinary men, such as Napoleon, place themselves outside morality. They act, after all, like physical causes such as fire and water. Indeed anyone who steps out of the position of subordination—for that is what morality is—becomes to that extent immoral. Whoever by the use of his intelligence injures others, or even so much as restricts their freedom, is to that extent immoral. Every virtue exerts compulsion, just as every idea acts like a tyrant when it first enters the world."

67. *Riemer* 19.3.1807

"Whatever Nature undertakes, she can only accomplish it in a sequence. She never makes a leap. For example she could not produce a horse if it were not preceded by all the other animals on which she ascends to the horse's structure as if on the rungs of a ladder. Thus every one thing exists for the sake of all things and all for the sake of one; for the one is of course the all as well. Nature, despite her seeming diversity, is always a unity, a whole; and thus, when she manifests herself in any part of that whole, the rest must serve as a basis for that particular manifestation, and the latter must have a relationship to the rest of the system."

68. *Riemer* 24.3.1807

"The formula of refinement [Steigerung] can be applied in the aesthetic and moral spheres as well.

"Love, as a phenomenon of the modern world, is a refined product. It is no longer the prime simple natural necessity and expression of nature, but something distilled and concentrated, condensed into itself as it were, and thus refined.

* A misquotation of the opening lines of Schiller's well-known *Song of the Bell*.

"It is naïve to disapprove of this mode of experience merely because it also can and does still exist in its simple form.

"We look in our kitchens and cellars for refinements of our experience; that is their whole purpose. Why then should it not be permissible and possible to refine this particular pleasure too, whether in artistic portrayal or as an immediate emotion?

"Every cook uses this distilling, concentrating process to make his soups and sauces more appetising."

69. H. Luden   16/24.5.1807

After the battle of Jena I took occasion to ask how his Excellency had fared during these days of shame and disaster, and Goethe replied: "I have no reason to complain. It was rather like a man looking down from a solid cliff into the raging sea, unable to help the shipwrecked, but out of reach of the breakers, with feelings which are even described by some ancient writer or other as very agreeable. That is how I stood, quite unscathed, letting the tumult pass me by." I must confess that at these words, which were indeed spoken with a certain complacency, I felt something of a cold shudder pass through me.

70. Riemer   1807

"In mediaeval doctrine there was a complete dichotomy between nature and ideal value. The ideal was purely spiritual and Christian, and nature was thought to be the domain of magicians and gnomes, all subject to the Devil. The world belonged to the Devil; this was still even Luther's view."

71. Christine von Reinhard   July 1807

I have already told you of our daily meetings with Goethe and of how fascinating it has been for me to contemplate this extraordinary and universal genius. I say contemplate, for despite all his advances our relations, so far as I am concerned at least, have never been cordial. There is in him too little spontaneity, a lack of naturalness, and this does not inspire confidence: on the contrary, it makes it impossible to speak one's heart. It would be presumptuous of me to try to judge him and to claim to have understood this unique being. I shall attempt nevertheless to give an account of the impression that this brilliant mind has made upon me, but to do so properly one would need his gift of observation and his bold spirit. It has been rightly said that Goethe always avoids individuality, and that is why he has never moved my heart : he glides above human suffering like an inhabitant of another sphere. He never talks about himself, and I have never seen him take an interest in the joys or sorrows of others. One seldom elicits from him any sign of approval or of displeasure. When one tells him of the troubles and disappointments of persons known to him, he treats these reports as interesting items of news, and quotes similar cases. Nothing moves him. He lives within the circle of his ideas and his knowledge, an immense circle embracing all the sciences, and he makes child's play of the most abstract matters. He is a passionate student of botany, chemistry, mineralogy, astronomy; nothing is unfamiliar to him. His present warhorse is his theory of colours, and my husband's brief account of it shows that it begins as chemistry and ends as philosophy. Accustomed as he is to adulation, no homage surprises him. In the course of a conversation during which he had expressed himself with unusual ardour and vigour, Karl told him that although from time to time he had been on more or less intimate terms with various distinguished men, he had never encountered in any of them such a wealth of ideas, such harmony, such loftiness of feeling, in fact such all-round perfection as in Goethe. He admitted that he had some difficulty in following him, as his mind was constantly having to revert to what he had just heard him say, and that he often felt quite dazzled by the truth and audacity of his conceptions. This compliment did not appear to surprise the poet, who replied that one must indeed be accustomed to his way of speaking if one wished to understand him; that he himself, for this reason, had renounced conversation and now disdained to talk at all except with men of his own level, as my husband was and as Schiller had been. He then praised the latter, without showing the slightest trace of any spirit of rivalry or seeking to suggest any comparison.

Goethe, like many superior men, willingly contents himself with a rather low degree of intellect in women, and almost likes them better if they are commonplace than if they have a more refined intelligence. In his dealings with people he follows the impulse of the moment and can always think of some principle to justify his whims and all their consequences. But the high-minded heroines of his works are neither moving nor attractive, because the poet has only adorned them with so many virtues and created them so lovingly in order to seem to have improved upon the handiwork of the Creator.

A reading of his poems, given by himself, is a real joy to listen to. His voice is sonorous, powerful, and well-modulated. His ardent gaze, his expression, his gestures, are appropriate and impressive. He prefers to recite ballads and poems of action. He had warned us that his chosen subjects were usually portrayals of some situation which he found striking, rather than effusions of feeling or aspiration.

72.   *Christine von Reinhard*   *July 1807*

Goethe said to my husband: "I should very much like you to make the acquaintance of my wife. I owe you a description of her, and in the first place I must tell you that she has read not a single line of any of my works. The intellectual world simply does not exist for her. She is born to keep house. In this sphere she relieves me of all cares; this is her kingdom, the element in which she lives and moves. In addition she likes pretty clothes and company and enjoys going to the theatre. But she is by no means without a certain sort of culture which she has acquired by being with me and especially by going to plays. In fact it is incredible what an education the theatre can be if one goes to it every night for ten years or so. After all, it has everything: the characters and their acting teach the spectators something about society and art and morality, and the free expression of opinion makes it all the more interesting and lively for them. I have noticed this with my son as well."

73.   *Riemer*   *28.8.1808*

Goethe's birthday. In the evening he talked about ancient tragedy and romantic* literature. Ancient tragedy is the tragic action of humanity. Romantic literature is not a natural and original thing but artificial, recherché, heightened, exaggerated, bizarre, to the point of travesty and caricature. Rather like a fancy-dress ball, a masquerade, with bright harsh lights. It is humorous (that is to say, ironic, e.g. Ariosto, Cervantes; thus

* The term "romantic" (das Romantische) is here being used in a wide sense to mean modern (including mediaeval) literature generally.

bordering on the comic or actually comic) or it immediately becomes so as soon as intelligence takes a hand in it, otherwise it is absurd and fantastic. The ancients are still limited (probable, human); the moderns capricious, impossible. Magic and enchantment in the ancients has style, but not in the moderns. Magic in ancient literature is nature viewed humanly, with the moderns on the contrary it is a mere brain-figment and fantasy. The ancients are sober, modest, moderate; the moderns quite unbridled and drunken. In a work of ancient literature we seem to see only an idealised piece of reality, a reality treated with grandeur (i.e. style) and taste; in a romantic work, something non-existent, impossible, to which fantasy imparts a mere pseudo-existence.

Ancient literature is plastic, true, and real; romanticism is delusive, like the pictures cast by a magic lantern, like the coloured image from a prism, like atmospheric colours. This is because romantic treatment superimposes a strange and wonderful veneer on completely commonplace material, the veneer being everything and the material nothing. Romantic literature borders on the comic (Wieland's *Huon and Amanda* or *Oberon*), ancient literature on the serious and dignified. Romanticism, where it comes near to the ancients in grandeur, as in the mediaeval Nibelung epic, occasionally does have style, that is to say a certain grandeur of treatment, but it lacks taste. So-called romantic poetry particularly attracts our younger generation, because it appeals to caprice, to sensuality, to impatience of discipline; in short to the passions of youth.

74. *F. von Müller* 2.10.1808

Goethe's audience with Napoleon lasted almost a whole hour. I had accompanied him as far as the anteroom and waited there till he came out.

The Emperor was sitting at a large round table having breakfast, with Talleyrand standing on his right. He beckoned Goethe to come nearer, and after looking at him closely asked him how old he was. On learning that he was in his sixtieth year he expressed his astonishment to find him still looking so energetic, and passed immediately to the subject of Goethe's tragedies. He also assured him that he had read *The Sorrows of Werther* seven times and as evidence of this delivered an extremely penetrating analysis of the novel, claiming however that

he had observed certain passages which rather confusingly introduced the theme of thwarted ambition in the hero into the main
story of his passionate love. "That is not realistic", he said, "and
it weakens the reader's impression of the overpowering influence of love upon Werther. Why did you do that?"

Napoleon supported his point with further arguments which
Goethe found so cogent and discerning that when talking about
it to me later on he would often compare the Emperor's criticism
to the professional opinion of a skilled tailor who soon discovers
the cunningly concealed seam in an apparently seamless sleeve.

To the Emperor he replied that this criticism was quite new
to him, but that he must acknowledge it to be perfectly justified.

Reverting to the subject of drama, Napoleon said : "Tragedy
should be a school for rulers and their peoples; there is no
higher achievement for a poet than that. You, for instance,
ought to write a tragedy about the death of Caesar—one really
worthy of the subject, a greater one than Voltaire's. That could
be the finest task you ever undertook. You would have to show
the world how Caesar would have been its benefactor, how
everything would have turned out quite differently if he had
been given time to carry out his magnificent plans. You must
come to Paris; I absolutely insist on it. We have a larger view
of things there! You will find abundant material there to inspire your works."

Each time he came to the end of anything he was saying he
would add : "Qu'en dit Monsieur Goet?"

And when Goethe finally took his leave, the Emperor was
heard to remark meaningfully to those standing by him :
"Voilà un homme!"

For a long time Goethe kept everything that had been said
during this audience a close secret, either because of his general
characteristic reluctance to disclose important matters which
concerned him personally, or for reasons of modesty and delicacy. But it was very quickly apparent that Napoleon's remarks
had made a profound impression on him, although he contrived
discreetly to avoid answering even Karl August's questions as to
the content of the conversation. In particular the invitation to
Paris gave him much food for thought for a considerable time.
He more than once asked my opinion as to what would be the
approximate cost of accepting it, and what the various necessary
arrangements for him in Paris would be, how he should divide
his time there and so forth. I rather think that later reflection

on the many discomforts which a stay in Paris would inevitably involve must have caused him to abandon the idea.

It was only long afterwards that he informed me of the details of the interview little by little, but not until eight years before his death could I induce him to make his still very laconic written record of it.

75. Ch. M. de Talleyrand   2.10.1808

Napoleon would sit long over breakfast : this was the time at which he liked to receive guests and talk. I have known several of these breakfasts last for over two hours. It was to them that he summoned the various important and distinguished men who had come to Erfurt to see him. Every morning he would read with satisfaction the list of new arrivals. As soon as he found Monsieur Goethe's name on it he sent for him.

"Monsieur Goethe, I am delighted to see you." "Sire, I see that when your Majesty is travelling, not even the humblest trifles escape your Majesty's notice." "I know that you are the leading tragic poet of Germany." "Sire, you do our country wrong : we think we have our share of great men : Schiller, Lessing and Wieland must be known to your Majesty." "I confess I know little about them; but I have read Schiller's *History of the Thirty Years War*, and I thought, if you will pardon my saying so, that any tragedies it might inspire would only be fit for our boulevards." "Sire, I am not acquainted with your boulevards; but it is there, I presume, that popular spectacles are given, and I am sorry to hear you judge one of the greatest geniuses of modern times so severely." "Your home is at Weimar; is that the place where the most famous men of letters in Germany meet?" "Sire, they enjoy considerable protection there." "I should be happy to see Monsieur Wieland." "If your Majesty will allow me to write and tell him so, I am sure he will come here at once." "While you are here you must go every evening to see what we are putting on at the theatre. It will do you no harm to see some good French tragedies acted." "Sire, I shall be very glad to go, and I must confess to your Majesty that it was my intention to do so; I have translated or rather imitated several French plays." "You are not as strict as we are in the rules of drama." "Sire, with us the three unities are not essential." "How do you like having us here?" "Sire, it is a very splendid visit, and one which we hope will be useful to our

country." "Are your people happy?" "They have high hopes."
"Monsieur Goethe, you ought to stay here until the end of our
tour and write something about your impressions of the magnificent show we are putting on for you." "Ah, Sire, it would
need the pen of some writer of antiquity to undertake such a
task." "Are you an admirer of Tacitus?" "Yes, Sire, very much
so." "Well, I am not, but we shall talk of that another time.
Write and tell Monsieur Wieland to come here: I shall go to
Weimar to return his visit, since the Duke has invited me there.
I shall be happy to meet the Duchess; she is a remarkable
woman. Monsieur Goethe, come to Racine's *Iphigénie* this evening. It is a good play; not one of my favourites, to be sure, but
the French think highly of it. You will see quite a number of
crowned heads in my parterre. Have you met the Emperor of
Russia yet?" "No, Sire, never, but I hope to be presented to
him." "He speaks your language well; if you write something
about our interview at Erfurt you must dedicate it to him."

I followed Monsieur Goethe and engaged him to come and
dine with me. On returning I wrote down this first conversation,
and during dinner, by putting various questions to him, I satisfied
myself that my record of it is entirely accurate. After dinner
Monsieur Goethe went to the theatre, and I took pains to secure
him a seat near the stage.

76. *Caroline Sartorius*   *15.10.1808*

Goethe had invited the famous actor Talma and Mme Talma
to lunch, and the host and his guests seemed to embark on a
positive competition to outdo each other in charm. Goethe's
command of French is not quite perfect, but a mind such as his
is not easily hampered by any language of which he has even
a moderate knowledge. M. and Mme Talma pressed him to
come to Paris and to stay with them. All France, they said,
would envy them the good fortune of having the author of
Werther in their house; not a lady in Paris would rest till she
had seen him; on every dressing-table, in every boudoir he
would find his book, which was still constantly re-read, constantly re-translated, and as full of the charm of novelty as it
had been thirty years ago. There was no sort of subtle flattery
that they did not lavish on him, with that easy French politeness
which never sounds vapid or obsequious. Goethe answered with
serene urbanity, but would not commit himself to any promise

and remarked jestingly that to cause such a sensation in Paris at his present age would be a burden of pleasure too heavy to support. Talma then came out with the plan of a tragedy into which he intended to convert *Werther*. This adaptation did indeed seem to be rather crude stuff. But Goethe's inexhaustible good humour survived the mutilation of his brain-child, and finally he merely remarked with an almost imperceptibly ironic air that he would be obliged if they would send him their tragedy when they had finished it, so that he might have it translated and performed in Weimar.

No doubt the point of this was not entirely lost on Talma, who exclaimed: "Mon Dieu, qu'avez-vous besoin de notre pièce, vous qui feriez cent fois mieux que nous?" "C'est qu'on n'aime pas à refaire ce qu'on a fait une fois," replied Goethe. Meanwhile his servant had brought him a bulky letter; he opened it, glanced through it, and had it put by the window without further mention. Talma now asked rather indiscreetly whether it was true, as was generally asserted, that the novel was founded on fact. I was apprehensive of what the effect of this question might be, and glanced at Goethe, but his face showed no sign of annoyance, and he answered amicably: "This question has often been put to me, and I usually answer that Werther was two persons combined, one of whom perished and the other remained alive, rather as in the Book of Job—'My lord, all thy sheep and thy servants are slain, and I only am escaped alive to tell thee'." We loudly applauded this admirable bon mot; then Goethe added more seriously, and with an unfathomable expression on his face: "But one can't come unscathed through writing a book like that". Hitherto he had spoken French, but this he said in German, and turning to my husband asked him: "Traduisez celà à nos amis, monsieur". Talma, well acquainted as he was with the traces of great passion, easily grasped Goethe's meaning without understanding his words. Goethe then at once resumed his former light-hearted tone. "One usually has to pay dearly for one's youthful follies", he said, "but I am one of the happy few who still reap a rich harvest from them even in their later years; to begin with it is to them I owe so many delightful and interesting acquaintances, as has been the case today; and the day before yesterday the Emperor Napoleon awarded me the Cross of Honour; and now another decoration has just arrived for me from the Tsar Alexander." And with that he showed us the packet which his ser-

vant had brought him: it contained the great ribbon of the
Order of St. Anne, with a star set with brilliants. Then he withdrew to change his clothes, for he had been invited to court.

77. Caroline Sartorius   16.10.1808

For our last evening the poet had saved up the best thing he
had to offer us: his poems. He appeared at the dinner table
with a handful of papers which he put down beside him, and
was in an extremely good humour.

After dinner he began to read aloud and recite by heart, and
went on till one o'clock at night; he really excelled himself that
evening. Poets have always been fond of wine, women and
song, and our friend, who lives in a perpetual spring, is still inspired to splendid poetry by the first two even in the autumn of
his life. Thus he had a sweetheart this summer in Carlsbad to
whom he sang his sweetest songs, and he read us these sonnets,
none of which has yet appeared in print. They were all beautiful,
but the finest are those in which he makes the beloved herself
speak; their delicacy is quite incomparable, and indeed I suppose there has never been a poet with such profound insight
into the feminine soul.—Later he recited all sorts of occasional
poems, many of them from his earlier years, which are unpublished and cannot be published since they contain so many personal allusions, but are so full of whimsicality that they soon
sent us into fits of laughter; I think I have never laughed so
much in my life.

I can well believe that Goethe shows this side of himself only
to a few people and only seldom; but to judge by this occasion I
have never met a more charming man.

78. F. von Müller   14.12.1808

He is now making a quite thorough study of early French
literature again, in order to be able to carry on serious conversation with the French. "What an infinite cultural history they
had behind them already", he exclaimed, "at a time when we
Germans were still unlicked cubs! Germany is nothing; though
each individual German is a great deal. And yet the latter themselves think it is the other way round. The Germans will have
to be transplanted, scattered all over the world like the Jews,

before the abundance of good that is in them can be developed fully, to the benefit of all nations."

79. H. Steffens 31.12.1808

At table Goethe was in a very good humour; the talk revolved round a number of subjects, and the spontaneous witty sayings of our famous host were an entertainment for us all. He also succeeded in making charming conversation to the ladies.

Finally he turned to Zacharias Werner, who had hitherto taken little part in the discussion. "Well, Werner," he said in his calm but rather imperious manner, "have you nothing to entertain us with, no poems to read us?" Werner dived into his pocket, and spread out such a pile of crumpled dirty paper in front of him that I was filled with apprehension and inwardly deplored this request of Goethe's, which seemed likely to bring our interesting conversation to a complete stop just when it was in full swing. So now Werner began to rant out a series of sonnets to us in his usual appalling way. In the end there was one that did attract my attention. It was a sonnet about the exquisite spectacle of the full moon floating in the clear Italian sky. He compared it to an elevated host. I was disgusted by this perverse simile, which made an unpleasant impression on Goethe as well; he turned to me, outwardly composed but fighting down an inner exasperation. "Well, Steffens," he asked, "how do you like that?" "Herr Werner", I replied, "was kind enough a few days ago to read me a sonnet in which he lamented the fact that he had gone to Italy too late and too old. I think I understand how right he is. I am too much of a scientist to relish such a substitution of ideas. So inappropriate a comparison detracts as much from the mystic symbol of our religion as it does from the moon itself." Goethe now completely let himself go, and talked himself into such a rage as I had never before witnessed. "I detest this perverse religiosity", he cried. "Don't expect any sort of support for it from me. It shall not raise its voice in any shape or form on the stage, not on this stage at any rate!" When he had thus vented his feelings at some length and in more and more stentorian tones, he grew calmer. "You have spoilt my meal", he said gravely. "You know that I cannot bear such absurdities. You have tempted me into forgetting myself in front of the ladies."—He now completely regained his composure, turned to the ladies with apologies, and

began a conversation on some indifferent topic; but he soon
rose and left the room, and it was obvious that he had been
deeply offended and wanted to recover his peace of mind in
solitude. Werner looked absolutely annihilated. Shortly after
we had risen from table I went into Goethe's room : he was
completely calm and good-humoured, seemed to have quite
forgotten the scene at table, and embarked in his favourite lecturing manner on a detailed exposition and discussion of certain
optical phenomena.

80.   Riemer   20.2.1809

"Wit always presupposes an audience. And that is why one
cannot keep a joke to oneself. One is not witty for oneself. One
enjoys all other feelings for oneself alone : love, hope, and so
forth.—Wit is always regarded as the sign of a cold nature; it is
merely that of a reflective mind which can hover freely and
detach itself from objects. (Accordingly it is said that wit spares
no one, not even one's friends.)

"Wit is an aspect of the play-instinct. Play reveals the great
freedom of the mind. Play demands not reality but illusion.
Illusion is closely akin to ideality. It is as it were an image, a
picture of the ideal. In fact it is the ideal itself, embodied or
revealed in a minimum of reality."

81.   J. D. Falk   28.2.1809

"If I were to write down the sum total of what is worth knowing in various branches of knowledge that I have studied all my
life long, the resulting manuscript would be so small that you
could take it home like a letter in an envelope. It is the custom
with scholars in this country either to debase their subjects in
order to earn a living, or to grind them completely into profes-
sorial dust, so that we Germans have to take our choice as it
were between a shallow popularised philosophy or an incomprehensible rigmarole of high-sounding transcendentalism."

82.   M. H. Hudtwalker   May 1809

I sometimes found him very quiet, but never haughty or un-
friendly, provided one did not thrust oneself on him. He particularly liked the society of young people, if they were unpretentious, which at that time admittedly I was not, but at any rate

I had myself well enough in hand to avoid being too forward.

On Sunday evening he was with us from seven till eleven and talked a great deal. And how he talks! Hitherto I have some-times thought it possible to differentiate between Goethe the man and Goethe the poet, but now I have come really to love him for himself as well. Anyone who is speaking to him feels unconsciously raised to his level, and imagines that he himself is Goethe. He values everything, is acquainted with everything, has an opinion on everything that can possibly interest a human mind. Most fascinating of all is to hear him talk about subjects from natural history, especially about flowers. His touching, al-most childlike tenderness of feeling, so well known to his readers, here shows itself more enchantingly than any poem can express. He is a very animated talker, and one friend of mine who is so deaf that he cannot hear his words assures me that he can under-stand a great deal of what Goethe says merely from his gestures. The expression of his eyes is absolutely captivating, and when they even fill with tears—for such is his fiery enthusiasm and his moral sensitivity that this quite often happens—then I am sure there is not a young man who would not willingly embrace him nor a girl who does not long to fall into his arms.

83. J. D. Falk   14.6.1809

On another occasion, in the summer of 1809, I visited Goethe one afternoon and again found him sitting in his garden in the fine weather. He had a small garden table in front of him, and on it stood a long-necked glass jar in which a little live snake was busily moving about. He fed it with a quill and philosophised about it daily.* He claimed that it knew him already and would move its head nearer to the edge of the jar as soon as it caught sight of him. "What wonderfully intelligent eyes!" he went on. "There are certainly a number of developments on their way with a head like that, but of course not many of them have arrived. It's just impossible with that clumsy wriggling body. Nature has left this elongated jointed organism with no hands or feet, although she really owed it both, having given it this head and these eyes; she does in fact often default in this way, leaving something undone for the time being, but taking it up again later if conditions are favourable."

* Riemer considers that this anecdote is an invention by Falk, since "Goethe found snakes repulsive" (Riemer, op. cit., I, 27).

84. *Riemer*   23.6.1809

Goethe's poetic works, as he himself remarked, were like the sloughed-off skins of past or passing states. People then picked up these empty husks and made them into shoes and clothes and so on and wore them out. He himself once said that his works were merely fragments from former existences—an old cast-off hat here, a pair of boots there, and so forth.

85. *Pauline Gotter*   21.7.1809

Although his works are splendid and great in every way, they still cannot compare with his conversation: to hear him talk is the purest delight I have ever experienced. But I think he can also be very dangerous company, and I assure you that I have had to muster all the poor wits I possess to keep firmly reminding myself that all the sweet words he whispered in my ear were not meant for me personally, but for any young girl. I was less afraid that my vanity might be aroused than that my heart might completely run away with my head, as I heard him entreat me with the utmost tenderness and the most exquisitely turned compliments for permission to kiss my hand—he who is always so formal and stiff and reserved and condescending to everyone else.

86. *B. R. Abeken*   15.8.1809

I wish you could have seen and heard how good-humoured, indeed how absolutely exuberant Goethe was at dinner; it is impossible to describe it. But I have never known a young man converse even on trifling topics with such vivacity and skill as this Goethe who is now in his sixtieth year. He and Wieland and Knebel are old and familiar friends, so the conversation was easy and intimate. Among other things certain Weimar actresses were discussed, in one of whom the younger ladies present found a great many faults, especially in respect of her outward appearance and figure. Goethe defended her and contrived to give a very comical demonstration of how, if a little were removed from her person here, a little added there and so forth, she might in the end be made to look very buxom and shapely. This sent old Wieland into such fits of laughter that he kept begging Goethe to spare his sides and finally collapsed, gagging himself with his napkin and putting it over his head.

87. K. A. Varnhagen von Ense 1809

Goethe once said: "I a heathen? Well, after all, I had Gretchen executed and Ottilie starve to death;* isn't that Christian enough for these people? What more do they want in the way of Christianity?"

88. (?) F. A. Wolf (reported by H. Laube) 1809

"As to whether the *Elective Affinities* is true or founded upon fact", said Goethe, "I answer that every work of literature is true, unless it exaggerates, and none exaggerates if it makes a lasting and deep impression. The rest should be a matter of indifference to the public; one is not bound to gratify mere curiosity. With me the main thing has always been to make use of experience; it was never my way to invent out of the air, I have always regarded the world as a greater genius than myself."

89. J. D. Falk 1809

On one occasion we talked about Heinrich von Kleist and his play *Kätchen von Heilbronn*. Goethe disapproves of his northern acidity and morbid over-insistence. "No mature mind", he said, "can possibly take any pleasure in such highly contrived themes as Kleist uses in his work. Even in his *Michael Kohlhaas*, pleasingly narrated and ingeniously put together though it is, the whole story is monstrously ungainly. Only a writer entirely possessed by esprit de contradiction could take up one singular case of this sort and attempt with such morbidly systematic thoroughness to make it seem specially significant. There is in nature an ugly, disquieting element, with which literature, however artistic the treatment, can neither deal nor come to terms." And he spoke again of the gaiety and the grace of the Italian tales he had been reading: their philosophy of life was both happy and meaningful, and in these gloomy times he turned to them all the more eagerly.

He mentioned in this connection that the happiest of those tales also owed their existence to dark days in which plague was ravaging the land. He paused and then went on: "I have a right to criticise Kleist, because I was fond of him and I furthered his ambitions; but whether it is because he was obliged by con-

* i.e. Gretchen in *Faust* and Ottilie in *The Elective Affinities*.

temporary events to interrupt his education, as so many young men now are, or whether it is for some other reason : the fact is, he is turning out to be a disappointment. His morbid disposition really is too bad; it is destroying him as a man and as a writer. You know what trouble I took to get his *Water-Pitcher* produced on the stage here, and how often I rehearsed it. That it failed nevertheless was entirely due to the fact that it lacks a swift-moving action, though for the rest its subject-matter is ingenious and humorous enough.

"But to blame its failure on me, and even to contemplate, as I understand he did, sending a challenge to me in Weimar on this account, is behaviour which suggests that there is in him a serious perversion of nature, as Schiller would call it; and this is only excusable on grounds of an over-sensitive nervous system or of illness. As for *Kätchen von Heilbronn*", he went on, turning to me, "I know you are well disposed towards Kleist, so you shall read it, and then give me a summary of the contents; I shall wait until you have done this and then decide whether or not I should be well advised to read it myself.* I read his *Penthesilea* recently and did not get on with it at all well. This tragedy borders very closely on high comedy in some passages, such as the one in which an Amazon warrior appears on the stage with one breast missing and assures the audience that all her emotions have taken refuge in the other she still has. If this notion were to occur in a popular Neapolitan farce, in a speech by Columbine to a ribald Pulcinello, I don't doubt that the public would find it highly effective; though even there such a joke, being associated with so repulsive an image, might well incur general disfavour."

90.   *Riemer*   *13.7.1810*

On the two ways of translating ancient and modern literature : freely, with an eye to the requirements and national genius of the people one is translating for, and faithfully, with an eye to the genius of the nation whose language one is translating from. One must not treat everyone as if they were women and children.

---

* According to a later report, Goethe was urged by Falk and others to have *Kätchen von Heilbronn* produced at Weimar, but after reading it he condemned its "damnable unnaturalness" and threw it straight into the fire.

91. Riemer   *5.8.1810*

"Man cannot maintain himself for long in the conscious condition or in consciousness; he must take refuge again in unconsciousness, for that is where his roots grow."

92. Riemer   *November 1810*

"Any living thing, as such, must be valued. All literatures, whether Italian or French or German, are like life taking shape in water, forming molluscs, polyps and so forth, until finally a human being comes into existence."

93. Henriette Herz   *1810*

When confronted by people who did not particularly interest him, Goethe was much too inclined to follow his mood of the moment, and seemed to regard their admiration for him as a due tribute which required not the slightest response on his part. No doubt the curiosity of insignificant visitors was often an intolerable nuisance to him and deprived him of valuable time which he felt he could have used more profitably. But I have also sometimes seen him surrounded by a group of men of acknowledged distinction and young men of promise, all ardently longing to hear him merely express some view or opinion, all hanging on his lips: and the prize they took away with them at the end of this long evening, to which they had perhaps been looking forward all their lives, was no more than a long-drawn-out "Ah—yes!" or "Really?" or "Hm!" or, at best, "I dare say, I dare say".

94. Elisa von der Recke   *June 1811*

What commended his late wife Christiane to me was that I never once heard her speak maliciously of other people; and her conversation, so far as my acquaintance with her went, was always such that I found it quite easy to understand how her unpretentious, clear and entirely natural intelligence should have appealed to our friend Goethe. When he introduced her to me he said: "Let me commend my wife to you by testifying that since she took her first step across my threshold I have owed her nothing but happiness".

95. *Riemer* 27.6.1811

"One loves best at the time of life when one still believes that one is alone in one's love and that no one else has ever loved so much or ever will."

96. *Riemer* 20.7.1811

"Insufficiency is productive. When I wrote my *Iphigenia* I had studied Greek materials, but insufficiently. If I had done so exhaustively, the play would never have been written."

97. *Riemer* 7.9.1811

He loved for example to protract the conversation unduly, or keep repeating some remark or reverting to it again and again, if he noticed that it bored some person who in any case had no reason to put on airs of being a know-all and quick in the uptake. He also used to adopt this or some similar manoeuvre when he felt disinclined to discuss something and wanted to get rid of the importunate visitor.

Bettina von Arnim experienced this for herself in the autumn of 1811 when she kept calling on him in the evening and would dearly have liked to chatter to him about her love or something or other—che so io! He continually thwarted her by drawing her attention to the beautiful comet which at that time was visible in its full magnitude and splendour in the evening sky, and by bringing out one telescope after another and descanting at some length upon this meteorological phenomenon. An absolutely baffling defence! The long-tailed meteor was like a whisk for this ever-returning fly, a rod to stave off this grown-up and already married child who would so gladly have sat on his knee.

98. *L. A. Frankl* 8.9.1812

The two great masters, one of language and the other of music [Goethe and Beethoven], had gone for a walk together further up the valley [at Carlsbad] in the hope of a more uninterrupted talk. But wherever they went there were people out walking, who made way for them to the right and to the left with respectful salutations. Goethe, annoyed at this interruption, said : "It is maddening, I cannot get away from the

GOETHE IN 1811

bowing and scraping anywhere here". Beethoven replied with a quiet smile: "Never mind, your Excellency, perhaps they're bowing and scraping to me!"

99. *F. von Müller* 16.12.1812

Today he was in a solemn and festive mood on account of the moon's occultation of Aldebaran, that beautiful fixed star in the sign of Aries. It was as if some highly significant event were taking place in his own life.

"The reason why I value astronomy so highly", he said, "is that it is the one and only science that rests on generally acknowledged, unchallengeable foundations, and can therefore advance with complete certainty further and further into infinity. Astronomers are the most sociable of solitaries: across the lands and seas that separate them they exchange their data with each other, and these are the rock on which they can continue to build."

100. *J. D. Falk* 25.1.1813

When Goethe heard that I had seen the dead Wieland on the previous day and in consequence spent a wretched evening and even worse night, he gave me a thorough scolding. "Why should one", he said, "allow one's cherished recollections of the features of men and women who have been one's friends to be ruined by a disfiguring mask? After all, such a sight forces an alien impression on one's imagination, a quite false impression in fact. I took good care not to see Herder or Schiller or the Dowager Duchess Amalia in their coffins. Death is a very mediocre portrait painter. For my own part I want all my friends to be preserved in my memory as living and breathing images, not as the masks he makes of them. So I beg you all, if the time should come, to do just the same in my case. And I must confess that that is exactly what I like so much about Schiller's way of dying. He came to Weimar unannounced, with no fuss, and he made no fuss when he left us. I have no use at all for pomp and circumstance in death."

101. *J. D. Falk* 25.1.1813

On the day of Wieland's funeral I noticed a kind of solemnity in Goethe's manner that is rarely to be seen in him. His mood was tender, one might almost say mournful : his eyes shone frequently, and there was even something different about his expression and his voice. Perhaps it was for this reason that our conversation that day took a turn towards supernatural matters such as Goethe normally disdains or at least personally declines to discuss; strictly on principle, I think, because in accordance with his natural tastes he prefers to confine his attention to the present and to the delightful phenomena which art and nature offer to our eyes and minds in the spheres of experience which are accessible to us.

It was clear that Goethe took survival after death for granted, as something self-evident. "There can be no question, in any circumstances", he said, "of nature permitting the disappearance of lofty spiritual forces such as Wieland; she does not use her capital so wastefully. Wieland's soul is a natural treasure, a jewel of the first water. In addition, his long life has increased rather than diminished this native intellectual excellence. Raphael was scarcely in his thirties, Kepler not much over forty, when they both suddenly brought their lives to an end, whereas Wieland—"

"What !" I interrupted in some astonishment, "do you then speak of death as if it were an autonomous act?"

"I do quite often take the liberty of so speaking", replied Goethe, "and what is more, if you have no objection, I will explain my ideas on this matter to you in full, since I am permitted at the present time to do so."

I begged him not to withhold them from me, and he began :

"As you well know, ideas which lack a firm foundation in the world of the senses, whatever other value they may have, carry no conviction for me, because in my dealings with nature I wish to know, not merely to surmise and believe. Now as to the personal survival of our souls after death, my view of the matter is as follows. Survival by no means contradicts the observations I have made in many years of studying our own nature and that of all other natural beings; on the contrary, these observations even give it fresh proof. But of course, as to how much or how little this personality of ours deserves to survive, that is another question, and a point that we must leave to God. For the time being I will only say this much : my assumption is that there are different classes and hierarchies among those ultimate primal components of all beings, those primordial points as it were of all natural phenomena, which I am inclined to call souls, because the animation of the whole universe proceeds from them, or even

more inclined to call monads—why not let us stick to this Leib-
nitzian term! It would be hard to find a better one to express
the simplicity of the simplest of beings.

"Now experience shows us that some of these monads or
primordial points are so tiny, so insignificant, that they are
suited at best to a subordinate and servile existence; but that
others are uncommonly strong and powerful. Accordingly it is
the habit of the latter to snatch anything that approaches them
into their sphere of influence and transform it into something
appertaining to them, that is to say into a body, into a plant,
into an animal, or—still higher up the scale—into a star. They
go on doing this until the micro- or macrocosm of which they
contain the spiritual potential comes into outward physical
being as well. It is only these stronger monads that I should like
to call souls. It follows from this that there are world-monads
or world-souls, just as there are ant-monads or ant-souls, and
that both kinds are in their primal origin if not wholly one and
the same, at least essentially akin. Every sun, every planet,
carries within itself a higher potential, a higher purpose, by
virtue of which its evolutions must proceed just as regularly and
according to the very same law as the evolution of a rose through
leaf and stem and corolla. Call this an idea or a monad as you
please, it is no matter to me; suffice it to say that this potential
is invisible, and precedes the visible development from it which
takes place in nature. And we must not be misled by the masks
which this idea adopts in its intermediate, transitional stages. It
remains exactly the same process of metamorphosis or natural
capacity for transformation which develops a leaf into a flower,
a rose, or an egg into a grub and the grub into a butterfly. For
the rest, the inferior monads obey a higher one simply because
they have to obey it, not because it gives them any particular
pleasure to do so. All this, too, is a very natural process. Consider this hand of mine for example. Its component parts are
constantly at the service of the principal monad which was able
to bind them indissolubly to itself when they came into being.
By means of them I can play this or that piece of music; I can
move my fingers about as I please on the keys of a piano. Thus
of course they transmit to me an experience of intellectual
beauty; but they themselves are deaf, only the principal monad
hears.

"The moment of death, which for this reason is also very
appropriately called a dissolution, is the very moment at which

the reigning principal monad releases all its hitherto subject monads from their faithful service. I regard both coming into being and passing out of being as autonomous acts of this principal monad, the real essence of which is quite unknown to us. But all monads are by nature so indestructible that they themselves do not cease or forfeit their activity at the moment of dissolution; on the contrary, at that very same moment they are continuing it afresh. Thus they pass out of their old situation only to enter upon a new one immediately. At the time of this change everything depends on the strength of the potential contained within this or that monad. Between the monad of a cultivated human soul and that of a beaver or bird or fish there is a world of difference. And thus we come round again to the hierarchy of souls, an assumption which we are bound to make if we are to achieve even a partial explanation of the phenomena of nature. After their bodily demise, each of our monads goes where it belongs, into water, air, earth, fire, or the stars; in fact the mysterious impulse that carries it there simultaneously holds the secret of its future destiny. There is no question of its being destroyed; it may, however, be seized as it passes and held subject by some powerful and at the same time evil monad. That risk indeed is one that may well give us pause, and for my own part I can think of nothing in natural philosophy alone that can altogether dispel this fear."

As he was speaking, a dog gave tongue in the street, barking repeatedly. Goethe, a born dog-hater, rushed to the window and shouted at it: "Try all your tricks, you mock-mongrel, you'll not get the better of me!" Most surprising for anyone unfamiliar with the interconnections of Goethe's thought; but for anyone who is, it was a highly appropriate flash of whimsicality.*

"If we are to embark upon speculation", said Goethe, continuing his discourse, "then I really do not see why the monad to which we owe Wieland's appearance on our planet should be unable in its new condition to enter into the highest combinations that are possible in this universe. I should not be in the least surprised, indeed I should find it entirely in keeping with my views, if one day, many millennia hence, I were to meet this Wieland again as a world-monad, a star of first magnitude, and could watch his delightful radiance reviving and refreshing everything that approached him. For after all, if we consider the

---

* Riemer was sceptical of this anecdote: "Goethe", he declares, "was quite incapable of such idiotic behaviour" (op. cit., I, 25).

eternity of this universe, the only possible destiny we can assume monads to have before them is that they too will eternally participate in the joys of the gods as blessed collaborators in the work of creation. The process of the world in making is entrusted to them. Bidden or unbidden, they come of their own accord from every direction, from every mountain, from every sea, from every star, who shall stay them? I myself, as you see me here, am sure that I have existed a thousand times already and may hope to return a thousand times again."

"Forgive me!" I interposed at this point: "I am not sure that a coming again without consciousness of the fact can be called a coming again. For one only comes *again* if one knows that one has been here before. And might it not take us nearer the truth we seek if we were to suppose that in the centre of creation there is a loving Principal Monad, who uses all the subordinate monads of this whole universe in just the same way as our soul uses those lesser monads which are subject to its service?"

"I have nothing against this idea as an article of faith", replied Goethe, "but I usually do not ascribe any exclusive value to ideas which are not based on any perception of the senses. It would be all very well if we really knew about our own brains and their connections with Uranus and the thousands of intertwining threads that carry our thoughts to and fro! But as it is we are never aware of the lightning flashes of our thoughts until they actually strike. We have knowledge only of ganglia, of cerebral nodes; we know next to nothing of the nature of the brain itself. So what can we claim to know about God?

"In one of our earlier discussions I described man as 'nature's first conversation with God'. I do not doubt that on other planets a much loftier, profounder and more intelligent form of this conversation may take place. For the time being we have only a thousandth part of the knowledge it requires. To begin with we lack self-knowledge, which comes before knowledge of anything else. Strictly speaking I cannot have any knowledge of God beyond what is warranted by the rather limited scope of my sense-perceptions on this planet, and that after all is in every respect little enough. But it by no means follows that these limitations of our study of nature also set limits to faith. On the contrary, the immediacy of divine intuitions within us is such that it may very well come to appear that our knowledge is but in part, especially here on a planet whose whole connection with the sun has been severed, and on which all philosophy must therefore remain imperfect, requiring for this very reason that faith should supplement and complete it. My study of colours has already given me occasion to observe the existence of 'primary phenomena', whose divine simplicity should not be disturbed and impaired by our useless experiments, but surrendered to the sphere of faith and metaphysical reason. Where knowledge suffices we of course do not need faith, but where the power of knowledge fails or seems insufficient, we should also give faith its due. Provided only we start from the principle that knowledge and faith are not meant to cancel each other out but to complete each other, we shall surely be on the right road to truth in all things."

It had grown late when I left Goethe that evening. As I took my leave he kissed me on the forehead, which at other times it is never his custom to do. I was about to go downstairs in the dark, but he would not allow it, and held me firmly by the arm till he had rung for someone to light me down. And he even warned me at the door to be careful and to beware of the raw night air.

102.   Riemer   *15.2.1813*

"Christianity puts everyone back into the state of nature (i.e. of original equality) without giving him the appropriate faculties. Consequently all the individuals who are really more powerful are endangered, for they are not allowed to use their powers. And consequently, under this system, all the inferior rabble can sit very pretty, because no one can touch them."

103.   W. von Kügelgen   *24.4.1813*

On the morning of the entry of the King of Prussia and the Tsar of Russia into Dresden, Goethe had simply arrived with friendly informality at our house, and as my father was out looking for him elsewhere, he asked my mother's permission to remain with her and watch the expected procession from her window, unmolested by the crowds. He added that he would not trouble her in any way, that he would not even speak, and begged her to pay no attention to him whatsoever.

My mother had the impression that he himself wanted to be left alone. Accordingly she assigned a window to him, sat down in another with her work, and did not bother him with any conversation. So there he stood, a magnificent lofty figure in his long coat, with his hands on his back, gazing placidly down at the gay thronging multitude. He looked very happy, and my mother sensed how grateful he was to her for tactfully leaving him to himself, for she knew what persecution had already been inflicted on her strange guest by the admiring importunities of literary ladies. He was usually surrounded by a considerable cortège, and since he had arrived quite alone my mother assumed that he had succeeded, perhaps with the help of the crowds, in eluding his retinue of adorers and had sought refuge in our house, where he might have peace to allow the solemn impressions of today's historic event to sink into his mind. She therefore called me away as well, for I had been moving nearer and nearer to the great man and staring at him like someone seeing a whale or an elephant for the first time. But he drew me close, put his hand on my shoulder and asked me various questions, inquiring, for example, whether I was looking forward to seeing the Emperor of Russia. I said yes, I was looking forward to it, "because he is my godfather". And to be sure, I had hitherto lived under this happy illusion, merely because my name was also Alexander. But my mother at once gave the needed explanation, and Goethe then asked a number of things about Russia. So she had got into conversation with him after all.

During this there was a violent peal at the bell. I ran to open the door, and an unknown lady thrust her way in, as tall and stately as a tiled stove and just as hot. She cried out to me in haste: "Is Goethe here?" Just "Goethe", without further ado! A stranger she might be, and I a small boy she had never met, but she vouchsafed him no further qualification, and I scarcely had time to utter my monosyllabic affirmative, before she sailed into my mother's room like a majestic three-decker, practically running me down, and without firing a single shot of customary salutation. Sweeping up to her idol with outspread arms she exclaimed: "Goethe! Oh, Goethe, I have been looking for you everywhere! How could you do it? I was so worried!" And she overwhelmed him with joyful greetings and reproaches.

The poet, meanwhile, had slowly turned round from the window. Every trace of good humour had vanished from his face, and he stood there as stern and stony as a pillar of justice. Indicating my mother, he said very pointedly: "Frau von Kügelgen is also here". The lady made a slight bow, but turned her fire back on to her friend, quite failing to notice his annoyance, and delivered one full broadside after another, declaring how delighted she was, how she had at last got her grappling-irons into him and would not let go of him again that morning. Goethe's embarrassment was visible. He fastened his coat up to the neck, and when my father, with whom the lady was acquainted, entered and for a moment distracted her attention, he suddenly slipped away.

104. S. Schütze   May–June 1813

When I arrived in his house I heard talking in the next room, and when I asked whether the Herr Geheimrat had company, the servant replied : "He's talking to himself".

105. A Prussian artillery-officer   18.11.1813

In Weimar I paid a visit to my old former war-comrade and benefactor, Geheimrat von Goethe. He was, as always, extremely kind to me and even invited me to dinner, so we spent a couple of hours over a bottle of good old Rhine wine, chatting very pleasantly and recalling the days of the 1792 campaign and the siege of Mainz. But there was, frankly, one thing that now did not greatly appeal to me about Goethe, and that was his lack of patriotic enthusiasm about our recent brilliant victories and the expulsion of Napoleon from Germany. Towards all this he maintained a remarkably cool and critical attitude, and even waxed very eloquent in the praise of the Emperor Napoleon's many brilliant qualities. I naturally had not nearly enough skill of speech to be able to enter into an argument with so famous a poet and savant as Goethe, so I could only reply that we Prussian soldiers fortunately took a quite different view of the matter, that we hated Napoleon as the oppressor of our fatherland and would gladly shed our blood to rid Germany of the danger of him for good and all.

106. H. Luden   13.12.1813

"Don't think for a moment," said Goethe, "that I am indifferent to great ideals such as freedom, the nation, the fatherland. No; we carry these ideals within us; they are a part of our nature, and no man can divest himself of them. Moreover, I am deeply interested in Germany. It has often been a bitter grief for me to think of the German people, so praiseworthy in its individuals and so pitiful as a whole. If one compares the German people to other nations one can only feel embarrassed, a feeling which I try in various ways to overcome; and in science and art I have found the wings that can raise one above it. For science and art belong to the world, and the barriers of nationality vanish before them. Nevertheless the consolation that they afford is still only a poor consolation, and no substitute for the proud consciousness of belonging to a great and powerful people, respected and feared by others. Nor is there more comfort to be found in the mere thought of Germany's future. This is something I believe in as firmly as you do. The German people does indeed hold promise of a future, and it has a future. The destiny of the Germans, as Napoleon says, has not yet been fulfilled. If their sole task had been to break up the Roman Empire and build a new world and a new order on its ruins, they would long ago have perished. But the fact that they have continued to exist and to be so energetic and effective persuades me that they must have a great future before them, a mission to fulfil which will be that much greater than the mighty work of destroying the Roman Empire and shaping the Middle Ages, in that they have now reached a higher level of culture. But the hour of opportunity will be one that no human eye can foresee, and no human power can hasten its coming or bring it about. In the meantime all we can do as individuals is that each of us, according to his talents and tastes and position, should increase and consolidate the culture of his people, disseminating it through the nation in all directions, not only downwards but also, and more particularly, upwards—so that we may not lag behind other peoples but be leaders among them at least in this; so that intellectually we may not wither, but remain fresh and lively; so that our courage may not fail and we may not be found wanting, but still have the strength for any great deed when the day of glory dawns."

107. *Riemer*   26.3.1814

"Men remain productive (in poetry and art) only so long as they are religious; then they become merely imitative and repetitive, which is what we are in relation to the ancients. Their inventions were all matters of faith, but we, fantastical as we are, can only imitate their achievements fancifully."

108. Riemer　　　　　　　　　　　　　　　　　　*3.5.1814*

"Hypochondrism simply means sinking into subjectivity. If I give up external objects, it is impossible for me to believe that they count me as an object; and my belief that they do not regard me as an object is my reason for giving them up."

109. F. von Müller　　　　　　　　　　　　　　　　*30.5.1814*

"A man should adopt some edifying habit or other which can increase his enjoyment on pleasant days and renew it on dull days. For example he should get into the daily habit of reading some pages from the Bible or Homer, or looking at some fine pictures or medallions, or hearing some good music."

110. S. Schütze　　　　　　　　　　　　　　　　　*1806/14*

The most remarkable thing was the way his mood differed almost every time one saw him, so that anyone who thought he had grasped him on one occasion had to admit on the next that he had lost him again. The Goethe one encountered was sometimes gentle and calm, sometimes forbiddingly irritable (he was usually also irritable when something was troubling him), sometimes withdrawn and taciturn, sometimes eloquent and even loquacious, sometimes all epic tranquillity, sometimes—though more rarely—all fiery excitement and inspiration; sometimes he was full of ironic jests and mischievous banter, sometimes he scolded and stormed, sometimes he was even arrogant. The fact that we find this changeability of his so amazing proves merely that we know too little about human nature in general. In Goethe this great variety or number of moods was something quite natural and even necessary; for how could he have achieved the universality at which he aimed, and entered so easily into so many different situations and states of mind, if he had not been endowed not only with imagination but also with great emotional flexibility? These changeable sympathies, for all his freedom and calm of mind, were needful to him as a medium of understanding and as a basis for any new creation. But such a degree of mental mobility has its effects in everyday life as well. Goethe certainly practised exceptional self-control; but his determination to keep up appearances was sometimes affected by some aftermath of the hour before or some mood of the

moment, and when he was a guest here, without special obligations, he would let himself go much more freely than when he
was a host in his own house. It could really be quite alarming
when he joined the company in an obviously bad humour and
wandered from one corner of the room to another. When he was
in his silent mood one never knew who should speak next, unless
perhaps someone saved the situation by telling a story. In these
circumstances, and in view of his general inclination to shut
himself off from the outside world, it was wise and commendable
in our hostess (Johanna Schopenhauer) to have hit upon the
idea of placing not far from the door a table with drawing-
materials at which he could sit down whenever he pleased if he
happened not to be in the mood for talking. Here he produced
a large number of landscapes, which were of no particular
interest to real painters but were preserved by our hostess as
highly honourable relics.

But he was all the more charming when he felt sociable and
carried on a light-hearted discussion in some small circle, where
everyone in turn contributed his mite. He was usually not ostenta-
tiously witty or overflowing with ideas, indeed he even eschewed
them, preferring for the most part a tone of good-humoured
irony: he would seem to be praising something, but its total
absurdity would at once become obvious. In this way censure
was transformed into a delicate pleasure, and imperfection into
renewed enjoyment. He could not bear sudden irrelevances and
random turns in the conversation. I often used to rush in headlong in this way, tempted by momentary bright ideas, and I
noticed that he would then always pass his hand over his face.

What he liked still more was to expound a theme at length
and at ease, with the others often doing no more than signify
assent or ask questions, while he himself really lead and developed the conversation. His charm would increase still further
when he gave himself over entirely to the epic vein, in an
account of the Roman carnival for example or some other
reminiscence of Italy. One could then listen to him for hours on
end in complete forgetfulness of the other guests. The calm clear
style of his description, his almost comically half-solemn tone
of voice, the vividness with which he conjured everything up
before one's eyes—all this not only fascinated us but filled us
with a great sense of well-being, a great relish for life: one felt
that one's outlook was widening and one's heart taking possession
of a happier world. Here was clearly to be seen the essential

purpose of Goethe's muse : to turn even this life into a delightful garden of Eden, and to make its best possible employment the whole task of our wisdom.

He talked much more about visual art than about works of literature. To the latter he was married, but the former never ceased to be his mistress. In addition, the whole realm of nature and the whole of life lay outspread before his mind. In the course of conversation one might happen to mention the most out-of-the-way phenomenon, but it would still be within his ken. I once spoke of how one could listen to the silence as the noises of day died gradually down. And sure enough, he had once long ago sat out on a hill one sultry summer evening, giving ear to the gently whispering sounds that meet and mingle in the air until the midnight stillness falls. On another occasion he asked me whether I too had sometimes been lucky enough to dream that I was flying, and what form the dreams took, because he would very much like to arrive in this way at some more general view of the matter. He himself, he said, always flew round in a circle high up in the room or in a hall. I replied that my flights varied, they were sometimes lower down, sometimes higher up, perhaps as high as the ceiling. I mentally noted that his way of flying again revealed his tendency towards calm epic contemplation, but of course I should not have liked to make this remark to him out loud.

Goethe was, for all his naturalness, nevertheless rather fond of formality and ceremony. Perhaps this was partly also a relic of the strict etiquette of former times. When he entered the room he would walk stiffly, looking neither right nor left, straight through the assembled company to his hostess, and having gravely paid her his compliments he would then incline himself in a slight bow to the other guests all round him. It was not his way to glide lightly and quickly over a topic from one brief remark to the next; rather he would gently dismiss it with a half-murmured word. Otherwise he would usually speak rather slowly, inclining towards the deeper pitch of the voice, with the kind of leisurely dignity that holds a subject at arm's length and keeps other people at their distance as well. The practical expression of this defensive aloofness was frequently a phrase such as "That is indeed the case", or "I dare say it will be so".—Even an entertaining event often had to be conducted ceremoniously. There was a scene like this one evening when he was giving a reading, but solemnity on this occasion very nearly turned into comedy. For Goethe had brought some Scottish ballads with him and offered to recite one rather long one himself, but stipulated that the refrain at the end of each verse should be spoken by the ladies in chorus. The dramatic declamation began, the ladies held themselves in readiness and joined in at the right moment; they got through the first verse successfully enough, but when the same words recurred a second and third time, one of them was overcome by an involuntary fit of the giggles. Goethe stopped, lowered the book and glared at them all with the flashing eyes of Jove the Thunderer. "In that case I shall not read", he declared curtly. We were considerably startled; but Johanna Schopenhauer stepped forward with renewed protestations of obedience and pledging herself for the good behaviour of the others. So on we struggled—and upon my word! It was so comical to see that roomful of ladies all rhythmically wagging their chins simultaneously and to order, that the whole weight of Goethean authority was needed to keep the company in the required serious and ceremonious frame of mind. In good-humoured moods, too, Goethe would sometimes stray into a kind of facetiousness which he kept up to the point of tedium, or some endless badinage on one and the same subject. For example he once tormented us for an entire evening by insisting that we should inform him by guesswork of the plots of the new plays which he had just been rehearsing in the theatre and about which we knew nothing whatsoever. We occasionally got isolated details right, rather as when one sees properties being assembled before a performance and infers from a sword that the play will contain an officer, or from a hunting-knife that there will be a huntsman; but it was impossible to arrive at anything which made sense as a whole, and we sat on suffering tortures of utter boredom. Surely, we wondered, he himself realises how forced this whole thing is?—But that is how it is with great minds: one of the marks of their superiority to others is that they occasionally carry it too far, especially if they have long been pampered with adulation and submissiveness.

111. Arthur Schopenhauer   *1808/14*

This Goethe was such a thoroughgoing realist that he was absolutely not to be persuaded that objects as such only exist in

so far as they are thought of by the cognitive subject. "What!"
he once said to me, with his Jove-like eyes flashing, "you mean
to tell me that light only exists in so far as you see it? No! You
would not exist if the light did not see you."

I once said to Goethe, as I was lamenting the disillusionments
and vanities of life: "After all, an absent friend is no longer
himself when he is present". To which he replied: "Yes, because
you yourself are the absent friend, and he is only a creation of
your mind; whereas when he is present he has his own individuality and follows his own laws, which do not always cor-
respond to whatever your ideas happen to be at the moment".

112.   A. Schopenhauer (reported)   *1808/14*

Schopenhauer quoted with great satisfaction Goethe's opinion
of *Don Giovanni*, to the effect that the gaiety in this opera is
only on the surface, but that there are depths of prevailing
seriousness, and that it is precisely this double character that
Mozart's music so wonderfully expresses.

113.   A. Schopenhauer (reported)   *1808/14*

As to Goethe's opinion of Schopenhauer, it may be judged
from an anecdote according to which, one day at the tea-table,
when Schopenhauer was standing sulkily at the window with
his back to the company, Goethe said to the giggling young
ladies: "My dears, leave him in peace! That man will outgrow
all of us one day."

114.   Riemer   *1808/14*

My conversations with Goethe, both at table or during working hours, were often about ancient or modern languages. From
Greek I would frequently quote to him some gnomic saying or
apophthegm in which we found much food for thought and
numerous applications. One such adage was a couplet from the
Anthology which animadverts upon the vanity, nullity and
absurdity of the world and all human affairs—an ancient
preacher's *vanitas vanitatum*, which goes something like this:

Πάντα γέλως, καὶ πάντα κόνις, καὶ πάντα τὸ μηδέν,
   Πάντα γὰρ ἐξ ἀλόγων ἐστι τὰ γεινόμενα.

All is a farce, and all things are muck, and all things are
*   nothing;*
Nothing that happens makes sense: all is the doing of
*   fools.*

This so particularly appealed to him that he liked to allude
to it in his expectorations about the general course of events,
and would merely utter the opening syllables πάντα γέλως like
a motto or clue.

115. S. Boisserée   *8.8.1815*

He confessed that poems would come suddenly into his mind
ready-made, when they were good ones; but that he then had
to write them down immediately or he could never recapture
them; consequently he always took care not to think anything
out when he was going for a walk. It was unfortunate if he
could not retain a poem in his mind completely, because as soon
as he had to try to remember it it would be spoilt again. Also
(he said) he hardly ever made alterations. And it was equally
unfortunate if he dreamt poems, these were usually unrecover-
able. An Italian poet (Petrarch) had had a leather doublet made
for this reason, so that he could write on it in bed.

116. W. Grimm   *28.8.1815*

He has an oddly diffident nature, indeed a strange nervous
reluctance to let anything come within arm's length of him.
When it was his birthday in Frankfurt, no one in the house said
anything about it, but as he was sitting at table a fine serenade
of horns was heard on the Main, and when he asked what it
was his servant merely said: "Why, Herr Geheimrat, it's your
birthday today". Meanwhile they had placed a dish in his room
full of beautfully arranged expensive fruit such as pineapples
and so forth; beside it they had put some genuine Persian
articles (because of his current interest in later Oriental culture)
which I think included a dagger, and then they watched him as
he entered the room. At first, when he saw it, he was very nervous and glanced to and fro, thinking someone was about to
spring out of hiding to congratulate him, then looked into the
next room to see if any group of people had assembled for the
purpose, and when at last he found everything empty and silent,
he was moved to tears by this kindness.

117.   S. Boisserée   *8.9.1815*

"Yes, I certainly rather incline to pantheism as a philosophy of nature; it's quite clear to me that one gets further with it than with any other system. The way nature is made, the Trinity couldn't improve on it. It's an organ with le bon Dieu playing and the Devil blowing the bellows."

118.   S. Boisserée   *15.9.1815*

"An art attains to supreme heights when its subject is a matter of indifference and the art itself truly absolute, with the subject-matter merely its vehicle."

119.   F. L. K. von Biedenfeld   *4.10.1815*

Goethe talked a lot about poetry, and among other things he said : "Once you feel the urge and the need to write, you must get into the way of putting whatever comes to your lips or your pen straight down without hesitating and selecting. You must refrain from all self-criticism when you first write something down, because otherwise, when one is young, one often loses one's finest inspiration, the richest flowerings of the imagination, which no amount of reflection and critical scrutiny can restore. It is only when one has really finished the act of poetic procreation that one must begin one's technical business as a writer. Both the work and its author benefit from this procedure and the latter experiences his sweetest pleasures twice over."

120.   Riemer

The aversion which he was traditionally supposed to feel for dogs was by no means as strong as is commonly assumed, nor had it any significance at all other than that Goethe simply was never particularly fond of this species of animal.

He did, however, once get on quite well with a dog. In later years his own son had a fine English mastiff which he brought with him from the university, and Goethe not only took quite a liking to it, he even regretted, when this animal for various reasons had to be removed, that he had not first had a model or a cast made of it, which he might have put by his door as a seemly and dignified guardian, like the Molossian hounds in King Admetus's palace.

Moreover, and above all, Goethe was a human being in the fullest sense, and as such he could only take real satisfaction in human beings, as his proper study and pleasure. Animals only interested him as more or less close organisational approximations to man, provisional forerunners of the eventually manifest lord of creation. He did not despise them, indeed he even studied them, but chiefly he pitied them as masked and muffled creatures unable to express their feelings intelligibly and appropriately. And for him the dog, too, belonged to this category. He even used to regard it as inferior to the cat in grace of bodily movement and independence of character, and would humorously describe the latter as a fallen princess of the lion-race. Accordingly cats were permitted to walk openly and unabashedly in his garden, and had no need to fear his approach.

121. V. Cousin   *20.10.1817*

Goethe received me in a gallery full of busts in which we walked to and fro. His gait is as calm and unhurried as his speech; but certain rare emphatic gestures betray an inner excitement beneath this placid exterior. His conversation, rather chilly at first, became gradually animated. As he walked he would stop to gaze at me or to meditate, to trace his thoughts in increasing depth, to find a more precise expression or to give an example and details. The gestures are rare but vivid, the general demeanour grave and imposing. He put forward not one paradox, and yet there was novelty in everything he said to me. A flash of imagination from time to time; much wit in the details and in the development of his ideas, and a veritable genius in their actual substance. I think what is most characteristic of his mind is its wide range.

It is impossible for me to convey the charm of Goethe's spoken words: he gives individuality to everything, and yet the magic of the infinite as well: his language combines precision with scope, clarity with force, abundance with simplicity, and is full of an indefinable grace. In the end I was completely under his spell and hanging on his lips. He passed effortlessly from one idea to another, shedding on each a vast and gentle radiance which both illuminated and enchanted me. His mind unfolded itself before me with the purity, the ease, the tempered brilliance and energetic simplicity of the mind of Homer.

122. Dorothea von Schlegel   *28.11.1817*

Goethe once declared to a visitor that he was an atheist in
science and philosophy, a pagan in art, and a Christian by sen-
timent.

123. Caroline, Baroness von Egloffstein   *29.4.1818*

We were fortunate in having a beautiful summer morning for
our excursion to Dornburg,* which I had undertaken with a
few friends, including Chancellor von Müller. We arrived at the
castle, and after we had waited for a little in the room into
which we had been shown, Goethe appeared and greeted us
with unusual cordiality. It was at once obvious to us how much
he had benefited both mentally and physically from his stay in
such charming surroundings, where he could enjoy peace and
freedom. His great eyes shone with a gentler radiance, and a
pure calm happiness lay upon his fine classical features. He had
put off the stiff mask which embarrassment and decorum usually
obliged him to assume, and stood before us now in the whole
splendour of his personality.

After a number of humorous remarks, he gradually began to
talk about those matters which most deeply concern mankind.
He spoke with the greatest lucidity and warmth of religion and
moral culture, which should, he declared, be the chief purpose of
political institutions. Among other things, he said: "Our
capacity to ennoble every experience of our senses, and to bring
the most lifeless matter into a living union with intellectual ideas,
is the surest guarantee of our supernatural origin; and attracted
and fascinated as we are by the myriad phenomena of this
earth, we are nevertheless compelled by a deep longing to raise
our eyes again and again to heaven, for a profound and inexplicable feeling persuades us that we are citizens of those worlds
which shine mysteriously above us, and that to them we shall
eventually return. The function of religion is to reconcile the
laws of that spiritual kingdom with the sensuous world of man;
morality has tried to achieve this, but it became flaccid and
servile when the attempt was made to subject it to the uncertain
calculus of a merely hedonistic theory. It is to Kant's everlasting
credit that he apprehended and expounded the supreme signifi-

* A Grand Ducal residence in the country near Jena, at which Goethe
often stayed.

GOETHE IN 1817

cance of morality. Its purpose has been to mitigate the type of barbarity which seeks to live by no laws but its own, and to encroach unscrupulously upon the interests of others. It was in order to set bounds to this barbarity and unscrupulousness that political communities were formed, and all positive laws are an imperfect attempt to restrain individuals from taking the law into their own hands at each other's expense. If we survey the behaviour of mankind for the last few thousand years, we shall discern in it certain formulae, recurring constantly in various guises, which have exercised a magical power over whole nations as well as over individuals, and which must be regarded as the infallible sign of a higher power that guides all things."

These remarks impressed themselves so strongly on my memory that I was able to write them down word for word on returning to Weimar.

124. F. von Müller   29.4.1818

At about eight o'clock in the morning we drove out from Weimar to Dornburg, in bright spring sunshine. We arrived at about eleven.

(*Müller gives an account of Goethe's remarks which is almost identical with the preceding account by Caroline von Egloffstein, and then concludes*): We listened attentively to every word that flowed with such eloquence from his beloved lips, and did our best, by contradictions and objections, to make him talk with greater and greater vividness. It was as if the great outlines of world history were passing before Goethe's inner vision, and as if his powerful intellect were engaged in reducing them to their simplest elements. With every new thing he said there was something increasingly majestic, I would almost say prophetic, about his whole manner. Fact and fiction intermingled, and his features radiated the sublime tranquility of a sage. And for all this he remained childlike, gentle and sympathetic, far more than usually patient in answering our queries and objections, and his thoughts seemed to be floating up and down as if in some pure untroubled ether.

But the precious hours slipped away all too soon. "My dear young friends", he said, suddenly rising from his seat, "you must let me hurry away and be alone again, down there with my stones; for after such a conversation old Merlin must commune again with the primal elements." Full of pleasurable excitement we gazed long at his retreating figure, as, wrapped in his light grey cloak, he walked solemnly down into the valley, pausing now by this rock or by that, or beside some particular plant, and testing the rocks with his mineralogical hammer. The shadows of the hills were lengthening already, and in them, like some spectral being, he gradually vanished from our eyes.

125. Riemer   *June 1818*

"Man is a strange creature, to be sure! When it was explained to me how a kaleidoscope works, I lost all interest in it. God could cause us considerable embarrassment by revealing all the secrets of nature to us : we should not know what to do for sheer apathy and boredom."

126. E. Genast   *27.8.1818*

On the morning of the twenty-seventh of August Goethe's faithful servant Karl was ordered to bring up two bottles of red wine and two glasses, and place them in the windows at opposite ends of the room. This having been done, Goethe began to pace round the room, stopping at regular intervals to empty a glass at each window in turn. After some little time Rehbein, who had accompanied him to Carlsbad, came in to see him.

GOETHE : "You're a fine friend! What date and day of the month is this?"

REHBEIN : "The twenty-seventh of August, your Excellency."

GOETHE : "No, it's the twenty-eighth and my birthday."

REHBEIN : "Oh, come now, I never forget your birthday. To-day is the twenty-seventh."

GOETHE : "You lie! Today is the twenty-eighth."

REHBEIN, *determinedly* : "The twenty-seventh."

GOETHE *rings, Karl enters.* "What date is it today?"

KARL : "The twenty-seventh, your Excellency."

GOETHE : "The devil take—get the calendar!" *Karl fetches the calendar.*

GOETHE, *after a long pause* : "Well, I'll be damned! So I've got drunk to no purpose."

127.   J. G. Cogswell   *28.8.1819*

I went first to Weimar to see Goethe, and as he was absent at Jena I followed him there. They say in Germany that he is proud and has no heart, but it has ever been my good fortune to see him when he showed none of his pride, and to be received by him as if he had a heart and a feeling one too. I know not when I was more touched at parting from a person to whom I was bound by no particular tie, than from him. "What brings you to Jena?" said he. "To take leave of you." "I thank you with all my heart for this mark of your regard. It delights me to find that you take such an interest in me in my old age, as to come so far to see me. Keep me, I beg you, in friendly remembrance." A little further conversation and I parted from him. He embraced and kissed me affectionately according to the German custom. This year he is just seventy, his birthday was celebrated in Weimar, August 28, and on that account he went away. "I am too old", he said, "to take delight in the anniversary."

128.   C. F. A. von Conta   *May 1820*

Goethe was in the happiest of spirits, talking willingly and at length of his earlier associations, most of all of his friend Schiller, of whom he said: "When I had not seen him for three days, I no longer recognised him, so gigantic were the strides he made in his process of self-perfection".

He blamed Schiller's untimely death on his methods of working. "I have always said", he declared, "that a poet should not set to work until he feels an irresistible impulse to create. And this is a principle which I have followed, and to which I owe my lusty old age. You can see here", he continued, "half a dozen pieces of work which I have begun; I do nothing to any of them unless it happens to attract me at the time, and I continue none of them for a moment longer than I feel so disposed.

"Schiller on the other hand did not accept this. He asserted that what a man wills must also be possible; and accordingly that was how he went about it. I will give you an example: Schiller set himself the task of writing *Wilhelm Tell*. He began by plastering every wall of his room with as many detailed maps of Switzerland as he could get hold of. Then he read travellers' descriptions of the country until he knew the scene of the Swiss

revolt like the back of his hand. At the same time he studied
Swiss history, and when he had collected all the material, he sat
down to work; and—" (here Goethe rose and banged his
clenched fist on the table) "—he *literally* did not get up from his
desk until *Tell* was finished. When fatigue overtook him he put
his head on his arm and slept. As soon as he woke up he would
ask—not, as has falsely been rumoured, for champagne—but for
strong black coffee, to keep himself awake. That was how *Tell*
was finished in six weeks; but that, too, is why it is all of a
piece!"

129.   F. von Müller   7.6.1820

Hocus-pocus by Goethe with a coloured goblet decorated with
a snake made of darker glass.* "This is a primary phenomenon,
for which one must not try to find any further explanation. God
himself understands it no better than I do."

130.   J. Ch. Lobe   *July 1820*

"It is the enviable good fortune of youth to be able to receive
impressions and enjoy experiences with full vividness and intensity. As critical understanding increases, the source of these
undulled pleasures gradually dries up. Every man is an Adam;
for every man is sooner or later banished from paradise—the
paradise of warm feelings."

131.   *Luise von Knebel (reported)*   24.8.1820

"Goethe is extraordinarily charming when he is in a good
mood, but sometimes he is out of humour, and then he becomes
very monosyllabic and one feels rather ill at ease with him;
but this is not very often the case." Frau von Knebel then began
to talk about Goethe's late wife, and praised her highly. "She
was a much envied woman, and consequently the victim of a
great deal of spiteful slanderous talk." And she went on to say
that Christiane had been a woman of excellent character, very
warm-hearted, and that they were all convinced that Goethe,
being the sort of man he was, could not possibly have found a
more suitable wife; she had devoted her entire life solely to him,
and in her dealings with him she had never thought of herself,

* An optical experiment; cf. No. 249.

her one aim always being to make things pleasant and comfortable for him. "And what is more, she had a most cheerful tem-
perament, she was able to raise his spirits, and knew him so well
that she could always adopt the right tone of voice, the exact
approach that would do him good. She was not a very well-
educated woman, but she had a great deal of clear native intelligence. Goethe has often told us that there were times when his
thoughts were much exercised by some topic, when ideas would
crowd and jostle too much in his mind and he would find himself wandering too far and becoming quite confused : at such
times he would go to her and simply put the matter before her,
and would often be astonished at the way her simple natural
astuteness always went straight to the right solution. He says he
has learnt many things from her in this way." Frau von Knebel
also recalled how deeply Goethe had felt his wife's death and
how even now he had still not got over it.

132.   J. G. von Quandt   December 1820

Goethe was a great intellect, but not an impish wit bubbling
over with bons mots. The force of his genius was not like elec-
tricity discharging itself in flashes and bangs. It is indeed probably rare for a man of great profundity to be an homme de
salon as well, notwithstanding Goethe's style, which most accur-
ately reproduces the tone of good society, especially in *Wilhelm
Meister* and *The Elective Affinities*.

133.   F. J. Frommann

The pleasure of reading his works is far excelled by that of
listening to him talk. He was a masterly raconteur; his stories
poured out all of one piece, and their charm was enhanced by
his expressive gestures and the way his eyes shone as he spoke.

134.   G. Bancroft   7.3.1821

*I was with Goethe for a half hour to-day. I tried to bring him
to talk of the German poets and mentioned Tieck. Goethe
remained silent. I mentioned the Schlegels: he observed merely
that they had written many pretty things. Byron's* Don Juan
*Goethe has read and admired its humour. "The humour of the
rimes," said he, "is capable only in your language, where words*

differently written are often pronounced alike. This peculiarity of your language has been cultivated and exercised by a series of comic writers, Swift and so on, and so on."

Goethe is still very industrious. He dictates often for several hours in succession. Professor Riemer says of him, he brings forth like the mice, who carry about in the womb young ones ready for delivery and others just beginning to exist.

135. Tsar Nicholas I   May 1821

When I met Goethe I was still very young, I did not want to become involved in conversation with him yet and merely listened to my elders talking. I never heard a word fall from his lips that was not full of meaning; he could talk on any subject with the originality of a genius, of a man full of ideas which were his own and not borrowed from anyone else. He asked me what I thought of the *Sorrows of Werther* and of Werther himself. This question, I confess, rather took me aback. How was I, a young man, to tell Goethe my opinion of his work ! But he insisted on an answer, and so I said that I considered Werther a weak character who fancied himself to be strong, and that Charlotte would probably have been unhappy with him. My answer entirely satisfied Goethe. In the course of further conversation he expressed his own opinion about *Werther*, remarking among other things that it had never been his intention to make suicide seem interesting, that on the contrary he regarded it as a morally reprehensible act.

136. R. P. Gillies   22.6.1821

My short morning's work was to compose three lines of as good German as I could muster, submitting that a humble student from Edinburgh, after a long journey, wished earnestly for the honour of a brief interview with the greatest of German poets.

Provided with this, I betook myself to the statesman's house, a sort of mansion such as a Duke's land-steward, in England, certainly would not have considered very distingué. I had time to wonder at the absence of all luxurious or costly appliances in the salle de réception. Some few busts and statues there were, it is true. But, alas! the dark oak-floor was uncarpeted, and if one had a feeling of cold even at midsummer, what must

*have been the atmosphere of that room in a dreary winter's day,
even supposing that the stove had its due supply of wood and
turf?*

*Now as the door opened from the farther end of the recep-
tion-room, and His Excellency's tall, gaunt form, wrapped in a
long blue surtout which hung loosely on him, slowly advanced,
he had veritably the air and aspect of a revenant. He advanced
in profound silence, in a mood, seemingly, of utter abstraction,
and after the manner of ghosts in general, he waited to be
spoken to! The spirit had been evoked from his other world,
had condescended to appear, and now the question was what
sort of conversation ought to be, or might be, without impro-
priety addressed to him? The plain truth was that I had set my
heart on seeing Goethe, but did not for a moment imagine that
my communications could have any interest for him, and in
sheer desperation I contrived to tell him this much, then fortunately made allusions again to my long journey and of my
great wish to settle, somewhere, at Weimar, for example. As it
happened, the best of diplomatists could not have managed
better. This was a practical point to which (with a half smile
at my broken German) he answered readily that nothing could
be more easy; Weimar was not over-populous, and he believed
that the court bookseller was at that moment charged to dispose
of a house and garden at a very low rent. To this he added:
"In days of yore, there were Englishmen here, who passed their
time pleasantly enough, and some of them I remember with
esteem and regret." I ventured to inquire whether Sir Brooke
Boothby had been among the chosen few? This question was a
lucky hit.*

*"I saw more of him," said he, "than of any other English
resident, and regretted his departure the most. You knew him
perhaps? Has he ever spoken to you about Weimar?"*

*"He told me about his having obtained a commission in the
Duke's cavalry, in order to have the privilege of appearing at
Court in boots instead of silk stockings."*

*"Quite right. His health was not good: he complained of our
cold winters, disliked silk stockings, and could ride better than
he danced."*

*This important fact disposed of, I mentioned that Sir Brooke
always had beside him a first edition of* Werther *and a few
other German books, from which he had made some translations. I then endeavoured to speak of the singular influence that*

Faust and Wilhelm Meister *had exercised on English authors; of Lord Byron's debt to the former in* Manfred, *and so forth; but to this his answers were in a tone of perfect indifference. He cared not a straw about praise and was inaccessible to flattery. About twenty minutes sufficed for my audience; but he was very courteous at parting, and said he should rejoice to hear that I could meet with an abode at Weimar suitable to my finances and views.*

137. C. G. Carus   21.7.1821

As soon as one entered Goethe's house, which was moderately large and built in a simple classical style, one could already guess the predilections of its owner from the wide, very gently rising stair and from the way the landing was decorated with the hound of Diana and the young faun of Belvedere. Further up, one's gaze was pleasantly greeted by a group representing the Heavenly Twins, and as one entered the anteroom one was welcomed by an inviting SALVE inlaid in blue on the floor. The anteroom itself was most richly decorated with engravings and busts, and at the back of the house, beyond a second gallery of busts, it opened on to an outdoor landing, gaily decorated with plants, from which a little stair led down into the garden.

At last a firm step approaching from the neighbouring room heralded the great man himself. Simply dressed in a blue cloth coat, wearing his boots, his hair short and lightly powdered, he walked towards me in an energetic upright posture and led me to the sofa. His seventy-two years have left little impression on Goethe; it is true that the arcus senilis is beginning to form in the cornea of both his eyes, but it does not detract from the fire of their gaze. In general his eyes are his outstandingly expressive feature, and it was chiefly in them that I perceived the whole tenderness of his poetic soul: that tenderness which otherwise—though apparently only with difficulty—he restrains, sheltering it behind frosty decorum from the importunate incursions of the world. But at certain moments, too, as the conversation developed and grew warmer, he would open his eyes suddenly, and from them the whole fire of a great visionary genius would shine with almost daemonic power.

So there I sat, facing him! A man whom I must admit to have had so great an influence on my own development had suddenly appeared before me, and I was all the more eager to

study and grasp in every detail this remarkable presence. The
customary preliminary talk was soon over, and I began to tell
him about my latest work on the primal components of the
skeleton. He often interrupted me with exclamations of approval
and a satisfied nodding of the head. "Yes, yes!" he said, "this
matter is in good hands...Well, well! Yes, yes!" It was in
general his habit to enliven all conversational pauses with these
words, which he uttered in a peculiarly good-humoured manner.

The servant brought some light refreshments. I found it a
moving situation to see Goethe pouring out wine for me and
sharing a loaf with me, eating one half himself and handing me
the other. As he did so he talked about my two pictures. Towards one o'clock I finally left, altogether warmed and delighted.

138.   F. Förster   24.7.1821

Goethe was always particularly charming and good-humoured
and sociable at lunch-time, though his guests never exceeded
the nine Muses in number. In front of him would be a bottle of
old Rhine wine which he would empty all by himself; the rest
of us were expected to help ourselves as we pleased from the
bottles placed before us. The presence of guests appreciably influenced the menu, for which he usually gave personal instructions. As a rule there were three or at most four courses, not
counting the soup : meat with vegetables (he was very fond of
a stuffato cooked in the Italian way), then fish (he liked trout
best), then a roast (usually poultry or game), and then—"for the
ladies", as he would say—a sweet such as Carlsbad strudel. He
himself preferred a piece of English or Swiss cheese instead of
the sweet. He did the carving with his own hands, even when
it was a difficult joint of game, and would sometimes lay a
selected morsel or the most delicate piece of trout on the plate of
some favourite lady guest. The old gentleman's predominating
mood during lunch was one of exceptional good humour, with
much teasing of his daughter-in-law; but occasionally the conversation also took a serious turn.

139.   Ulrike von Levetzow   August 1821

I met Goethe in 1821 in Marienbad; Mother had taken me
from my pension in Strasbourg to spend a few months with her
there. At that time Marienbad was still a tiny place, indeed it

scarcely existed yet, and the house we had taken was nearly the largest and finest. Goethe was also living there, and I can still remember the first meeting very clearly. Grandmother sent for me; the maid said she had an old gentleman with her who wished to see me, and I was not at all pleased at this, for it interrupted me in a piece of needlework I had just begun. When I entered the room my mother was there too, and she said: "This is my eldest daughter Ulrike". Goethe took me by the hand and looked at me kindly and asked me how I liked Marienbad. Having spent the last few years in Strasbourg at a French boarding-school, and being only seventeen, I knew nothing about Goethe, or what a famous man and great poet he was, so I was quite unembarrassed before this kindly old gentleman, and without any of the shyness that usually overcame me when I made new acquaintances. Goethe invited me the very next morning to come for a walk with him, in the course of which I had to tell him all about Strasbourg and my school; I complained in particular that I felt lonely without my sisters, from whom I had been separated for the first time, and I am convinced that it was this childlike frankness of mine that interested him; for from then on he spent a great deal of time with me. Nearly every morning he took me with him when he went out walking, and if I did not come he brought back flowers for me, for I suppose he very soon noticed that I took no interest in the stones he was often looking at, but that apart from this I was willing to learn; towards evening, too, he would often sit by the hour on a bench outside the door, telling me about all sorts of things. When I realised what a great scholar he was, he was already so well known and familiar to me that this could not possibly make me feel shy or embarrassed; and later too, it occurred to no one, not even to my mother, to see in our frequent association anything more than the pleasure taken by an old man who, by his years, could have been my grandfather, in the company of a child, which was after all what I still was. Goethe was such a kind, charming old gentleman, whose friendship a young person could well enjoy, especially when she took so lively an interest in all the things which he described to her in so agreeable a manner: flowers, stones, stars and literature.

That summer, Goethe also made me a present of *Wilhelm Meister's Travels*. When I read the book I noticed at once that it must be the sequel to something else [*Wilhelm Meister's Apprenticeship*]. I said: "Herr Geheimrat, I don't understand,

surely there must be something else before this". To which
Goethe replied: "Indeed, you are quite right; but that is something you must not read yet, I will tell you the story". And he
sat on a bench and told it me for hours on end. If I had had
any idea at the time that importance would be attached to it
later, I should have written it all down.

140. J. S. Grüner   26.8.1821

Goethe suddenly got out of the carriage to examine a stone,
and I heard him say: "Well, well! how did *you* get here?"—
a question which he repeated, and which, knowing nothing
whatever about mineralogy, I found almost ludicrous. How can
so learned a man, I thought, find that piece of stone so interesting?

141. Felix Mendelssohn-Bartholdy   4.11.1821

Two hours later, Professor Zelter came and told us: "Goethe
has arrived! the old gentleman has arrived!" At once we rushed
downstairs into Goethe's house. He was in the garden, just appearing round a hedge. He is very kind; though I don't think
he looks like any of his portraits. Then he had a look at his
interesting collection of fossils which his son has arranged, and
kept saying "Hm! Hm! That is very satisfying". Afterwards I
walked round the garden for another half hour with him and
Professor Zelter. Then we went in to lunch. One would not take
him for a man of seventy-three, but for a man of fifty. After
lunch Fräulein Ulrike, Frau von Goethe's sister, asked for a kiss,
and so did I. Every morning I get a kiss from the author of
Faust and *Werther*, and every afternoon two kisses from my
father and friend Goethe. Just fancy that! In the afternoon I
played to him for about two hours, partly Bach fugues and partly
improvisations.

142. L. Rellstab   8.11.1821

Goethe had an excellent grand piano in his reception-rooms.
We all assembled there again that evening; for he had invited
a rather large party in order to acquaint his Weimar friends,
especially those of them who were musical, with the extraordinary talent of this boy Felix Mendelssohn-Bartholdy about whom
Zelter had been telling him all day.

It was Goethe's usual habit, at least so far as I have observed, to wait until the whole company had arrived before showing himself; meanwhile his son and daughter-in-law acquitted themselves as host and hostess very charmingly. There was invariably a certain solemnity about the moment of the poet's appearance among his guests; for nearly always they included some who were seeing him for the first time, or at least had very seldom been near him, and even in the case of those who associated with him more or less intimately, their predominant feeling towards him was one of reverence. And such was the impression made on that evening too; there was a sudden hush as the aged poet opened the door; every eye turned towards him; all greeted him with a silent bow. His "Good evening!" was addressed to everyone, but in particular he went up to Zelter and warmly shook his hand. It is well known that they were on terms of intimate address, calling each other *du*. Felix Mendelssohn gazed up with shining eyes at the lofty poet's snow-white head; but the latter took his face affectionately between his hands and said : "Now you shall play us something, Felix!" Zelter nodded approval.

Goethe now approached the rest of us. After addressing a few kindly remarks to me, he began to talk about Felix Mendelssohn : "My friend Zelter has brought me this little pupil of his, whom I am sure you know already". I said I did; Goethe went on : "He is to give us a display of his musical talents first, but he is extraordinarily gifted in every other direction too. You know the doctrine of the four temperaments : every man is supposed to have all of them in him, but mixed in different proportions; in the case of this boy I would suppose that he has the absolute minimum of the phlegmatic and the maximum of the opposite."

The piano had been opened, and the candles placed on the music-desk. Felix Mendelssohn was about to play. "What shall I play?" he asked Zelter, to whom his attitude was one of complete childlike submission and trust. "Well, anything you can!" answered the latter in the light casual tone which everyone who knew him well will remember; "anything that isn't too hard for you."—It was finally agreed that he should improvise freely, and he asked Zelter for a theme. The latter asked him : "Do you know the song 'I dreamt one night of Jenny', etc.?" Felix said he did not. "Then I'll play it to you."

Zelter sat down at the piano and played with his stiff hands (he had several lame fingers) a very simple song in G major with a triplet rhythm. Felix repeated it once right through, and then played over the triplet figure several times with both hands in unison, as if to guide his fingers into the shape of the main figure and accustom them to moving in it quite automatically. Then he began, but he went straight into the wildest allegro. The gentle melody became a passionate theme which he introduced now in the bass and now in the treble and developed with fine countersubjects : in fact, he improvised in a headlong stream of fiery inspiration. With the unerring tact that characterised him even at that age, the young artist did not continue his performance for too long; and the impression it made was all the greater. There was an astonished, spellbound silence as after leaping powerfully on to a final chord his hands left the keys and came to rest.

Zelter was the first to break the stillness, in his casual humorous manner which I have already mentioned, by saying out loud : "Well, well ! I suppose the hobgoblin must have got into you ! What a steeplechase that was !" The boy's playing had, as may well be imagined, sent everyone into ecstasies of admiration, and Goethe especially was overjoyed with the little artist, whose childlike features wore an expression of mingled happiness, pride and embarrassment. He hugged him warmly, taking his head between his hands and caressing him with affected roughness, and said jokingly : "But you're not going to get away with that and no more ! You must play some more before we give you our full recognition." "But what shall I play, Herr Professor?" asked Felix (he always called Zelter "Herr Professor"). "What shall I play now?"

Goethe was very fond of Bach's fugues; and so Felix Mendelssohn too was set the task of playing a fugue by that venerable master. Zelter chose it from the volume of the fugues which was brought, and the boy, quite unprepared, played it with perfect assurance. Goethe's delight was increased by this amazing performance. Among other things he asked Felix to play him a minuet. "Shall I play you the most beautiful one in the whole world?" "Well, what might that be?" And he played the minuet from *Don Giovanni*. Goethe stood all the time by the instrument listening; his features shone with pleasure. After the minuet he wanted the overture to the opera; but this the performer flatly refused, declaring that it could not be played as it was written and that it would be wrong to alter a note of it.

But instead he offered to play the overture to *Figaro*. He began it with a lightness of touch, with an assurance and polish and clarity in the passage-work such as I have never heard since. Goethe became more and more good-humoured and kindly, jesting with the spirited and lively boy and teasing him. "So far", he said, "you have only played me pieces you know; and now let us see whether you can also play something you don't know. I'll put you to the test."

He left the room and came back a few minutes later with several manuscript sheets of music. "Here are a few things from my manuscript collection; now let us see what you can do. Will you be able to play this?" And he put a sheet on the music-stand. The notes were clearly written but small; it was Mozart's hand. It was not an easy manuscript to read, but the young artist played it at sight with absolute assurance, not making even the slightest mistake; the piece sounded as if he had known it by heart for years, so sure and clear and balanced was his rendering.

Everyone applauded, and Goethe maintained his bantering tone. "That's still not good enough!" he exclaimed. "Other people could read that too. But now I shall give you something that will puzzle you. Now watch out!" And thus jesting he selected another sheet and put it on the stand. This one indeed looked very strange : one could scarcely tell whether it was music or only a piece of lined paper covered with blobs of ink and in-numerable smudges. Mendelssohn laughed out loud with surprise. "What funny writing!" he exclaimed. "Who could possibly read that?" But suddenly he became serious; for no sooner had Goethe begun to say : "Now just guess who wrote that?" when Zelter cried : "Why, it's a Beethoven manuscript! One can tell that a mile away! He always seems to write with a broomstick and wipe his sleeve over the notes before they're dry. I have a lot of his manuscripts : they're easy to recognise." —But at the mention of this name Mendelssohn's face had suddenly become serious and more than serious : his features wore an expression of reverent awe. Goethe watched him with curiosity and visible delight. The boy went on gazing intently at the manuscript, and a look of amazement shone from his face, as a lofty concept of beauty, of profound and noble originality disentangled itself from the chaos of erased, obliterated, superimposed and inserted notes and words. But all this lasted only a matter of seconds; for Goethe wanted to make the test a severe one and leave the player no time for preparation. "There you are!" he cried. "Didn't I tell you it would puzzle you? Now try! Show us what you can do!

Felix at once began to play. It was a simple song; if clearly written, it would have been child's play, no problem at all even for a mediocre performer; but in this case he did need, if he was to distinguish the right notes and passages from the ten or twenty others that had been crossed out or partly or wholly obliterated, a rapidity and sureness of comprehension such as few can achieve. He played it through once, correctly on the whole, but pausing over particular notes and several times saying quickly as he corrected an error: "No, this is it!" Then he exclaimed: "Now I shall play it to you!" And this second time not even one note was missing; the vocal line he partly sang and partly played it in with the rest... After this exhibition of skill Goethe declared himself content. I need hardly add that abundant praise was again lavished on the young performer, and that Goethe veiled his with persiflage, pointing out that Felix had hesitated after all over this piece and not been quite sure of himself.

The aged poet foretold a very great future for the musical prodigy; he spoke with the warmest conviction of it to me, to whom he addressed several remarks to this effect. A phenomenon so rich in promise filled him with true artistic delight, and the fire of his enthusiasm was constantly rekindled as he talked. The boy had obviously very much taken his fancy.

143. Felix Mendelssohn-Bartholdy   10.11.1821

Every afternoon Goethe opens the piano and says: "I haven't heard you play yet today; make a little noise for me". And then he sits down beside me, and when I have finished (I usually improvise) I ask him for a kiss, or I just take one. You have no idea how good and kind he is, or what a rich collection of minerals, busts, engravings, little statues and large drawings this polar star among poets possesses. I would not say that his stature is impressive; he is actually not much taller than Father. But his bearing, his speech, his name—these are impressive. The tone of his voice is extraordinary, and he can roar like ten thousand warriors. Zelter was planning to leave for Jena on Tuesday and go straight to Leipzig from there. We were to go with him, but we decided to throw ourselves at his feet and beg for a couple of extra days in Weimar. Professor Zelter was dragged into Goethe's room, whereupon the latter broke out at him in his voice of thunder, berated him for wanting to take us with him to that dreary hole, ordered him to hold his tongue, to obey without answering back, to leave us here, to go to Jena by himself and then return, and so beset him from all sides that he is going to do everything that Goethe wishes. At this we all besieged Goethe, kissing his lips and his hands, and those who could not get near him stroked him and kissed his shoulders, and I think that if he had not been at home already we should have followed him home as the Romans followed Cicero after his first Cataline oration. Fräulein Ulrike von Pogswisch had also fallen on his neck too, and as he is flirting with her (she is very pretty) the whole thing had a very satisfactory effect on him.

So you see, if Goethe says to me: "My dear boy, tomorrow I am giving a party, and you must play to us too", I can't say no, can I!

144. *J. S. Grüner*   *31.7.1822*

Goethe was particularly fond of my son Ignaz; he said it was because the little boy looked at him in such a friendly way with his big eyes and gave such spirited answers to all his questions. Goethe would often ask him to tell him a story, for instance he once said: "Tell me a story about a cat". The boy was not at a loss and asked: "What sort of cat, a white one or a black one?" "Tell me about a white one." So the boy made his cat swim across a pond to an island and catch mice there, then swim back again, only to be shot by a huntsman as it came ashore.

"You see, my friend", said Goethe, "he takes the same way out as many authors do! They can think of no further suitable development for their theme, so they kill off their hero."

145. *J. S. Grüner*   *1.8.1822*

In my conversation with Goethe we referred to the *Sorrows of Werther* and the astonishing sensation which this work produced all over Germany the moment it was published. Goethe said: "Apparently one can't please everyone; some people tried to hold me responsible for the fact that a few students shot themselves. In Vienna a firework display was held in honour of

Werther, there was general silence, and at the end of a long pause a pistol-shot was heard. Novelty has its charms."

146.   F. Soret   21.9.1822

This evening Monsieur Meyer took me to see the celebrated Goethe, who received me kindly, though with a touch of coolness. Our conversation turned mainly on mineralogy, chemistry and physics. He appeared to be particularly interested in the phenomenon of polarisation. He showed me some apparatus constructed partly in accordance with his own ideas, and told me that he would like to carry out experiments with me in this field. I thought it very strange to see this great poet busy with scientific research and taking pleasure in the contemplation of motionless minerals after creating the passionate Werther.

Our visit lasted over an hour. Towards the end Goethe became more communicative and said very flattering things to me as we left. His face is still handsome and there is something especially majestic about his forehead and his eyes; he is tall and well built. For the last few years he has been thought too elderly for social life and no longer goes out, not even to call on their Highnesses; he receives them instead. But to see him one would hardly believe him to be old or infirm.

147.   F. von Müller   3.2.1823

"If", said Goethe, "I were so unfortunate as to have to belong to the opposition, I would rather stir up revolution and riot than wander gloomily round and round perpetually carping at the established order. I have never in my life cared to oppose myself bitterly and uselessly to the overwhelming current of the popular will or ruling principle; I preferred to withdraw into my own shell and live as I pleased inside it."

148.   F. von Müller   February 1823

(*17th*): Called on Goethe in the afternoon and found him already very sick, with his bedroom in complete darkness. At midday he had had a violent fit of fever, lasting two hours. He kept moaning repeatedly: "God Almighty, how ill I am! How one suffers, poor devil that one is! I haven't been so ill for years."

Then : "The gods are hard on us on these sick days—not that they treat us particularly kindly when we are well".

(20th–22nd): From Thursday till Saturday he kept getting better and then worse again. He was often in a stupor, and sometimes his mind half wandered, but always with intervals of quite lucid speech and communication. On Thursday he was able to spend quite some time with his elder grandson and even sang a little song to him. He frequently asked after people in whom he had previously taken comparatively little interest. Once he murmured to his servant Stadelmann : "You can't imagine how wretched I am, how terribly ill !" He kept exhorting the doctors to bethink themselves seriously about his condition, and hinted that he regarded their art with a certain scepticism. "Ply your trade !" he exclaimed. "It's all very fine, but I don't suppose you'll save me." Several times he asked for a hot bath, but this was considered too dangerous. Once when the doctors had been consulting together in undertones he said : "There go these Jesuits ! They can take counsel, to be sure, but they can't give counsel or save one's life." He lamented the way each of them at random prescribed "damnable stuff" for him to swallow. At midday on Saturday they let him drink a glass of champagne, without visible effect. He ate with great enjoyment a bergamot pear and some pineapple jelly. Once he remarked softly to himself : "I wonder indeed whether this unity will be able to reappear and reconstitute itself as a new unity, after all the disintegrations and tortures it has suffered?" To Ulrike von Pogwisch he said : "Oh, you can't imagine how these ideas torment me, how they cut across each other and tangle each other up !"

(23rd): Sunday was his worst day. Early that morning he said to his son : "Death is standing round me in every corner", and to one of the doctors he said several times : "I am done for". I am told that he once exclaimed : "Oh you Christian God ! How much pain you inflict on your poor human creatures, and yet you expect us to praise and thank you for it in your temples !"

(24th): In the afternoon he got very angry with the doctors, and shouted loudly for some Kreuzbrunnen to be brought to him, and said : "If I've got to die, at least I'll die in my own way". And he did in fact drink a small bottle of Kreuzbrunnen, with evidently beneficial results. From half past four until nine I was in the adjoining room, and his voice sounded quite son-

orous and powerful. I heard him demanding a full circumstantial account of the progress of his illness, as if it were some impersonal matter which had now been brought to a conclusion. He was jubilant that his keen sense of taste had detected some aniseed in one of his medicines and that in view of his rooted aversion to this herb they had decided to alter the prescription. He heard with satisfaction that they intended to give him arnica, and delivered quite happily a short botanical lecture on this flower, which he had often seen growing very profusely in Bohemia. He asked many times which of his friends had called to enquire after him. "Very obliging of the dear people, I'm sure." His condition visibly improved, and he urged his family to go to bed; they should think of themselves, he said; his own small needs were catered for. He himself began to recover hope; he said: "Tomorrow I shall drink plenty of Kreuzbrunnen again, and then I'll soon be a proper man again with regular habits". He asked if they had kept his diary up to date, and lamented that this had not been done.

149. *Eckermann* 10.6.1823

I arrived here a few days ago, and called on Goethe today for the first time. He received me in an exceedingly friendly way, and my impression of his personality was such that I count this as one of the happiest days of my life.

He at once began to talk about my manuscript. "I have just been meeting you already", he said. "I have been reading your essays all morning; they need no recommendation, they recommend themselves." He then praised the clarity of the exposition and the flow of the ideas, saying that it was all admirably well founded and well thought out. "I shall send it to the publishers at once with a letter", he added. I thanked him fervently.

We sat together for some time, talking quietly and affectionately. I rested my hand on his knees, I was so intent on looking at him that I forgot to speak, so insatiable was my gaze. He had such a powerful, brown face, full of wrinkles, and every wrinkle full of expression. And in his whole appearance there was such integrity and strength and tranquillity and greatness! He spoke slowly and unhurriedly, rather as an elderly monarch might talk. It was evident that he is sufficient to himself and far above any praise or blame. To be with him made me indescribably happy; I felt reassured and at peace, like one who has passed through much toil and expectation to the fulfilment of his dearest wish.

150.   *Eckermann*   *15.9.1823*

Goethe has arrived back safely from Marienbad. When we met he began at once to talk about my plans.

"I must tell you frankly", he said, "that I should like you to spend this winter with me in Weimar. I shall arrange lodgings for you somewhere near me; you shall not have a dull moment all winter. There is still a concentration in Weimar of many excellent people and things, and as you get to know the better circles here you will enjoy a society that is not inferior to the finest in any large city. We also have a choice library and a theatre which is essentially as good as the best in any other German town. So I repeat: stay with us! and not only this winter: make Weimar your home. There are gates and roads from here to everywhere in the world. You can travel in summer and gradually see all the places you want to see. I have been here fifty years and travelled all over the place! But I was always glad to come back to Weimar."

I assured him again that I was prepared to do anything that he thought would be best in my particular circumstances.

151.   *Eckermann*   *18.9.1823*

"The world is so large and rich and life so diverse that there will never be any lack of occasions for poems. But they must all *be* occasional poems; that is to say, reality must be their stimulus and their material. A particular case becomes general and poetic by the very fact that a poet treats it. All my poems are occasional poems, suggested by reality, based on it, rooted in it. I have no use for poems that are simply picked out of the air.

"Let no one say that reality lacks poetic interest; for a poet, after all, proves that he is one precisely by having the wit to present a common object from an interesting angle. Reality must provide the themes, the points to be made, the heart of the matter; but to shape all this into a beautiful living whole is the poet's business."

152.   *F. von Müller*   *23.9.1823*

His dissatisfaction at being cooped up here again after so

FRIEDRICH
VON
MÜLLER
(1779-1849)

JOHANN
PETER
ECKERMANN
(1792-1854)

happy a stay at Marienbad was very noticeable throughout the evening. When I urged him to go for drives every day, he said: "Who am I to go with? They all bore me. That Staël woman once told me: Il vous faut de la séduction; and she was quite right." When I mentioned Ottilie and Ulrike he replied: "Anyone whom one sees every day from morning to evening ceases to be seductive. Yes, I came home well and in good spirits; for three months I have felt happy, drawn from one interest to another, from one magnet to another, almost like a ball being rolled to and fro. But now—the ball is back in its corner, and I must bury myself in my badger's lair and get through the winter somehow or other." How sad it is to witness the inner torment of such a man, and to see how neither science nor art can restore the lost balance of his mind without the most terrible struggle.

153. F. von Müller   25.9.1823

He talked a great deal to me about Marienbad, especially about Frau von Szymanowska, who plays the piano so beautifully; he said of her that she was so lovely and charming that despite her enchanting music one is glad when she stops playing, just to hear her speak, and on the other hand one wants her to begin again, because her speech is so very exciting that it is only during her playing that one can hope to regain one's composure.

He had, he said, made friends with her so quickly, without any preliminaries, just as one feels at home at once in a pure mild climate. Then he went to his garden-room and fetched an example of her handwriting, from which he expounded her character; and then, with passionate solemnity, he read me the poem he had written to her, three beautiful stanzas.

154. F. von Müller   19.10.1823

He gave a brilliant analysis of the history of the Church as the product of error and tyranny. The doctrine of the divinity of Christ, first affirmed by the Council of Nicaea, had been (he said) a very useful and indeed essential aid to despotic government.

On personal survival Goethe expressed quite definite views. It was (he said) absolutely impossible for any thinking being to conceive a state of non-being, a cessation of thought and life; to this extent every man quite involuntarily carries the proof of immortality within himself. But as soon as one attempts to get outside oneself objectively, as soon as one tries to prove and conceptualise personal survival in dogmatic terms, and builds a philistine superstructure of argument on that inner knowledge, then one becomes entangled in contradictions. Man nevertheless feels constantly impelled to reduce the impossible to a hypothesis (a unity). Almost all laws are syntheses of the impossible, the institution of marriage for example. And yet it is good that this should be so, for the maximum possibilities are realised if the impossible is demanded.

155. Eckermann   3.11.1823

"Always hold fast to the present. Every situation, indeed every moment, is of infinite value, for it is the representative of a whole eternity."

156. F. von Müller   4.11.1823

Today at long last Madame Szymanowska's public concert took place. Afterwards we had supper at Goethe's house, and he was all kindness and charm. Among the various toasts that we drank, someone proposed one to Memory, and this caused Goethe to exclaim with some emphasis: "I do not admit the existence of 'memory' as you understand it: the word is a mere clumsy makeshift. When we have some great or beautiful or significant experience, we do not need to 'remind' ourselves of it, to chase and recapture and recall it to mind from somewhere outside ourselves as it were: on the contrary, it must from the very outset weave itself into our mind and become part of it: it must beget in us a newer and better self and thus live on in us for ever as a creative and transforming force. We should not long nostalgically for the past, for there is none to recover: there are only the elements of past experience perpetually growing and shaping themselves into something new. True longing must always be a creating, the making of a new and better thing."

157. Eckermann   16.11.1823

Remembering his promise to show me his Marienbad Elegy

again when we had a suitable opportunity, Goethe rose, placed a light on his desk and gave me the poem. I was delighted to have it before me once more. Goethe sat down again quietly and left me to examine it undisturbed. He seemed to go to sleep and I took the opportunity of reading and re-reading it several times.

"What you have there", he told me later, "is the product of an extremely passionate mood; when that mood was on me, I would not for all the world have had it cease, and now I would not want to feel like that again for any price.

"I wrote the poem immediately after leaving Marienbad, when my emotion was still fresh and intense. I wrote down the first stanza at eight in the morning when the coach made its first stop; then I went on composing as we travelled and at each stop I wrote down what I had in my head, so that by evening the manuscript was finished. That is why it has a certain immediacy and is all of one piece, which I dare say is to its advantage as a whole. Rather as a man stakes a large sum on one card, I staked on a present experience and tried to raise its value as high as possible without exaggerating."

158. F. von Müller   *25.11.1823*

According to Zelter, when someone once asked Haydn why his masses were so joyful and indeed almost jovial, the composer replied : "Because whenever I think of God [den lieben Gott] I always feel so indescribably happy". When I told this anecdote to Goethe, tears poured down his cheeks.

159. Eckermann   *31.12.1823*

"People speak of God", said Goethe, "as if this incomprehensible supreme Being, so far beyond the limits of our thought, were someone not much better than themselves. Otherwise they would not say der Herr Gott, der liebe Gott, le bon Dieu. To such people—and especially to priests, who mention him daily— he becomes a cliché, a mere name which means nothing to them at all. But if they deeply felt his greatness they would stop talking, and reverence would make them reluctant to name him."

160. Eckermann   *2.1.1824*

We discussed English literature, the greatness of Shakespeare, and the very disadvantageous situation of all the English dramatists who had succeeded that poetic colossus.

"I myself, of course", said Goethe, "was luckier fifty years ago in poor old Germany. I was soon able to come to terms with such existing tradition as there was; it could not impress me for long or be much of an obstacle to me. I very soon left German literature and the study of it behind me and concentrated on living and on creative writing. Thus I gradually advanced and continued my development and progressively fitted myself for the literary achievements of each period of my life. And in each phase of my development my ideal of excellence never far exceeded what I was actually capable of achieving at that stage. But if I had been born an Englishman and all those manifold masterpieces had borne in upon me with full force at the first awakening of my youthful imagination, I should have been overwhelmed and not known what to do. I could not have advanced with such light-hearted confidence, but would have had to reflect long and deep and look well about me before finding some sort of new way out."

The conversation turned to *Werther*. "That", said Goethe, "is another creature I fed, like the pelican, with my own heart's blood. There is so much in it of my own innermost feelings and thoughts that it could run to a novel of ten such volumes. And incidentally, as I have often remarked before, I have re-read the book only once since its publication, and have taken good care not to do so again. It's sheer high explosive! To read it fills me with an uncanny feeling, a dread of being involved once again in the pathological state of mind by which the novel was inspired."

161.   *Eckermann*   4.1.1824

"The public has really never been satisfied with me and has always wanted me to be something different from what it pleased God to make me. And they have rarely been satisfied with my creative efforts either. When I had toiled for a year and a day with all my heart and soul to produce some new work which would please the world, I would even be expected to thank the world for not actually disliking what I had written. If anyone praised me, I was not expected to accept the tribute with self-appreciative pleasure as my just due, but on the contrary to decline it with some modest formula which would humbly express the total unworthiness both of myself and of my work. This however was quite foreign to my nature, and I should have had to be a contemptible wretch to lie and dissemble in such a fashion. But since I was strong enough to show myself with complete truthfulness, just as I felt, I got the reputation of being proud, and I still have it to this day.

"Whether it was in religion or in science or in politics, I have always been getting myself into trouble by refusing to be a hypocrite and having the courage to speak my mind freely.

"I have believed in God and Nature and in the triumph of nobility over baseness; but that was not good enough for pious souls, they wanted me also to believe that three is one and one is three. But this offended my intellectual conscience; and be- sides, I could never understand how such a belief could be of the slightest use to me.

"And as for politics! I cannot tell you what I have had to suffer and put up with. I have been called all sorts of names which I do not care to repeat. The world is simply determined not to see me as I am, and averts its eyes from anything that might display me in my true light. Schiller, on the other hand— who between you and me was much more of an aristocrat than I was but took much greater care what he said than I did— enjoys the singular good fortune of being regarded as a warm friend of the people. I do not begrudge him his reputation in the least, and take comfort in the fact that others before me have fared no better than myself.

"It is true that I could not help disliking the French Revolu- tion, for its horrors touched me too nearly and revolted me day by day and hour by hour, whereas it was then not yet possible to foresee its beneficial consequences. Moreover I could not view with indifference the attempts that were being made in Germany to provoke similar events artificially, events which in France had been born of a great necessity.

"But at the same time I was no friend of arbitrary tyrannical rule, and I was absolutely convinced that it is never the people who are to blame for any great revolution, but the government. Revolutions are quite impossible so long as governments remain constantly just and constantly wide awake, and can thus antici- pate them by timely reforms instead of resisting until the neces- sary change is forced on them from below.

"A nation only benefits from something which has proceeded out of its own centre and its own total need, without imitating

any other nation. For what may be wholesome food for one
people at a particular stage of its development may turn out to
be poison for another. It is therefore folly to attempt to introduce
any foreign innovation for which one's own people does not
have a deep-rooted need, and all would-be revolutions of this
kind are ineffectual, for God is not with them : he withholds
his aid from such bungling enterprises. But if in any nation there
exists the genuine need for a great reform, then God is with it,
and it will succeed."

162.   Eckermann   27.1.1824

"I have always been held to be a man particularly favoured
by fortune; and, indeed, I have no wish to complain or to
deplore the course of my life. But at bottom it has been nothing
but toil and labour, and I think I can say that in my seventy-
five years there have never been four weeks in which I felt really
at ease. It has been like constantly rolling a stone and having
to heave it up again and again. There were too many external
and internal claims on my activity.

"My real happiness lay in my poetic meditations and crea-
tions. But these were very much disturbed and limited and
hindered by my worldly position. If I had been able to withdraw more from my involvement in public affairs and business,
and to live a more solitary life, I should have been happier
and could have done much more as a writer."

163.   Eckermann   25.2.1824

"I have no wish to be deprived of the happiness of believing
in a future life; indeed, I would say with Lorenzo dei Medici
that those who hope for no other life are dead for this one as
well. But these incomprehensible matters are too remote to be an
object of daily meditation; such speculations ruin the brain.
Moreover, anyone who believes in an after-life should enjoy his
good fortune in silence, but it does not entitle him to give himself airs. I have encountered foolish ladies who were proud of
their belief in immortality, and I had to put up with being cate-
chised by a number of them on this point in the most opinion-
ated manner. But I annoyed them by saying that I should have
no objection whatsoever to finding, after this life had ended, that
we are blessed with yet another; but that it would be my special

request not to have to meet in the hereafter any of those who had believed in it here below. For otherwise my torment would begin in real earnest! I should be surrounded by pious souls who would say: 'Weren't we right? Didn't we tell you? Hasn't it happened?' And thus even the Beyond would be one long bore.

"Preoccupation with thoughts about immortality", Goethe went on, "is a pastime for the aristocratic classes, and especially for women who have nothing better to do. But an honest man who hopes to achieve something while he is still here on earth and is working and striving and struggling every day to that end, will let the other world take care of itself and bestir himself usefully in this one."

164. *Eckermann*   *26.2.1824*

Goethe said that a genuine poet possesses an inborn knowledge of the world and can portray it perfectly well without having had much experience or scope for practical observation. "I wrote my *Götz von Berlichingen*", he told me, "as a young man of twenty-two and was amazed ten years later to find what an accurate picture of life I had given. I had, as you know, not yet experienced or seen anything of that kind; various human situations therefore had to be known to me by anticipation.

"In fact, I only enjoyed writing about my inner world until I got to know the world outside me. When I later discovered that the world was in reality just as I had thought, I was annoyed and lost all wish to write about it. Indeed, I am inclined to say that if I had waited until I knew the world before writing about it, my writing would have held it up to ridicule.

"If I had not already been carrying the world inside me by anticipation, I should have remained blind with my eyes wide open, and all my investigations and experiences would have been nothing but lifeless wasted effort. Light exists, and colours surround us; but if we had no light and no colour in our own eyes we should perceive no such thing outside us either."

165. *F. von Müller*   *27.3.1824*

Goethe's negating propensity and sceptical neutrality were again very much in evidence. In general, today, he was in that sardonic, sophistical, contradictory mood which is so displeasing in him.

166.   F. von Müller   31.3.1824

This evening Goethe was in a thoroughly good humour, restrained, communicative, informative, not in the least malicious or ironic or passionate or brusque.

167.   Eckermann   2.5.1824

Near Tiefurt we turned back into the Weimar road and had the setting sun straight ahead of us. Goethe was lost in thought for a while, then he quoted an ancient writer to me:

*Though it may set, the sun is the same sun, ever unchanging.**

"When one reaches the age of seventy-five", he continued, speaking without the least trace of sadness, "one cannot help occasionally thinking about death. To me this thought is in no way disturbing, for I am firmly convinced that the spirit within us is by nature quite indestructible; its activity continues from eternity to eternity. It is like the sun, which merely seems to our earthly eyes to sink and perish, though in reality it never does so, but shines on perpetually."

168.   Eckermann   2.5.1824

We talked of the many years he has spent as director of the theatre and the immense amount of time he had thus lost as a poet. "Indeed", said Goethe, "I could have used it to write several more good plays, but on reflection I do not really regret this. I have always regarded all my work and achievements as merely symbolic, and in the last resort it has been a matter of indifference to me whether I made pots or dishes."

169.   F. von Müller   6.6.1824

In the afternoon, after lunching at court, he sat in his shirt-sleeves drinking with Riemer, and for the former reason did not admit Countess Line von Egloffstein when she called. "Please ask her to come in the evening", he told Ottilie, "not when I

* Δυόμενος γάρ, ὅμως ἥλιός ἐστιν ἔτι. (Nonnus of Panopolis).

have friends here who make me feel profound or sublime." I have rarely seen him more witty and lively.

A few anecdotes which I told him led to a discussion of humour. Goethe said : "Only a man with no conscience or sense of responsibility can be a humorist. Of course we all have our humorous moments, but the point is whether humour remains a constant life-long attitude of mind."

I remarked that the reason was probably that the humorist's mood means more to him than the object; that he attaches an infinitely greater importance to the former than to the latter. "A very good comment", he replied, "in fact that is exactly what I mean.

"Wieland, for example, was a man of humour, because he was a sceptic, and sceptics take nothing very seriously. Wieland held himself responsible to no one, not to his family, nor to his prince, and he behaved accordingly. But a man who lives in bitter earnest cannot be a humorist. How dare a man have a sense of humour when he considers his immense burden of responsibilities towards himself and others?

"However, I have no wish to pass censure on the humorists. After all, does one have to have a conscience? Who says so?"

170. F. von Müller   *6.6.1824*

A propos of his poem *The Bride of Corinth* he remarked that a rich source of literary inspiration was certainly to be found in the contrast between paganism and Christianity, but that in fact there was nothing to be said for either religion.

He continued for some time with these oracular utterances, for example : "All tragedy is grounded in an irreconcilable antithesis. As soon as reconciliation takes place or becomes possible, the tragic element disappears."

171. F. von Müller   *30.6.1824*

Wild sarcastic attacks by Goethe on the mysteries of the Christian religion, especially the immaculata conceptio Sanctae Mariae, and the alleged immaculate conception of her mother St. Anne as well.

172. *Heinrich Heine*   *2.10.1824*

I was deeply shocked by Goethe's appearance—his face was yellow and mummy-like, his mouth toothless and in constant nervous movement, his whole body a picture of human decrepitude. Perhaps these are the effects of his recent illness. Only his eyes were clear and shining. These eyes of his are the one thing now worth visiting in Weimar. I was very much touched by Goethe's deeply human solicitude for my health. In many respects I recognised him as the Goethe who is above all else concerned with life, its beautification and preservation, and in general with peculiarly practical aims. This contrast between his nature and mine struck me very forcibly.

173. *H. Heine (reported by M. Heine)*   *2.10.1824*

Goethe received my brother with characteristic gracious condescension. Their conversation concerned itself, if not quite with the weather, at least with very everyday matters; they even talked about the avenue of poplars between Jena and Weimar. Then Goethe suddenly asked Heine : "What are you working at just now?"

The young poet answered without a moment's hesitation : "I am writing a *Faust*".

Goethe was rather taken aback and inquired with a touch of sarcasm : "Have you no other business in Weimar, Herr Heine?"

Heine replied at once : "Having crossed your Excellency's threshold, all my business in Weimar is at an end". And with that he took his leave.*

174. *F. von Müller*   *18.11.1824*

A visitor from Frankfurt was announced, but Goethe refused him admission. "One must get people out of the habit of calling on one unexpectedly; these visits always start one on new trains of thought which are not one's own, one has to think oneself into the situations of these people. I don't want anyone else's thoughts, my own are quite enough, more than enough for me to deal with."

---

* The authenticity of this anecdote has been questioned.

175. F. von Müller   *17.12.1824*

We talked about Byron's *Conversations*. "I am reading them
for the second time now", said Goethe. "I should not like to
be without them, and yet they leave one with a distasteful
impression. How often he chatters on merely about some
wretched triviality, how oversensitive he is about every foolish
journalistic criticism, what a dissolute life he led with his dogs
and apes and peacocks and horses; no logic or system in it at all.

"It is only when he concerns himself with concrete observations that Byron's judgment is excellent and clear. Reflective
thought is not his strong point: when he attempts it, his
opinions and arguments are often childish.

"He is much too patient with people who accuse him of
plagiarism—merely skirmishing in his defence instead of bringing up heavy artillery and blowing his opponents sky-high. Do
not all the achievements of a poet's predecessors and contemporaries rightfully belong to him? Why should he shrink from
picking flowers where he finds them? Only by making the riches
of others our own do we bring anything great into being. And
did not I, for my Mephistopheles, adopt the Book of Job and
one of Shakespeare's songs?—Byron was for the most part a
great poet without knowing it; he seldom felt any happy appreciation of himself."

176. F. von Müller   *December 1824*

One December evening in 1824 Goethe remarked with reference to Klinger: "One should not see old friends again; one no
longer has any common ground with them, one has come to
speak a different language and so have they. A man who takes
the cultivation of his mind seriously should beware of such
encounters, for the disharmony they reveal can only have a
disturbing effect, and one clouds one's unspoilt memory of the
earlier relationship."

177. Eckermann   *10.1.1825*

Because of his keen interest in the English nation, Goethe had
asked me to introduce to him from time to time all the young
Englishmen residing here. Today at five o'clock he was expecting me with Mr. Hutton, an officer in the Royal Engineers, of

whom I had been able to give a very good preliminary report. We arrived therefore at the appointed time and after we had waited for a few minutes Goethe came in and greeted us cordially. "I am assuming that I may talk to you in German", he said to Mr. Hutton, "as I hear that you already have a good command of our language." Mr. Hutton replied with a few polite words, and we were asked to sit down.

Mr. Hutton's personality must have made a favourable impression on Goethe, whose great charm and affability were at their height today in his treatment of this foreign visitor. "It was very sensible of you", he said, "to come over and stay with us in order to learn German, for here you can easily and quickly become familiar not only with the language, but also with the elements on which it is founded—our soil and climate and social behaviour, manners, customs, constitution and so forth—and you can return to England with a mental picture of these."

Mr. Hutton replied that interest in the German language was now considerable in England and was spreading daily, so that by now there was scarcely any young Englishman of good family who did not learn German.

"We Germans, however", answered Goethe politely, "are half a century ahead of your country in that respect. I have been studying the English language and English literature for the last fifty years, so that I know your writers and your national way of life and institutions very well. If I were to come over to England I should be no stranger.

"But as I said, your young fellow-countrymen are acting very wisely nowadays in coming here to learn our language too. For it is not only that our own literature merits this in itself, it is also undeniable that anyone with a good knowledge of German can now dispense with many other tongues. I do not mean French, for it is the language of society and particularly necessary when travelling, because everyone understands it and one can get along with it in any country in lieu of a good interpreter. But as for Greek, Latin, Italian and Spanish, one can read the finest works of these literatures in such good German translations that except for quite special purposes one has no need to spend a long time laboriously learning these languages. Germans have a natural gift for appreciating the peculiar qualities of any other nation and for entering into a foreign way of thinking. So this and the great adaptability of our language combine to make German translations extremely faithful and perfect. And one cannot, I think, deny that in general a good translation takes one a long way."

Goethe then asked Mr. Hutton what German literature he had read. "I have read *Egmont*", replied the latter, "and enjoyed the book so much that I came back to it three times. And *Torquato Tasso* also gave me great pleasure. I am reading *Faust* now, but I find it a little difficult." Goethe laughed at these last words. "Well, indeed", he said, "I should not have recommended you to take up *Faust* at this stage. It's crazy stuff, and goes right out beyond the usual range of human sensibility. But since you have started it on your own without asking my advice, I must leave you to fend for yourself. Faust is so strange an individual that very few men are able to enter into the experiences of his mind and heart. And Mephistopheles too is a very difficult character, with his irony, and being as he is the product of a very considerable observation of the world. But you must see how you get on, and what light it all sheds in your mind. *Tasso*, on the other hand, is much nearer to the ordinary emotions of mankind, and it is also written with a formal completeness which makes it more easily intelligible."

"Nevertheless", replied Mr. Hutton, "*Tasso* is considered difficult in Germany, so that I have caused surprise here by saying I was reading it."

"The essential thing with *Tasso*", said Goethe, "is that one must have grown out of one's childhood and must have moved in good society. Any young man of good family who has sufficient intelligence and delicacy, and enough of the kind of outward culture that one acquires by associating with highly cultivated members of the upper classes and the nobility, will not find *Tasso* difficult."

We conversed on these and similar matters until it was time to go to the theatre, when we stood up, and Goethe said goodbye to us very courteously.

As we went home I asked Mr. Hutton how he had liked Goethe. He answered: "I have never met a man who could combine such entirely charming kindness with so much innate dignity. He is always great, whatever efforts he may make to lower himself to the level of others."

178.   *Eckermann*   *18.1.1825*

"*Hermann and Dorothea* is almost the only one of my longer

poems that I still enjoy; I can never read it without being interested and moved. I am particularly fond of it in the Latin translation, in which it seems to me to take on a new dignity, as if it had returned to its original form."

179. Eckermann   *24.2.1825*

"Lord Byron should be considered from three angles: as a man, as an Englishman, and as a great talent. His good qualities derived above all from the human side of him; his bad qualities from the fact that he was an Englishman and an English peer; and his talent is an incommensurable quantity.

"All Englishmen, as such, are essentially incapable of reflection; distractions and party politics make it impossible for them to complete the quiet processes of culture. But as practical men they are great.

"Thus Lord Byron was never able to get round to thinking about himself, and consequently he is never a success in any reflective vein. But he does succeed in everything he produces, and indeed it may be said that in his case inspiration takes the place of reflection. Poetry was a constant necessity to him! And when it was an expression of his humanity, above all when it came from his heart, it was all excellent. He produced his best things as women produce beautiful children: unthinkingly and without knowing how.

"He was a great talent, a born talent, and I thought there was more of the true poetic force in him than in anyone else I have known."

180. George H. Calvert   *27.3.1825*

In 1825, Americans were seldom seen so far inland. In his whole life, Goethe had not probably met with six. The announcement of one for the unbusied moments of after-dinner, was, I dare say, to the ever-fresh student and universal observer, a piquant novelty. His attitude and expression, as I entered, were those of an expectant naturalist, eagerly awaiting the transatlantic phenomenon.

Goethe was then in his seventy-sixth year; but neither on his face nor figure was there any detracting mark of age. Kindly and gracefully he received me; advancing as I entered, he bade me be seated on the sofa, and sat down beside me. In a few moments I was perfectly at ease.

At such an interview the opening conversation is inevitably predetermined. How long had I been in Europe; the route by which I had come; the sea-voyage. When he learned that for fifteen months I had been a student at Göttingen, he inquired with interest for several of the professors.

Opportunities of converse with the wise have ever been esteemed, by men eager for improvement, among the choice human privileges. What a position was mine at that moment— seated beside one wiser than the wisest of the seven sages of Greece! Yet, in this interview with the chief of teachers, it was not Goethe who taught me, it was I who taught Goethe.

The news of the election of John Quincey Adams to be President of the United States had just reached Germany. Goethe wished to understand the mode and forms of election. This I explained to him in full: the first process through electors, and then, as in this instance, the second by the House of Representatives. In saying that the people did not directly choose, but voted for a small number of electors, and that these then voted for one of the candidates, I used the word "gereinigt (purified)" to describe how the popular will, to reach its aim, was sifted through the electoral colleges. The term "gereinigt" pleased Goethe much.

Thinking that a stranger, with not even the claim of an introductory note, should be content after sharing with Goethe a brief fragment of his time, before half an hour had expired I rose and took my leave.

Back into the park I strolled, now no longer lonely: I was accompanied by the image of Goethe.

181.   Eckermann   27.4.1825

"It really is very odd how easily one can find oneself at cross purposes with public opinion! I simply have once and for all acquired the reputation of being no lover of the people, though what I have ever done against the people I cannot recall. To be sure, I am no lover of the revolutionary mob which is out to kill and burn and plunder and merely uses the so-called public good as a façade for motives of the basest egoism. I am no friend to such persons, any more than I am a friend of Louis XV. I hate all violent upheavals, because they destroy as much good as they gain. I hate those who carry them out as well as those who give cause for them. But does that make me an adversary of the people? Is mine not the attitude of every right-thinking man?

"You know how delighted I am at every prospect of improvement the future offers us. But, as I said, I hate all violent and sudden transitions with all my soul, for they are not natural.

"I am a lover of plants; I love the rose as the most perfect flower that nature has to offer here in Germany; but I am not fool enough to expect my garden to be producing it for me already at the end of April. I am content now if I can find the first green leaves; content if I see the stem forming itself leaf by leaf as the weeks pass; I am glad when I see the bud in May, and happy when June at last gives me the rose itself in all its splendour and fragrance. If anyone cannot wait that long, he should go to the hothouses.

"Then again it is said that I am a server of princes, a prince's slave, as if such phrases had any meaning! Am I then the servant of a tyrant, of a despot? Do I serve a man who lives only for his own pleasures, at his people's expense? Such rulers and such times, thank God, lie far behind us now. I have been intimately associated with the Grand Duke for half a century, and for half a century we have worked and striven together; but I should be a liar if I claimed to recall a single day on which the Grand Duke did not have in mind some action or plan that would do good to his people and improve the lot of his individual subjects. As for himself, what did his princely station ever bring him but toil and trouble! Does he live or dress or eat better than any wealthy private citizen? One need only visit a German seaport to find well-to-do merchants with better kitchens and cellars than his.

"This coming autumn we shall celebrate the day on which the Grand Duke will have reigned and ruled for fifty years. But when I come to think of it, how else has he ever ruled but by constantly serving? What has his reign been but service to great ends, service to his people's welfare? So if I must perforce be a prince's slave, at least I take consolation in only being enslaved to one who is himself enslaved to the general good."

182. *Eckermann*   *12.5.1825*

"There is all this talk about originality, but what does it

amount to ? As soon as we are born the world begins to influence us, and this goes on till we die. And anyway, what can we in fact call our own except the energy, the force, the will ! If I could give an account of everything I have owed to great pre-decessors and contemporaries, there would be little else left."

183. Eckermann   *25.12.1825*

"Shakespeare gives us silver dishes filled with golden apples. The study of his plays may perhaps bring us the silver dish, but the trouble is that we have nothing to put in it but potatoes."

184. C. Schuchardt   *ca. 1825*

At the time when I was working for Goethe as his secretary, he was preparing the final edition of his works; he dictated to me a good deal of new and revised material for it, including [Book II of] *Wilhelm Meister's Travels*, and I had occasion to admire his intellectual energy and assurance and clarity despite his advanced years. He dictated as confidently and fluently as many another man could only have done out of a printed book.

I should not have paid particular attention to this if it had all taken place quietly and without any disturbance or inter-ruption from outside. But during his dictation the barber and hairdresser would call (Goethe had his hair singed every other day and dressed daily) and so would the library attendant, and from time to time Goethe's former secretary Rat Kräuter : all these had permission to enter unannounced. Or the manservant would announce a stranger, with whom Goethe, if he admitted him, would converse briefly or at greater length; and now and then some member of the family would come in. The barber and the hairdresser would tell him what had been happening in town, the library attendant would give a report on the library, and so forth. As soon as someone knocked and he boomed out his powerful "Come in !" I would finish the last sentence and wait until the visitor left again. Then I read out as much as I thought he would need in order to pick up the thread and the dictation proceeded until the next interruption as if nothing had happened. This was really too much for me and I looked all round the room to see if I could discover some hidden book or sketch or rough copy into which Goethe glanced as he passed (for as he dictated he used to walk incessantly round the table and round me as I wrote), but I was never able to find the least trace of any such thing.

When I expressed my amazement at this to Hofrat Meyer, who had been Goethe's friend for many years and whom I saw daily, he treated the fact as something quite familiar to him, and told me of another instance : one day while they were driving slowly from Jena to Weimar Goethe had recited the whole of the novel *The Elective Affinities* to him as a spoken narrative, with as much fluency as if he had had a printed copy of it in front of him; and yet at that time not a word of it had existed in writing.

Another thing that quite often happened in the course of these dictations was that Goethe would suddenly stand still, rather as one does when one unexpectedly sees a group of people or some other object in front of one which momentarily distracts the attention. He would at once seem to be artistically shaping and grouping what he saw. With outspread hands and leaning slightly to one side he would poise it and place it until its position was aesthetically correct. Having achieved this he would usually exclaim : "Exactly ! Exactly so !"

185. Eckermann   *29.1.1826*

Germany's leading poetic improviser, Dr. Wolff from Hamburg, has been here for several days and has already displayed his rare gifts in public. This evening I discussed him with Goethe.

"He is certainly talented", he said, "there is no doubt of that. But he suffers from the general disease of the present day, which is subjectivity, and I should like to cure him of it. I set him an exercise to try him out. 'Describe to me', I said, 'your return to Hamburg.' This he was quite prepared to do immediately, and he began at once to talk in harmonious verse. I could not help admiring him, but I felt unable to praise him. What he described to me was not his homecoming to Hamburg but merely the emotions of any homecoming of a son to his parents, to relatives and friends, and his poem might just as well have been a return to Merseburg or Jena as a return to Hamburg. But what a fine town Hamburg is, with a character quite of its own, and how rich a scope for the most particular descriptions lay open to him, if only he had known how to grasp the object properly and had dared to do so ! If he can break through to the objective style, his fortune is made; he has it in him, for he is not lacking in imagination.

"When a man tries to learn to sing, his vocal organs furnish him with a range of notes which are all natural and easy; but the others, which are not within that range, he at first finds extremely difficult. But he must master them if he is to become a singer, for they must all be at his command. It is just the same with a writer. So long as he merely expresses his limited range of subjective feelings, he is still no true poet; but he becomes one as soon as he can make the world his own and express that. And he then has an inexhaustible store and need never turn stale, whereas on the contrary a subjective writer will soon have poured out the little that is in him, and will end in mannered fanciful nullity.

"There is all this talk about the study of the ancients, but all it amounts to is to say: Turn your attention to the real world and try to express it, for that is what the ancients did when they were alive.

"All epochs undergoing a process of retrogression and dissolution are subjective, but all epochs of advance have an objective tendency. Our whole modern age is retrogressive because it is a subjective age. This is evident not only in literature but also in painting and many other things. But all serious work is directed away from the inner world towards the world of reality, as you may see in all the great epochs which were genuinely active and progressive, and all objective in character."

186. Eckermann   *16.2.1826*

I showed Goethe a poem which was one of his own, but written so long ago that he had no recollection of it. It had been printed in 1766 and was on the subject of Christ's descent into Hell. He remarked: "I was hard up for subject-matter in those days, and could count myself lucky to find anything to compose poetry about. Only the other day I chanced upon some verses in English which I wrote at that time, lamenting the shortage of poetic themes. And we Germans really are badly off: our early origins are too obscure, and our later history is of no general national interest because there is no one ruling dynasty. My *Götz von Berlichingen* was a lucky hit; that at least was bone of my bone and flesh of my flesh, and it was possible to make something of it.

"But for *Werther* and *Faust* I again had to have recourse to my own fancy, there being nothing much in the way of tradition. I used the world of devils and witches only once, and then turned to the tables of the Greeks, glad to have squandered my northern inheritance. But if it had been as clear to me as it is now how many masterpieces have existed for hundreds and thousands of years, I should never have written a line, but taken up some other occupation."

187. F. von Müller   1.5.1826

We talked about the drinking of tea. "It's always poison to me", said Goethe. "And yet what would women do without it? Making tea is a kind of function or imaginary occupation, especially in England. And there they sit, all looking so comfortable and so pale and so beautiful and so tall, and we must just let them go on sitting there."

188. S. Boisserée   17.5.1826

Wednesday, 17th. Slept till nine. Note to Goethe; he sent for me at once. Eleven o'clock : found him in his study at the back. Warm welcome. Looking well, rather listless in conversation—his hearing rather poor; and then from time to time tending to forget things in the immediate past. He reads *Le Globe* with great interest, indeed current events occupy his mind a good deal.

The son is a blunt unsophisticated fellow, a little bit common; he treats me with honest friendliness. We had lunch together in the big anteroom. Today was the first time for a fortnight that the old man has taken a meal in the front room. A fortnight ago his daughter-in-law fell from her horse, scratching her face to pieces and injuring her knee and wrenching various muscles; she is still bedridden. The old man has not seen her yet.

189. F. von Müller   17.5.1826

On May 17th I met Sulpice Boisserée at Goethe's; he was a very welcome visitor.

Ottilie was not yet able to show herself in company; Goethe was still shunning the sight of her disfigured face, "for I can never" (he said) "get unpleasant impressions of that sort out of my mind afterwards, they permanently spoil my memories. My sensory receptivity happens to be so peculiarly constituted that I can remember all outlines and shapes with extreme clarity and distinctness, but am on the other hand very acutely affected by anything misshapen or imperfect. The finest and most valuable engraving has only to have a stain or a crack on it and I can never bear to look at it again. This idiosyncrasy is of course often distressing, but I have no reason to complain about it, since it is intimately bound up with other more agreeable characteristics of my nature. For after all, if I did not have such keen receptivity and impressionability, the characters in my works could not be so vividly depicted and sharply individualised. When I was younger this ease and precision of perception deluded me for many years into thinking that I had a vocation and talent for drawing and painting. Only later did I realise that I lacked the gift of conveying my impressions to others with equivalent intensity."

I replied that I supposed he had perhaps also been deterred by the difficult and time-consuming mechanical and technical training that he would have needed; but he denied this, declaring that where there is true talent it will break through despite all obstacles, and find the right ways and means to its proper development.

190.   K. H. Ritter von Lang   *(?) Summer 1826*

My return journey took me to Weimar, where I let the devil tempt me into announcing myself to that old Faustus of his, Herr von Goethe, in a letter full of bowing and scraping and humble duty. My visit was accepted for half past twelve.

A tall, aged, ice-cold, stiff Imperial Free City official emerged in a dressing-gown to receive me, motioned me to be seated with a gesture reminiscent of Don Juan's statue, remained mutely unresponsive to my various attempts to strike a chord in him, nodded assent to everything I told him about the ambitious undertakings of the Crown Prince* of Bavaria, and then suddenly uttered the following words: "Tell me, I suppose you also have a fire-insurance company in your Ansbach district?" Answer: "Certainly".—I was thereupon invited to describe to him in precise detail what procedure is adopted when fires

* Ludwig I.

actually occur. I replied that it depended on whether the fire
was extinguished or the place or house actually burnt down.
"Let us have the place burnt down completely, if you please."
So I set warmly to work and consigned everything to the flames,
with the water-hoses vainly spouting and the magistrates vainly
shouting : next day off I go with my official survey, I have the
damage estimated, the estimate pared down as much as possible,
then beautiful new sketch-plans prepared which lie about in
Munich for a year and a day, while the poor victims of the
conflagration languish in temporary huts and basements, and
then after two or three years I pay out the minute sum of com-
pensation that has finally been negotiated. Old Faustus listened
to all this and said : "Thank you". Then came the further enquiry : "What's the population, then, of a district like that where
you live?" I told him : "Rather more than 500,000 souls".
"Well, well!" he said. "Hm! hm! That's quite a lot." (It was
of course more than twice the population of the entire Grand
Duchy of Weimar.) I remarked : "At present, as I have the
honour of being with you, there is one soul the less down there.
I am, however, about to set off on my return journey, and I will
take my leave." Whereupon he held out his hand, thanked me
for honouring him with my visit, and accompanied me to the
door. I had the feeling that I had been putting out a fire and
caught my death of cold.

191.   J. Schwabe   *(?) 28.8.1826*

On one of Goethe's birthdays Frau Melos and her little five-
year-old daughter were among the large crowd of people who
had come to congratulate him. As soon as Goethe saw them he
walked over to them, held out his hand to the child and said :
"Well, Marie, are you going to wish me many happy returns
too?" "Yes, your Excellency!" said Frau Melos; "and Marie
has learnt a poem as well, which she would like to recite to you
later on." "Oh, I must hear that at once!" he said, and taking
little Marie into a neighbouring room which the distinguished
company had left unoccupied, he sat down and took her on his
knee. "And now tell me what you've learnt." Marie began :
"*I was sitting on the hillside—*" "*And I watched—*" prompted
Goethe. "*And I watched the little birds*", Marie went on. "*They
were leaping—*" "*They were cheeping*", prompted Goethe
again, and in this way he and the little girl went right through

the whole of this charming song,* after which he took the child
back to her mother and turned to his other guests. In the afternoon he sent Marie a dish of fruit and sweetmeats from the
birthday table.

192. G. Downes   *31.8.1826*

*On the evening of Goethe's weekly party we were invited to
tea in his garden at an early hour, which afforded us the enjoyment of the leviathan's society in the privacy of his own domestic
circle. We found him in a blue frock and straw hat, sauntering
about with a friend.*

*At the tea table Goethe was agreeable and animated. In re-
counting the following anecdote, his whole frame was at times
pervaded by an electric thrill, evincing the ardour of eighteen
rather than of eighty. "Mr S., an Englishman, residing at Berlin, was one day enjoying the prospect from a spire. In the yard
of a house he descried with his telescope a girl of such sur-
passing beauty that he resolved, if possible, to become acquainted with her. On descending, however, he vainly endeavoured to discover the house, and he therefore re-ascended
the spire and marked the spot with greater precision. This novel
description of steeple chase was at length successful. He was
rich—she poor—and she consented to become his bride, although
under the strange stipulation that she should never unveil her
face in company." So far Goethe.*

*It has been said that his colloquial style possesses peculiar
brilliancy: on this, none but a German can be competent to
pronounce. To me it appeared exceedingly plain, and unambi-
tious. He spoke with great vivacity and seemed very impatient
of interruption:* "My dear creature," *said he to a friend who
had interposed to correct some misstatement, real or apparent,*
"it is most kind of you, but would you let me finish my story."

193. J. G. von Quandt   *1826*

A further proof of Goethe's perfect tact is that after I had had
the misfortune to break both my legs he made no mention of
this accident in any of his letters to me. I suffered indescribably
under bad surgical treatment for three years, and I had to go

* The original (in Swiss dialect) runs "*Ufm Bergli bin i gesässe,/Ha
de Vögle zugeschaut./Hänt gesunge, hänt gesprunge ...*" etc.

through a great mental struggle every time anyone pitied me; for vain pity merely revives vanquished pain. Even the compassion of a friend cannot gladden the sufferer; for it means, after all, that the friend is suffering too, a fact in which one can take no pleasure. Goethe knew this very well. When a lady in Weimar, who had visited me in Dresden, began to give him a detailed description of my state, he at once interrupted her: "Don't spoil my imagination! In my mind's eye Quandt stands before me as a fully active vigorous man."

194. F. Förster   1826

"A young painter from Berlin", said Goethe, "has just sent me a landscape from which one may see that he quite certainly has the gift of poetic sensibility and a talent for composition and execution; and nevertheless I feel that both the artist and his picture are quite alien to me. The painter here takes us into a winter landscape, and it seems that the ice and snow in it are not enough for him: he outbids or outwinters even the winter, so to speak, by various repulsive additional features. A procession of monks in the snow, barefoot friars into the bargain, are following the coffin of a departed brother, who is being carried on a black-draped bier to his grave in a ruined monastery. All these things are negations of life. First we have the death of nature, the winter landscape: I do not acknowledge winter. Then monks, fugitives from life, men buried alive: I do not acknowledge monks. Then a monastery, a ruined one to be sure, but I do not acknowledge monasteries. And finally, to crown all, even a dead man: but I do not acknowledge death."

195. *August von Goethe to Ernst von Schiller*   17.9.1826

My father has since yesterday been so upset by the thought of the impending ceremony [the enshrinement of Schiller's skull in the library] that I have had fears for his health. He sent for me this morning at six and told me, with tears in his eyes, that it was impossible for him to attend today's solemn act in person. So I am representing him.

196. A. Stahr   18.9.1826

Once, on the birthday of one of his grandsons, a band of small boys were playing at robbers and soldiers. The robber chieftain had just been taken prisoner and locked into one of the rooms in the garden house when the aged Goethe, then nearly eighty, emerged and spoke to the boys. "What are you?" he asked the nearest of them. "Robbers!" "Where's your captain?" "In prison!" "And aren't you ashamed to leave your captain in prison instead of freeing him?" "Yes, but the others have locked the door!" "Are you stout fellows going to let a little thing like that stop you freeing your captain?" And thus encouraged, the loyal young bloods, with loud hullabalooing, smashed in the door and brought out the prisoner, while the old gentleman, smiling complacently, returned to his den of meditation.

197. F. Grillparzer   *September–October 1826*

(*September 29th*): I finally reached Weimar and took a room at the "Elephant", an inn then well known all over Germany, the antechamber, as it were, of Weimar's living Valhalla. From there I sent the waiter to Goethe with my card and the enquiry whether I might come and pay my respects. The waiter brought back the reply that His Excellency had guests and therefore could not see me now, but would expect me that evening for tea.

In the early evening I went to Goethe's house. I found in the drawing-room a fairly large company waiting for the still in-visible Geheimrat. At last a side door opened and he himself entered. Dressed entirely in black and wearing the star of his order, holding himself almost rigidly erect, he stepped among us like a monarch giving audience. He exchanged a few words with this guest and that, and finally approached me too; I was standing at the opposite side of the room. He asked me whether Italian literature was much studied in Austria. I answered him truthfully that the Italian language is of course widely known, since all persons holding public appointment are officially re-quired to learn it; but that Italian literature, on the other hand, is entirely neglected. "For reasons of fashion", I said, "we are showing a greater interest in English literature, in which, for all its excellent qualities, there is nevertheless an element of coarse-ness, and in the present state of German culture, especially of literary culture, this seems to me a rather harmful influence." I do not know whether he liked this remark of mine or not, though I rather think the latter, as this was the period of his correspon-dence with Lord Byron. He moved away from me, spoke to other people, came back to me again, talked I can no longer remember about what, then finally left the room; we were dismissed.

I confess that I returned to my hotel in a very uncomfortable state of mind. It was not as if my pride had been hurt; on the contrary. Goethe had treated me more kindly and attentively than I had supposed he would. But to see the ideal of my youth, the author of *Faust*, *Clavigo* and *Egmont*, transformed into a ceremonious minister graciously entertaining his guests to tea—this was indeed a fall from the clouds. I should almost have preferred him to have heaped insults upon me and thrown me out of the house. I almost regretted having come to Weimar.

(*October 1st*): We were just arranging to visit various places of interest in Weimar, and Chancellor Müller, who had no doubt noticed my dejection, was just assuring me that Goethe's ceremonious manner was nothing but an effect of the embarrassment he himself always felt on meeting a stranger for the first time, when the waiter came in with a card bearing an invitation to luncheon with Goethe for the next day. I therefore had to prolong my visit, and I cancelled the horses which I had already ordered for the following morning.

At last came the fateful day and its lunchtime, and I went to Goethe's house. The guests who had been invited besides myself were already assembled, and it was an exclusively male company; Goethe's daughter-in-law (of whom I later became so fond, as well as of her daughter who died so young) was not in Weimar at the time. As I crossed the room, Goethe came to meet me and was as charming and warm as he had lately been ceremonious and cold. The depths of my heart began to stir. But when we went to take our seats at table, and this man who had come to be for me the embodiment of German literature and indeed, in his remoteness and immeasurable superiority, an almost mythical person, took my hand to lead me into the dining-room, I suddenly became a boy again and burst into tears. Goethe did everything he could to camouflage my foolishness. I sat beside him at table, and he was more good-humoured and talkative, as the guests later assured me, than he had been known to be for a long time. The conversation, animated by him, became general. But Goethe also often turned to address me in particular; and yet I can no longer remember what he said, apart from a witty remark about a new periodical. I unfortunately made no notes on this journey. The only characteristic thing I can still remember about what happened at table is that in the heat of conversation I distinguished myself as usual by fiddling with the piece of bread beside me and turning it into ugly crumbs. Goethe then swept every one of these with the tip of his finger into a tidy little heap. I did not notice this until later, and then desisted from my handiwork.

As we were leaving, Goethe asked me to come the following morning to have myself drawn. For it was his habit to have the portrait of any of his visitors who interested him drawn in black crayon by an artist specially ordered for the purpose. These portraits were mounted in a frame which hung there for them in the reception-room, and they were changed in turn every week. I too was selected for this honour.

(*October 2nd*): When I presented myself next morning, the painter had not yet arrived. I was therefore shown into the little garden, where Goethe was walking up and down. The reason for his rigid posture in the presence of strangers now became clear to me. Old age had not passed over him without a trace. As he strolled in the garden, one could clearly see that his head and neck and the upper part of his body had an awkward stoop. And this was what he wanted to hide from strangers; hence the artificially erect attitude which made so unpleasing an impression. To see him now holding himself naturally, wearing a long house coat, with a little cap on his white hair to shade his eyes, was somehow infinitely touching. He looked half like a king and half like a father. We talked as we walked up and down. He mentioned my *Sappho*, of which he seemed to approve, though here, to be sure, he was in a sense paying a compliment to himself, for in that play I had more or less ploughed with his heifer. When I lamented my isolated situation in Vienna, he said what he has since told us in print: that a man cannot achieve anything without the companionship of others who are equal or akin to himself. If he and Schiller had become what the world recognises them to be, they owed it largely to this stimulating interchange in which each completed the other. By this time the painter had arrived. We went into the house and I was drawn. Goethe had retired to his room and emerged from it now and again to inspect the progress of the portrait, with which, when it was finished, he expressed himself satisfied. When the painter had been dismissed Goethe made his son bring down various items for display from among his treasures.

There was his correspondence with Lord Byron, everything that related to his acquaintance in Carlsbad with the Empress and Emperor of Austria, and finally the Imperial letters of privilege which made his complete works copyright. This last document he seemed to value particularly, either because he liked the conservative attitude of Austria, or because he regarded it as a curiosity, in contrast to other literary phenomena in that country. These treasures were preserved in semi-oriental fashion, everything that belonged together being wrapped in a separate silk cloth, and Goethe treated them with a kind of reverence. Finally he bade me goodbye in the friendliest possible manner.

In the course of that day Chancellor Müller suggested to me that I should visit Goethe in the evening. I should find him alone and my visit would be by no means unwelcome to him. It was not until later that it struck me that Müller could not have said this without Goethe's knowledge.

And now occurred the second of my Weimar follies. I felt afraid of spending a whole evening alone with Goethe, and after much hesitation and irresolution, I did not go.

(*October 3rd*): When I took my leave of Goethe on the fourth day of my stay, his manner was kind, but less warm. He expressed surprise that I was leaving Weimar so soon, and added that if I would let them hear from me at a later date, it would give them all great pleasure. "Them", in the plural, not him. And since then, indeed, he has done me less than justice; for after all, despite all the disparity between us, I do consider that I am the best writer to have appeared since himself and Schiller. But I need hardly say that this has in no way diminished my love and reverence for him.

On the day of my departure the whole of Weimar gave me a farewell dinner out at the shooting-club, and Goethe had sent his son to join us.

198. Eckermann   27.12.1826

"People want to know which town on the Rhine is the setting for my *Hermann und Dorothea*! As if it were not far better to imagine any town they like! They want truth, they want reality, and that is just what spoils poetry."

199. Eckermann   *12.1.1827*

After a pause for conversation and some refreshments, Goethe asked Madame Eberwein to perform a few songs. She first sang Zelter's setting of Goethe's beautiful poem *Um Mitternacht*, which made a profound impression. The *Erlkönig* was also loudly applauded. Madame Eberwein ended the evening by giving us, at Goethe's request, some songs from the *Westöst-licher Divan*, in her husband's setting. Goethe particularly liked the passage "Jussufs Reize möcht ich borgen (Joseph's beauty I would borrow)". "Eberwein", he remarked to me, "excels him-self at times." Finally he asked for the song "Ach um deine feuchten Schwingen (Moist west wind, thy wings I envy)" which was also calculated to evoke deep emotion.

When the company had left, I stayed behind for a few moments alone with Goethe. "I noticed this evening", he said, "that those poems from the *Divan* no longer mean anything to me. Both the oriental element in them and the passion in them have ceased to be part of my life; they have been dropped at the roadside like a cast-off snake-skin. The poem *Um Mitternacht*, on the other hand, is one that I still find meaningful : it is alive in me and lives on with me still.*

"As a matter of fact it quite often happens that the things I have written become totally alien to me. I was reading a piece of French the other day and I thought as I read : This man is talking quite good sense, I should say much the same as this myself. And on closer inspection it turned out to be a passage translated from one of my own works !"

200. Eckermann   *17.1.1827*

"I have met people", said Goethe, "who simply could not reconcile themselves to Schiller's early plays. Prince *** once expressed himself to me about *The Robbers* as follows : 'If I had been God', he said, 'about to create the world, and had at that moment foreseen that Schiller's *Robbers* would be written in that world, I should have refrained from creating it'." We could not help laughing. "What do you think of that?" said

* The poems *At Midnight* and *Erlking* appear on pp. 305 and 80 respectively of *Selected Verse* (Penguin Books). A selection from the *West-Eastern Divan* appears on pp. 230 to 269; for the two poems quoted, see pp. 245 and 251.

Goethe. "That was certainly an aversion that went rather far, and I found it scarcely comprehensible."

"But it is one not shared in the least", I replied, "by our younger generation, and especially by our students. The finest, maturest plays by Schiller and other poets can be performed and you will see very few young people or students in the theatre, or none at all; but if you put on Schiller's *Robbers* or Schiller's *Fiesco* the house will be almost entirely packed with students." "It was exactly the same fifty years ago", said Goethe, "and I dare say it will be no different fifty years hence. When something has been written by a young man, it will be young men who appreciate it most. And let us not imagine that the world makes such progress in cultivation and good taste that even youth must already have outgrown the crudity of an earlier epoch! The world in general may advance, but youth has always to begin at the beginning and pass individually through the epochs of the world's culture."

201.   *Eckermann*   18.1.1827

"I have never deliberately studied nature for poetic purposes. But my earlier activities as a landscape artist and later as a scientist constantly obliged me to make precise observations of natural objects, and thus I gradually learnt nature by heart, right down to its smallest details, so that when as a poet I need anything, it is at my disposal, and I seldom fail to be true to life. Schiller lacked this gift of observation. The Swiss local colour in his *Wilhelm Tell* was entirely based on what I told him; but he had such a remarkable mind that even out of these accounts he could make something realistic."

202.   *Eckermann*   18.1.1827

"We do not become free by refusing to acknowledge anything higher than ourselves, but precisely by respecting what is above us. For by respecting it we raise ourselves to its level, and by acknowledging it we prove that we too have something higher in us, and are worthy to be its peers."

203.   *Eckermann*   21.1.1827

"The very essence of dilettantism is to be unaware of the

difficulties inherent in a thing, and to keep embarking on projects which lie beyond one's capacity."

204. *Eckermann*   *29.1.1827*

"To write prose, one must have something to say; but a man who has nothing to say can of course compose verses and rhymes, for in these one word suggests the next, and the final product, though it is in fact nothing, nevertheless looks as if it were something."

205. *Eckermann*   *31.1.1827*

"It is becoming increasingly clear to me that poetry is a common heritage of mankind, and that it manifests itself at all places and times in hundreds and thousands of individuals. One of them writes a little better than another and floats on the surface for a little longer than the other, that is all. Each of us must simply tell himself that the gift of poetry is not so very rare a thing, and that no man has any particular cause for self-congratulation when he has written a good poem. But of course, if we Germans refuse to look out beyond the narrow circle of our own milieu, we shall fall all too easily into this pedantic self-complacency. That is why I like to take a look at the work of other nations, and I would advise everyone else to do the same. National literature means little nowadays, the era of world literature is at hand, and each of us now must help to hasten its arrival."

206. *Eckermann*   *1.2.1827*

"I have tried my hand at pretty well every branch of science; but my efforts were always directed solely towards the earthly phenomena which surrounded me and which could be perceived directly by the senses. That is why I have never devoted myself to astronomy, because in this field the senses are no longer sufficient: one must have recourse to instruments, calculations and the formulae of mechanics, which are a lifetime's work in themselves and never appealed to me."

207. Eckermann   *21.2.1827*

At table Goethe talked long and admiringly about Alexander von Humboldt, whose work on Cuba and Columbia he had begun to read and whose views on the project of a cutting through the Isthmus of Panama seemed to interest him quite particularly. "Humboldt", said Goethe, "has considerable expert knowledge and has suggested several alternative points at which this plan could perhaps be more expeditiously executed than at Panama, by making use of several rivers which flow into the Gulf of Mexico. All this of course is for the future and a great spirit of enterprise to decide. But this much is certain, that if they succeed in cutting such a canal that ships of any tonnage and size can be navigated through it from the Gulf of Mexico to the Pacific Ocean, the results would be of incalculable benefit to the whole civilised and non-civilised world. But I should be surprised if the United States let slip the opportunity of getting such a project into their own hands. It is to be expected that this youthful state, with its decided tendency to expand westwards, will also in thirty or forty years' time have occupied and peopled the vast tracts of land beyond the Rocky Mountains. It is also to be expected that all along the Pacific coast, where very safe and spacious natural harbours already exist, there will be a gradual growth of very important commercial cities, for the furtherance of large-scale trade between the United States and China and the East Indies. This, however, would make it not only desirable but virtually necessary for both merchantships and men-of-war to maintain a more rapid communication between the western and eastern shores of North America than has hitherto been possible by the tedious, unpleasant and expensive route round Cape Horn. So I repeat, it is absolutely indispensable for the United States to contrive a passage from the Gulf of Mexico through into the Pacific Ocean, and I am certain they will succeed in doing so.

"I should like to live long enough to see it, but I never shall. I should also like to live to see a junction cut between the Danube and the Rhine. But this enterprise, too, is so gigantic that I doubt if it will be carried out, particularly as our resources in Germany are so limited. And thirdly and lastly I should like to see the English in possession of a canal through Suez. These are three great things I wish I could be alive to see;

it would be worthwhile holding out for another fifty years or so for the sake of them."

208. *Eckermann*   *28.3.1827*

"Thoughts that are the same as our own leave us unmoved; but it is contradiction that makes us productive."

209. *Eckermann*   *11.4.1827*

"There are some things in nature which are accessible and others which are inaccessible. This distinction must be made and well considered and respected. It is useful even to be aware of it all, though it remains very difficult for us to discern the point at which one category ends and the other begins. A man unaware of the distinction may waste his whole life struggling to explore the inaccessible, and never getting anywhere near the truth. But the man who does distinguish, and is wise, will confine himself to the accessible area, within which he will range in all directions, and consolidate his position. By so doing he will even succeed in making one or two inroads into the inaccessible sphere; though here in the end he will still have to confess that many things can only be understood up to a certain point, and that there is still something mysterious behind nature which it is beyond the power of the human mind to fathom."

210. *Eckermann*   *18.4.1827*

"I cannot help being amused", said Goethe, "by the laborious efforts of aestheticians to reduce that inexpressible quality which we call 'beauty' to a theoretical concept by means of a few abstract words. Beauty is a primary phenomenon, and although it never manifests itself directly, its reflexion is visible in a thousand different utterances of the creative mind, and is as manifold and varied as nature herself."

I remarked that I had often heard it said that nature is always beautiful, and that she is the despair of the artist because he is seldom quite able to equal her.

"I know very well", replied Goethe, "that nature is often incomparably enchanting, but I do not by any means agree that she is beautiful in all her aspects. Her intentions, to be sure, are always good, but the conditions which she requires in order to achieve a perfect manifestation of herself are not always favourable.

"The artist's relationship to nature is twofold: he is both her master and her slave. He is her slave inasmuch as he must work in an earthly medium in order to be intelligible, but her master in so far as he subordinates this earthly medium to his higher intentions and makes it serve them.

"The artist desires to communicate with the world by creating something which possesses wholeness; this whole however is not something he finds in nature, but a fruit of his own mind—or, if you prefer, the product of a fructifying divine afflatus.

"If we take a mere cursory glance at a landscape by Rubens, it all looks as natural as if it had been copied straight from nature. But in fact it is not. So beautiful a picture has never been seen in nature, and neither has any of Poussin's or Claude Lorrain's landscapes, which also strike us as very natural but for which we shall search reality in vain."

211. Eckermann   3.5.1827

After Stapfer's highly successful French translation of Goethe's dramatic works, an equally excellent review of them appeared last year in the Paris periodical *Le Globe*: it was by Monsieur J. J. Ampère, and pleased Goethe so much that he repeatedly spoke of it with great appreciation and frequently returned to the subject.

"Monsieur Ampère", he said, "writes from a very elevated standpoint. German critics like to approach such matters philosophically; their way of viewing and reviewing a work of literature is such that their attempts to elucidate it are intelligible only to philosophers of the same school as themselves, and much more obscure for everyone else than the work they are trying to explain. But Monsieur Ampère, on the contrary, goes about his business in the most practical and human fashion. As one who knows the job himself thoroughly, he draws attention to the kinship between the product and its begetter, and discusses the poet's various works as the fruits of different epochs of his life.

"He has profoundly studied the changing course of my worldly career, and my changing states of mind, and has even been able to discern things which I did not put into words and which were only to be read between the lines, so to speak. How right he is in observing that during the first ten years of my court life and official activities at Weimar I produced virtually nothing, that I was driven by sheer desperation to Italy where a new creative enthusiasm seized me and I took up the story of Tasso, in the hope that by treating this appropriate theme I might rid myself of such Weimar memories and impressions as were still an affliction and a burden to me. And thus he most felicitously describes *Tasso* as 'a refined and intensified *Werther*'.

"His remarks on *Faust* are brilliant, too, for he points out that not only the hero's gloomy discontented striving but also the mockery and bitter irony of Mephistopheles are elements in my own nature."

Goethe praised Monsieur Ampère very frequently in these and similar terms; we conceived a strong interest in him, we tried to imagine his personality, and although unsuccessful in this, we did at least agree that he must be a man of mature years to have acquired so thorough an understanding of how a poet's life and his work interact with each other.

We were therefore greatly surprised when Monsieur Ampère turned up in Weimar a few days ago and revealed himself to us as a high-spirited youth of not much more than twenty.

212. *J. J. A. Ampère*   *April–May 1827*

Goethe finds it a little difficult to speak French, but he does so correctly; his difficulty is noticeable only in the way he pauses after every word. This is indeed not without a kind of charm, and often even adds weight to what he is saying. He is of average height, tall rather than short; his face is noble and at times very expressive, his manner is serious; he has a prominent nose, his mouth has lost almost all its teeth, but his complexion looks robust.

213. *J. J. A. Ampère to Madame Récamier*   *April–May 1827*

Goethe is an extraordinary man, and is being charming to me. He is interested in everything, has ideas about everything, admires everything that is at all worthy of admiration; and as he sits there in his snow-white dressing-gown looking like a big white sheep, with his son and daughter-in-law beside him and his two grandchildren playing with him—as he talks about Schiller and their common labours, about what the latter wanted to do and would have done, about his own works, his plans and his memories—he is the most fascinating and lovable of men. He has a naïve awareness of his own renown which is never disagreeable, for he takes constant notice of other talents and is truly sensitive to everything good that is being done in all branches of art.

He worships Molière and La Fontaine, admires *Athalie* and appreciates *Bérénice*. As to Tasso, he claims to have done a great deal of research and says that his treatment of the subject is quite close to the historical facts. He asserts that the story of the poet's imprisonment is an invention, as you will be glad to hear; he believes that Tasso and the princess were in love with each other, but always at a distance, always romantically, and that there was no question of these dreary and absurd proposals of marriage that occur in M. Alexandre Duval's version.

I have read in manuscript a very remarkable work which he is about to publish: an episode or rather an interlude which he intends to include in the still unwritten sequel to *Faust*. It is, as he entitles it himself, a phantasmagoria, and more or less untranslatable; but though much of it is bizarre and obscure, it is full of profundity, poetry and grace. Everything is in it, from the siege of Troy to the siege of Missolonghi; Greek mythology, the Middle Ages, modern times, Lord Byron. It is a dream full of meaning, and this conception, in which for better or for worse everything is original, has emerged from the mind of a man nearly eighty years old.

214. *Eckermann*   3.5.1827

We had been equally surprised to learn in the course of further conversation with Monsieur Ampère that all his collaborators on *Le Globe*, which we had often admired for its wisdom, moderation, and high cultural maturity, were merely young men like himself.

"We who live here in Central Germany", remarked Goethe to me, "have had a hard time of it to acquire what little wisdom we possess. For when all is said and done we do live a pretty wretched isolated life! From the people as such we get very little cultural nourishment, and all the talents and brains among us are scattered all over Germany: one in Vienna, one in Berlin, another in Königsberg, another in Bonn or Düsseldorf, all hundreds of miles apart, so that any personal contact and personal exchange of ideas is a rare thing. But imagine a city like Paris, where all the finest minds of a great kingdom are together on one spot, all learning from each other and refining each other by daily intercourse and controversy and emulation. Imagine, too, that this is not the Paris of a dull uncultured age, but nineteenth-century Paris, where for three generations men such as Molière, Voltaire, Diderot and others like them have been pouring out a richer intellectual currency than is to be found on one and the same spot anywhere on earth. Consider this and you will understand how an intelligent man like Ampère, growing up amid such abundance, may well achieve great things by the age of twenty-four. A nation in which individual talents are to be speedily and happily developed must be one in which a great many ideas and sound cultural values are already in circulation.

"Take the case of Burns. He is great simply because the old songs of his forefathers were still alive on the lips of the people, because they were sung to him in his cradle so to speak, because he grew up among them as a boy and the high excellence of these models so impressed itself on his sensibility that he had in them a living basis on which he could advance further. And secondly he owes his greatness to the fact that his own songs at once found receptive ears among his people, that at once the reapers and the sheaf-binders sang them to him in the fields, and his boon companions greeted him with them in the ale-house. Small wonder he could achieve something in those conditions! When I was a young man, how many of our own equally fine old songs were alive among the people, the real country people? Herder and his followers had to start collecting them to save them from oblivion. They have been written down and printed and put in libraries, thus sharing the general fate of German poets. Which of my own songs is still alive? Perhaps one or two of them are occasionally sung by some pretty girl at her piano, but among the people as such not a voice is raised. Imagine my feelings when I remember hearing passages from Tasso's work being sung to me by Italian fishermen!

"We Germans go back no further than yesterday. For the last hundred years, to be sure, our culture has made quite good progress; but another couple of centuries may still go by before intellect and the higher civilised values become so well established and widespread among our fellow-countrymen that they will pay the same homage to beauty as the Greeks did, that a beautiful song will move them to enthusiasm, and that it will be possible to say that they have long left barbarism behind them."

215. *Eckermann* 6.5.1827

The conversation turned to Goethe's play *Torquato Tasso* and he was asked what idea he had tried to express in it.

"Idea?" said Goethe, "none, so far as I know! I had Tasso's life and my own life to draw on, and by the compounding of two such strange and peculiar characters my mind conceived the image of Tasso, to whom, as a prosaic contrast, I opposed Antonio; I had plenty of models for the latter as well. As for the further particulars of court life and love affairs, they were the same at Weimar as at Ferrara, and I can truly say of my version of the story that it is bone of my bone and flesh of my flesh.

"But what strange people the Germans are! They make life so much more difficult than it need be by their profound thoughts and ideas which they look for in everything and read into everything. Why on earth will you never have the courage to surrender yourselves to your impressions, to allow yourselves to be delighted, moved, uplifted—even to allow yourselves to be taught something new, to be inspired and emboldened to some great achievement! Why must you always assume that nothing is any good unless it is some sort of abstract thought or idea?

"They come to me for instance and ask: what idea did you try to embody in *Faust*? As if I knew the answer myself and could put it into words! The life I portrayed in *Faust* is rich and many-coloured and very various, and a fine thing it would have been, I must say, if I had attempted to thread that on to the thin string of a single pervading idea!

"On the whole", Goethe went on, "it has not been my way as a poet, to struggle to incorporate abstractions. Perhaps the only large-scale work which I am conscious of having composed on the basis of a central idea is *The Elective Affinities*. That has made the novel intelligible, but I will not claim that it has made it any better. On the contrary, I take the view that the more incommensurable and elusive to the intelligence a work of literature is, the better it is."

216. Eckermann   *15.7.1827*

"There is always a lot of talk about aristocracy and demo-
cracy, and the truth is quite simply this: in youth, when we
have no possessions, or attach no value to stable ownership, we
are democrats. But when in the course of a long life we have
acquired property, we not only want to be secure in the possession of it, we also want our children and grandchildren to enjoy
this acquisition undisturbed. Consequently we are always aris-
tocrats in our old age, without exception, whatever may have
been our youthful leanings towards the contrary view."

217. Eckermann   *15.7.1827*

"It is an excellent thing that the close contact nowadays between the French and the English and the Germans gives us
the opportunity for a corrective interchange of views. That is
the great advantage of world literature, and it will become
increasingly evident. Carlyle has written a biography of Schiller
and arrived at a general judgment of him which it would be
hard for a German to form. We on the other hand have a clear
understanding of Shakespeare and Byron and can perhaps
appreciate their merits better than the English themselves."

218. Eckermann   *25.7.1827*

Goethe received the other day a letter from Sir Walter Scott
which greatly pleased him. It seems that he had written first to
the great English [*sic*] novelist, and that this letter is Scott's
reply. He writes:

"*To the Baron* [sic] *von Goethe, etc. etc., Weimar.*

"*Venerable and much respected Sir,—I received your highly
valued token of esteem and have been rarely so much gratified
as by finding that any of my productions have been fortunate
enough to attract the attention of Baron von Goethe of whom
I have been an admirer ever since the year 1798 when I became
a little acquainted with the German language and soon after
gave an example at once of my good taste and consummate
assurance by an attempt to translate Baron of Goethe's Götz von
Berlichingen, entirely forgetting that it is necessary not only to
be delighted with a work of genius but to be well acquainted with*

6—G

the language in which it is written before we attempt to communicate its beauty to others. I still set a value on my early translation however because it serves at least to show that I know how to select an object of admiration although from the terrible blunders into which I fell from imperfect acquaintance with the language it was plain I had not adopted the best way of expressing my admiration.

"It gives to all admirers of genius and literature delight to know that one of the greatest European models enjoys a happy and dignified retirement during an age in which he is so memorably honoured and respected. Fate destined a premature close to that of poor Lord Byron who was cut off when his life was in the flower and when so much that was hoped and expected from him was cut off for ever. He esteemed himself as I have some reason to know happy in the honour which you did him and not unconscious of the obligations which he owed to One to whom all the authors of this generation have been so much obliged that they are bound to look up to him with paternal reverence.

"I have entreated my booksellers to find some means of conveying to you a hasty and of course rather tedious attempt to give an account of the life of that remarkable person Napoleon who had for so many years such a terrible influence in the world which he ruled. I hope you will forgive the faults of the composition in consideration of the author's wish to be as candid towards the memory of this extraordinary man as ever his insular prejudices would permit. I do not know but what I owe him some obligations since he put me in arms for twelve years during which I served in one of our corps of yeomanry and notwithstanding an early lameness became a good horseman, a hunter and a shooter. Of late these faculties have failed me a little as the rheumatism, that sad torment of our northern climate, has laid its influence in some degree on my bones. But I cannot complain since I see my sons pursuing the sport since I have given it up. For the rest I have enough to live in the way I like notwithstanding some very heavy losses and I have a stately antique château to which any friend of Baron von Goethe will be at all times most welcome, with an entrance hall filled with armour which might have become Götz von Berlichingen's castle itself and a gigantic bloodhound to guard the entrance.

"As this opportunity of addressing you opens suddenly by a chance traveller and must be instantly embraced I have not time to say more than to wish Baron von Goethe a continuance of health and tranquillity and to subscribe myself with sincerity *and profound respect His much honoured and obliged humble servant*

"Walter Scott.

"*Edinburgh, 9th July 1827.*"

Goethe, as I have said, was delighted by this letter. For the rest, he thought that its contents did him so much honour that he must ascribe a large part of them to the courtesy of a man of rank and high cultivation.

"I am now greatly looking forward", he went on, "to his Life of Napoleon which he promises to send me. I have heard so many contradictory and passionate reports of it as to be certain in advance that it will at least be a very significant book."

219. *F. von Müller*   *5.9.1827*

This morning Goethe was so agreeably affected by the visit of Shukovsky and von Reutern that I have scarcely ever known him to be more charming and kindly and communicative. Everything that was in him to say to these friends he said, everything that could possibly give them pleasure or warm their hearts or be of service to them, all the opinions, suggestions, approval and affection they needed he gave them. He seemed to be breathing a new life-giving air, long-desired and refreshing.

220. *F. von Müller*   *7.9.1827*

To-day, by comparison with the day before yesterday, he was a quite different person. Perhaps it was something to do with the presence of Meyer, in front of whom Goethe seemed reluctant to show his feelings. To-day he struck me as very Mephistophelian, very cold and unloving and contemptuous of everything.

221. *W. Zahn*   *7.9.1827*

It was on the 7th of September 1827, when I was still an unknown young man, that I passed through Weimar on my way to Berlin. All my thoughts revolved round Goethe, and I decided to pay a call upon this great celebrity. But he was not a very easily accessible person. Daily besieged as he was by visitors, he maintained a certain seclusion. The painter and poet August

Kopisch, the discoverer of the Blue Grotto at Capri, told me
how he had written a long letter to the prince of poets in which
he had requested an audience, but to which he had received no
answer. Another of my acquaintances—his name escapes me
for the moment—had even ventured into the house, and tiptoed
nervously into the courtyard to look around for one of the servants. But he met only two boys, the poet's grandsons, who were
rushing around wildly and making a great hubbub. Then suddenly a window was flung open and the object of his longing
leaned out. With flashing eyes and the voice of a lion he shouted
down: "Will you young blackguards stop that noise!" Thus
roaring, he slammed the window shut. The boys fell silent, and
my friend took to his heels in terror. I was undeterred by these
unfortunate anecdotes, and set out boldly, although I had neither
a name nor a single line of introduction to show for myself.

In the hall I was met by a servant, to whom I gave my name:
"Zahn, painter and architect". "Painter and architect", repeated the servant mechanically, eyeing me with some doubt.
"Tell his Excellency: lately arrived from Italy." "Lately arrived
from Italy", he repeated, and withdrew, only to return at once
and ask me to follow him. We ascended a fine, wide staircase.
My guide opened the door, admitted me, and I found myself
in a handsome reception room.

After a few moments Goethe entered. By countless repetitions
it has become trite to remark that the poet in his nature and
bearing resembled the father of the Greek gods; but no one
could deny that the man who now stood before me was a unique
figure. Old age only made his lofty, powerful, awe-inspiring
person even more splendid. Under his mighty brow shone two
great dark eyes, and his bronzed countenance bore the stamp of
high distinction and genius. He bade me sit down opposite him,
and with his rich expressive voice, in which there was nevertheless an occasional tinge of Frankfurt dialect, he asked: "Been
in Italy, then?" "For three years, your Excellency." "And visiting the underground sites near Naples, perhaps?" "That was
the very purpose of my journey. I had lodged myself very comfortably in an ancient house at Pompeii, and during two summers
the excavations took place under my very eyes." "Delighted you
say so! Glad to hear it!" said Goethe, who was fond of a condensed manner of speaking and liked to leave out the personal
pronouns. He shifted his chair nearer to me, and then continued
with some emphasis: "The Vienna and Berlin academies ought

to send young men out there : told them so already several times.
Make them study ancient paintings and those wonderful underground places. All the better if you've done so on your own
initiative. Yes, yes, antiquity must still be the model for every
artist. But let's not forget the main point : got some drawings
in your luggage, I suppose?" "When these ancient murals were
discovered, I usually took tracings of them immediately, and I
have tried to copy them in colour. Would your Excellency perhaps care to see a few of them?" "Oh, indeed, indeed!" Goethe
broke in. "Delighted, most obliged! Come back again to lunch.
Have my lunch at about two. Got some other people coming
who are interested in art. Looking forward very much to seeing
your pictures. Good morning to you, my young friend!" And
he offered me his hand and pressed mine warmly.

When I presented myself again at the appointed hour, I passed
through a series of rooms all decorated in the same taste, and
entered the dining-room, where I found Goethe and his other
guests already assembled; the latter included Chancellor von
Müller, Professor Riemer, Eckermann, and Hofrat Meyer. All
the guests, and Goethe himself, were in formal dress. I sat between Goethe and Fräulein Ulrike von Pogwisch, who was a
great favourite with the poet, for he often addressed her, and
obviously took pleasure in her replies. Opposite us sat Frau
Ottilie, the poet's daughter-in-law and Ulrike's sister. I found
the food absolutely delicious and the wine at least equally good.
In front of every guest stood a bottle of red or white wine. I
wanted to keep a clear head for dessert, so I poured water into
my wine. Goethe noticed this and remarked disapprovingly :
"Where did you learn that bad habit?" The conversation was
general, lively, and never came to a halt. Goethe led it in masterly fashion, but without ever restricting anyone else. Round
him sat his walking encyclopedias, to whom he appealed from
time to time, for he did not like to weigh himself down with the
ballast of mere bookish erudition. Riemer represented philology,
Meyer the history of art, and Eckermann unwound himself of
an endless string of quotations on every conceivable subject.
In the intervals of these, he hung with bated breath on the
words of the master, which he seemed to be learning by heart
at once, like the utterances of an oracle. The conversation was
chiefly about Italy and its artistic treasures. Goethe was able to
loosen even my shy awkward tongue and induce me to talk of
my studies in the Vatican. Everyone present had rapturous

memories of Rome and praised its glories enthusiastically. Goethe had emptied a whole bottle, and was still pouring himself another glass from the second as coffee was being handed round. Then we rose. Tables were pushed together and white cloths spread over them, and there I unrolled my drawings and explained them. They were all coloured copies of frescoes from Pompeii, which had been brought up again to the light of day from under thirty feet of ash. Goethe looked lovingly and reverently at every picture, and made very subtle and striking comments on them, which proved to me how profound was the insight of this great genius into the nature of art and the mysteries of the Hellenic mind. Suddenly we heard behind us a firm military tread, and when I turned I saw a man of medium height, in an officer's cap, and a short gold-braided green velvet hunting-tunic. It was the Grand Duke. He had come through the garden and entered by the back door, of which he always had the key. Goethe greeted him characteristically with the remark: "Just in time for lunch, your Royal Highness!" Karl August had in his hand a short meerschaum pipe at which he used to puff constantly wherever it was possible, but now he let it go out, for Goethe loathed tobacco. And though the Grand Duke usually called his old friend *du*, today he adressed him courteously as *Sie*.

It was my intention to continue my journey the following morning, but Goethe urged me to stay for another fortnight at least and to visit him daily. The Grand Duke invited me to lunch next day, but Goethe answered for me and said: "No, at lunchtime Zahn belongs to me". And Karl August did not dispute the point. Most of the guests had already taken their leave, and I too was about to go, but Goethe held me back, declaring: "Appetite not exhausted yet. Must show us a few more pictures." In the meantime he had taken off his formal attire and fetched out his comfortable house coat. Then he sat down in an armchair, the others stood round him, and his grandsons Walter and Wolfgang, who had just come in, snuggled up close to their grandpapa while I showed him the pictures... He sank into silent contemplation and then exclaimed: "Yes, the ancients are unrivalled in any branch of the divine arts. Believe me, gentlemen, I think I have achieved something too, but compared to one of the great Attic poets such as Aeschylus or Sophocles, I am nothing after all."

222. *W. Zahn* *8–10.9.1827*

On these unforgettable evenings Goethe used to be particularly fond of talking to me about his stay in Italy. The great poet was exceedingly devoted to Rome, he knew every little street in it, and all the little street-corner taverns, not least because it is in these that the best wine can be had, as is well known. "Yes", he said, "I made good use of my time, I didn't fritter it away paying calls, I studied the city and the people very thoroughly. You know how the words go in my *Roman Elegies* :

> *Pay what respects you please! At long last I am safe*
> > *now from you*
> *Elegant ladies, and you, gentlemen of the* grand monde ! . . .
> *Now you'll be hard put to it to track me down in this*
> > *refuge*
> *Where beneath Cupid's wings, royally sheltered, I dwell!*

And do you know the Osteria alla Campana?" he went on to ask. "The Bell Tavern? Certainly. We German artists celebrated your birthday there only last year." "Do they still serve good Falerno?" "Excellent!" "And what does the kitchen have to offer?" "Oh, one gets *stuffato*, a sort of stew, and macaroni, and a mixed fried dish that they call *fritti*." "It's all as it was in my time!" said Goethe with a satisfied smile. Then he went on : "That osteria was my usual haunt. It was here I met the Roman girl who inspired the *Elegies*. She would come along escorted by her uncle, and we would arrange our meetings under the good fellow's nose by dipping a finger in the spilt wine and writing the time on the table. Do you remember?

> *Here was our table, and Germans, at home here, sat*
> > *revelling round it . . .*
> *Stamped on my mind's eye, I still gazed at that*
> > *sweet figure four!"*

223. *W. Zahn* *September 1827*

One day, when I was again having a meal with Goethe, a deputation arrived from the Crossbow Club which has existed in Weimar for three hundred years, and solemnly invited his Excellency, as they did every year, to be present at their annual celebration. Goethe had hitherto always declined to attend it, but this time, after reflecting for a moment or two, he accepted, to everyone's surprise. "Very well!" he declared, "I shall come, but Zahn must come too." Goethe was born under a lucky star. Even at this festival he hit a bull's eye with his crossbow, whereupon we sat down to a sumptuous breakfast at the shooting-range. Goethe was in the best of spirits and invited everyone to a great banquet that evening. A large company was present and the noble wine flowed copiously. He watched with enormous relish as one guest after another succumbed to pitiful befuddlement. On him alone the wine had no effect.

My most enjoyable hours in Goethe's company were on certain evenings when we were quite alone. On these occasions I would even see the great man in his dressing-gown. We would eat cold roast meat and wash it down with bottle after bottle, and sometimes it would be midnight and after before he dismissed me, although his usual bedtime was between nine and ten. He asked endless questions and succeeded in bringing out the best in me and eliciting all my closest secrets, so that I was often amazed at myself. During these precious hours he would become absorbed in the golden memories of his abundant life, and open his great and noble heart for me to see—a heart no less great than his intellect. It knew no shadow of envy, but embraced all mankind with warm benevolence, and it had moved him to help hundreds of people by good deeds and good counsel, though always quietly and in secret.

224.   F. von Müller   20.9.1827

"The great thing in translating is on no account to become involved in a hand-to-hand fight with the foreign language. One must go to the limits of translatability and respect the untranslatable: for it is precisely the latter that gives every language its value and character."

225.   F. von Müller   23.9.1827

"I must confess that I should have little use for an eternity of blessedness if I could not spend it solving new problems and overcoming new difficulties. But that has been well taken care of: one need only look at the planets and suns, there will be plenty of nuts to crack there."

226. *Eckermann* 26.9.1827

Goethe had invited me this morning for a drive up the Etters-berg; it was a beautiful day. We reached the most westerly summit; the broad valley of the Unstrut, full of villages and little towns, lay before us in the brilliant morning sun.

"This is a good place!" said Goethe, ordering the carriage to stop. "I think we should perhaps see if we can eat a little breakfast in this good air."

We got out and walked up and down for a few minutes while Friedrich unpacked the breakfast which we had brought, and laid it out on a grassy hillock. We sat down with our backs to the oak-trees, and thus had the wide view over half Thuringia in front of us all the time as we devoured a brace of roast partridges, and new white bread, and washed them down with a bottle of excellent wine, drinking it from a flexible fine golden cup which Goethe on such excursions usually carries with him in a yellow leather case.

"I have often been up here", said Goethe, "and I hope this is not the last time we shall both spend a pleasant day on this spot. We must come to it more often in future. One shrivels up in a narrow indoor life. Here one feels free and great, like great Nature that lies spread before one's eyes, and as one ought properly always to be."

227. *Eckermann* 26.9.1827

"I have never had much respect for mere princely rank as such, unless there was some sound human nature and sound human value behind it as well. In fact I have always been so glad to be as I was and have always felt so distinguished that if I had been made a prince I should not have found the change so very remarkable. When I was given the diploma of nobility, many people supposed I should feel myself elevated by it. But between you and me, I thought nothing of it—nothing at all! We Frankfurt patricians always considered ourselves equal to the nobility, and when I held the diploma in my hands I had in my own opinion acquired nothing more than what I had long possessed."

228.   *Ottilie von Goethe (reported)*   *17.10.1827*

One day Goethe announced to his daughter-in-law that there would be a guest for lunch, but did not tell her his name, which he had never omitted to do before, and did not introduce the guest when he arrived. Mute bows on both sides. During the meal Goethe said comparatively little, presumably in order to give free rein to his very talkative guest, who unfolded his thoughts with great logical acumen and in oddly complicated syntax. His increasingly animated exposition with its quite new terminology, its intellectually elliptical style of expression and its strange philosophical formulae, finally reduced Goethe to complete silence, though the guest did not notice this. The hostess also listened silently, no doubt glancing at her papa (as she always called Goethe) in some surprise. When the meal had come to an end and their guest departed, Goethe asked his daughter-in-law: "Well, how did you like him?" "How very strange he is! I don't know whether he's brilliant or crazy. He didn't seem to me to be a very clear thinker." Goethe smiled ironically. "Well, well! We have just had lunch with a man who is now the most famous of modern philosophers—Georg Friedrich Wilhelm Hegel."

229.   *Eckermann*   *18.10.1827*

Hegel is here; Goethe has a very high esteem for him personally, though he does not greatly relish some of the fruits of his philosophy, and this evening he gave a tea party in his honour. In the course of conversation the nature of dialectics was discussed. "Basically", said Hegel, "it is merely a regulated, methodical cultivation of the esprit de contradiction, which is an inborn gift in every man and particularly valuable for distinguishing the true from the false."

"But let us hope", interposed Goethe, "that such intellectual arts and skills are not too much misused for the purpose of turning falsehood into truth and truth into falsehood!"

"That does sometimes happen", replied Hegel, "but only with people who are mentally diseased."

"Well", said Goethe, "I personally recommend the study of nature as a prophylactic against that disease. For in nature we are dealing with something which is infinitely and eternally true, and which immediately rejects as inadequate everyone who does not show complete integrity and honesty in the way he observes and treats his subject. And I am certain that the study of nature would be a wholesome remedy for many a dialectical sufferer."

230. F. Förster (?) 1827

"It is true", said Goethe to me today, "that there is no nation like the English for plaguing me with visitors and sometimes boring me too with their mere idle curiosity; but I must also admit, and I have often experienced it myself, that when it comes to making the magnificently tactful gesture the Englishman is second to none. A month or two ago an Englishman who takes an interest in our literature sent me a translation of my *Faust** in very neat calligraphy, with the request that I should undertake to give an opinion on it. I replied very politely that I was prevented by an eye-complaint from reading manuscript and that he must therefore excuse me if I should be unable to meet his wishes in the near future. And lo and behold, yesterday I received from the noble lord a copy specially printed for me on vellum in magnificent large letters, with a note expressing the hope that it might be possible for me to read this writing without injuring my eyes. Dr. Vogel found me today reading this splendid gift, and he forbids me to lead my still inflamed retina into temptation for another four or five weeks. But I should nevertheless like to say a few kind words to the noble lord about his work and the courtesy he has shown me, so perhaps you will be good enough to take the translation with you and tell me of any notable passages you find in it and read them aloud to me."

Next day I turned up at the appointed hour and began by reading the *Dedicatory Poem*, which Goethe thought very successfully rendered. I then told him that I had been very disagreeably surprised to find that the translation omitted the wonderful opening scene in Heaven, and I remarked that the difficulties of translating this into English did not seem to me to be insuperable, to which Goethe replied: "I don't suppose the

* Förster, who was unreliable on factual details, appears to be referring to Lord Francis Leveson Gower's translation of *Faust* (cf. No. 231) a printed copy of which had, however, been received by Goethe in 1825. According to another report, an unidentified English translation of *Torquato Tasso* was sent to Goethe in 1827, specially printed large to spare his eyes, and Förster is probably confusing the two stories. The date, 1827 according to Förster, of his alleged discussion of Leveson Gower's *Faust* with the poet is also very uncertain.

noble lord was hampered by difficulties of translation but by religious or rather High Church scruples; perhaps not his own scruples, but those of his aristocratic circle. Nowhere in the world are there so many hypocrites and prigs as in England; I suppose it may have been different in Shakespeare's time." I next had to inform him that I did not think the rendering of Gretchen's song *There was a king in Thule* quite correct. The passage

> *Und als er kam zu sterben,*
> *Zählt er seine Städt im Reich,*
> *Gönnt alles seinem Erben*
> *Den Becher nicht zugleich**

runs in his lordship's version (no doubt merely for the rhyme's sake)

> *He called for his confessor,*
> *Left all to his successor . . .*

Goethe laughed heartily. "Called for his confessor!" he repeated. "We must point out to the noble lord that the King of Thule reigned before the Flood; there were no confessors then."†

He also asked me to report on [?Stapfer's] French translation, and sure enough there were plenty of curiosities here. "In sheer ignorance of our language", remarked Goethe, "the recent and latest translators of *Faust* are a match for their brilliant and famous compatriot Madame de Staël. That lady has undeniably deserved great things of both the German and the French nation, for her book *Sur la littérature allemande* made her fellow-countrymen acquainted with our achievements and secured recognition for the Germans in France. But when Gretchen faints in the church, crying out

> *Nachbarin, Euer Fläschchen!*

Madame de Staël's translation of these words is :

> *Ma voisine, une goutte!*

as if Gretchen were asking her neighbour for a flask of brandy and not for a bottle of smelling-salts."

* "And when he came to die he numbered the cities of his kingdom and withheld nothing from his heir, except only the cup." (Cf. *Selected Verse* (Penguin Books) pp. 38f.)

† This mis-translation does not, in fact, occur in Leveson Gower's version.

This reminded us of other amusing versions of the same kind. Faust's line

> *Heisse Magister, heisse Doktor gar!*

was once translated

> *On me nomme Maître—Docteur Gar.*

Faust says of Gretchen :

> *Und wie sie kurz angebunden war,*
> *Das ist nun zum Entzücken gar!*

Here the translator leaves out the "gar" altogether, but he takes "kurz angebunden" (i.e. pert) to mean "with her skirt drawn well up", and his version runs :

> *Et sa robe courte, juste,*
> *Vraiment, c'était à ravir!*

Once an Englishman expressed surprise that the father in the *Erlking* ballad was described as being so excessively concerned about the boy, when after all he had been blessed with so large a family. When it was pointed out to him that there is no mention of this in the poem he recited with his half-shut mouth :

> *Dem Vater grauset, er reitet geschwind,*
> *Er hält in den Armen das achtzehnte Kind.**

231. *A. B. Granville* 2.1.1828

At half-past ten precisely, Goethe made his appearance in one of his classically decorated withdrawingrooms, into which I had been but the moment before introduced. When he extended his friendly hand to welcome me to his dwelling, I stood absorbed in the contemplation of the first literary character of the age. The sound of his voice, which bespeaks peculiar affability, and the first questions he addressed to me respecting my journey, however, recalled me from my reverie. I found him in his conversation ready, rather than fluent, following rather than leading; unaffected, yet gentlemanly; earnest yet entertaining; and manifesting no desire to display how much he deserved the high reputation which not only Germany, but

---

* "The father shudders, he quickens his horse's pace, he holds his eighteenth child in his arms." Goethe's poem (cf. *Selected Verse*, pp. 8off.) reads: "das ächzende Kind" (the moaning child).

Europe in general, had simultaneously acknowledged to be his due. He conversed in French, and occasionally in English, particularly when desirous to make me understand the force of his observations on some recent translations of his works into that language. Faustus was one of these. The translation by Lord Francis Leveson Gower seemed not to have given satisfaction to the veteran author. He observed to me that most assuredly it was not a translation, but an imitation, of what he had written. "Whole sentences of the original," added he, "have been omitted, and chasms left in the translation, where the most affecting passages should have been inserted to complete the picture. There were probably difficulties in the original which the noble translator might not be able to overcome; few foreigners, indeed, can boast of such mastery of our prodigal idiom as to be able to convey its meaning with equal richness of expression and strength of conception in their own native language; but, in the case of the translation to which I allude, that excuse for imperfection does not exist in many of the parts which Lord Francis Gower has thought proper to omit. No doubt, the choice of expressions in the English translation, the versification, and talent displayed in what is original composition of his lordship's own well-gifted mind may be deserving of his countrymen's applause; but it is as the author of Faustus travesti, *and not as the translator of Goethe's* Faustus, *that the popular applause has been obtained."*

Throughout this interview, which lasted upwards of an hour, Goethe manifested great eagerness after general information, particularly respecting England and her numerous institutions.

232. F. von Müller   6.3.1828

The present complaints about Wellington's omnipotence as Prime Minister were absurd, he said; they ought to be glad that he had at last taken his rightful place. A man who had conquered India and Napoleon might surely be thought entitled to govern a dirty little island. "The man who holds supreme power is in the right; we must respect him and bow down before him.—But I am not going to bother my head at my age about the utter absurdity of world history; what is it to me whether this or that man dies or this or that nation perishes? I should be a fool to care."

Warum stehen sie davor? Können sie getroffhoren
Ist nicht Thüre da und Thor. Würden wohlempfangen seyn
Goethe 1828

GOETHE'S HOUSE IN WEIMAR

233. *Eckermann* 11.3.1828

"Man", said Goethe, "has his periods of doubt and darkness and his periods of illumination, and it is on this that his fate depends! We need the daily guidance of the daemonic spirit within us, always telling us what to do and impelling us to do it. But this friendly guiding hand leaves us, and we grope nervelessly in the dark.

"What a fellow Napoleon was! Always illuminated, always clever and decisive, and gifted at every moment with enough energy to carry out at once whatever he had recognised to be expedient and necessary. His life was the striding of a demigod from battle to battle, from victory to victory. Of him it could well be said that he was in a state of continual illumination."

I remarked that this seemed to me to have been more particularly the case when Napoleon was still young and his powers were still on the increase.

"For that matter", said Goethe, "I didn't write my love-lyrics or my *Werther* twice. The divine illumination which inspires extraordinary achievements will always be found to be allied with youth and productivity; and Napoleon, you know, was one of the most productive men who ever lived. One need not necessarily write poems and plays in order to be productive; there is a productivity of deeds as well, and in many cases its quality is significantly higher."

"You seem here", I said, "to be giving the name 'productivity' to what used to be called genius."

"Both are very closely akin", replied Goethe. "For what else is genius but that productive energy which brings forth deeds that can stand unashamed before God and nature and are for that very reason long-lasting and fraught with consequence? All Mozart's works are of this kind; they contain a procreative force which works on from generation to generation and is unlikely to be spent and consumed for a long time to come. The same is true of other great composers and artists. For there is no genius without this continuing productive power; and what is more, it does not depend on the man's particular occupation or art or profession—the same thing applies to them all. I should also add that the sheer number of a man's products or deeds is not a measure of his productivity. In literature we have poets who are considered to be very productive because they have published one volume of poems after another. But these persons are absolutely unproductive in my sense of the word, because what they have done has no life or durability.

"But you are quite right in saying that the really brilliant period of Napoleon's deeds was his youth. Ah yes, my dear fellow, we must be young if we are to do great things. And Napoleon is not the only one!—If I were a prince, I should never choose my leading ministers from among people who have gradually risen by mere birth and seniority and now, in old age, crawl slowly along their accustomed track; small wonder if scarcely anything sensible gets done that way. I should want young men!—but they would have to be capable men, gifted with clear-headedness and energy and full of good will and nobility of character as well."

It struck me as remarkable that a man who himself still held an important appointment at such an advanced age could be so decided an advocate of youth. I could not refrain from mentioning several distinguished Germans who, old as they were, still seemed to have quite enough youthful active energy to carry out very important and varied tasks.

"These men and others of their kind", replied Goethe, "are natural geniuses, and they have a special peculiarity. They experience a repetition of puberty, whereas other people are young only once.

"Every entelechy,* you see, is a piece of eternity, and the few short years during which it is bound to an earthly body do not make it old. If this entelechy is of a trivial sort, it will exert scarcely any influence during its period of bodily obscuration; on the contrary, the body will predominate, and when the body grows old, the entelechy will not hinder its decay. But if the entelechy is powerful, as it is in all men of natural genius, it will pervade and animate the body, and not only will it have a strengthening and ennobling effect on the physical organisation, but its superior spiritual strength will also be such that it will constantly try to assert its privilege of perpetual youth. That is why fresh periods of unusual productivity may still be seen to occur in exceptionally gifted men even when they are old; they seem from time to time to undergo a temporary rejuvenation, which is what I should like to call a repetition of puberty.

---

* A term adopted by Goethe from Aristotle, to mean the active spiritual principle or "soul" in an organism. In Aristotelian philosophy the "entelechy" was the capacity of the potential to become actual. (Cf. No. 101.)

"But youth is youth; however powerful an entelechy may prove to be, it will never quite prevail over the body, and it makes a considerable difference whether the latter behaves as its ally or as its opponent.

"At one time in my life I could make myself write a printed sheet every day, and I found this quite easy. Nowadays I suppose I must give up trying that sort of thing; and nevertheless, even in my old age, I have no cause to complain of unproductiveness. But things which when I was young I could do every day and in any circumstances, I can now only do at intervals and under certain favourable conditions. In that lucky period ten or twelve years ago after the War of Liberation, when the poems of the *Westöstlicher Divan* had me under their spell, I was so productive that I could often write two or three of them in one day, no matter where I was—out in the fields, or in a carriage, or in a hotel. And now I can only work at the second part of my *Faust* in the early hours of the day, when I am feeling revived and strengthened by sleep and not yet harassed by the absurd trivialities of everyday life. And even so, what does this work amount to? If I am very lucky indeed I can manage one page, but as a rule only a hand's-breadth of writing, and often even less if I am in an unproductive mood."

I asked whether this meant that there exists no way of inducing a productive mood or of intensifying one if it is not strong enough.

"This particular point", said Goethe, "is a very strange matter, and needs a lot of thought and explanation.

"All productivity of the highest kind, all important insights and inventions, all great thoughts which bear fruit and have consequences—all these are things beyond any man's control and subject to no earthly power. Man must simply look upon them as unexpected gifts from on high, as pure children of God which he must receive and venerate with gratitude and rejoicing. This kind of thing is akin to the daemonic, that superior force which does what it pleases with human beings and to which they unwittingly abandon themselves, in the belief that they are acting on their own impulses. In such cases a man can often be regarded as an instrument of some higher government of the world, as a worthy and chosen vessel of divine inspiration. In saying this I have in mind how often a single thought has changed the course of whole centuries, and how individual men, by the force that flowed from them, have made a mark upon their age which remained uneffaced in the generations that followed, and continued to exert its beneficent influence.

"There is, however, another kind of productivity in which earthly factors do indeed play a rather greater part and which is more susceptible to human control, although here too man still finds cause to revere something divine. I include in this category everything that appertains to the execution of a plan, all the intermediate links in a chain of thought whose beginning and end already radiantly exist; I include everything that constitutes the visible physical body of a work of art.

"Thus when the initial conception of *Hamlet* first came to Shakespeare—when the essence of the whole work presented itself to his mind as an unexpected impression, and in an inspired mood he surveyed its particular situations and characters and how it would all end—it came as a pure gift from on high, and he had had no direct power to bring it about, although it would of course never have been possible to have such an insight without a mind such as his. But the further development of the individual scenes, and the writing of the dialogue, were matters completely under his control, so that he could work at them daily and hourly and for weeks on end, just as it suited him. And in fact his plays all show the same constant productive energy, and in none of them do we ever come upon a passage which could be said to have been written when he was not in the right mood or not at the height of his powers. As we read him we get the impression of a man who was always thoroughly strong and healthy in mind and body.

"If, however, a dramatist's physical constitution is less robust and exceptional and if, instead, he is subject to frequent ailments and debilities, then the productivity which he needs for the daily construction of his scenes will certainly be very frequently reduced and will often, no doubt, desert him completely for days on end. If he then, by the use of alcohol for instance, tries to compel the productive mood to come to him when it is absent, and to heighten it when it is insufficient, this too may well be in some measure effective; but in all the scenes to which he has applied some such method of forced production, the fact that he has done so will be obvious and very detrimental.

"My advice therefore is that one should not force anything; it is better to fritter away one's unproductive days and hours, or sleep through them, than to try at such times to write something which will give one no satisfaction later on.

"It is true of course that wine does contain certain very important powers which stimulate production, but this all depends on what state one is in and what time it is, and something that is good for one man is bad for another. Rest and sleep also possess these stimulative powers, but so does movement. Water possesses them, and above all they are contained in the atmosphere. The fresh air of the open country is our proper element : there it is as if the spirit of God were breathing directly upon man and a divine power exerting its influence. Lord Byron used to spend several hours every day in the open air, sometimes riding on horseback along the seashore, sometimes sailing or rowing a boat, or bathing in the sea and swimming to exercise his strength : and he was one of the most productive men who ever lived."

We discussed the various misfortunes that had darkened Lord Byron's later life, till in the end a noble impulse, but an unlucky fate, had driven him to Greece and destroyed him altogether.

"You will in fact find", continued Goethe, "that in middle life a man's career often takes a different turn, and that whereas in youth everything favoured him and he succeeded in everything, it is now suddenly all reversed, and disasters and misfortunes follow one on top of the other.

"But do you know what I think it is? This disintegration of a man has to happen. Every exceptional man has a certain mission which he is destined to accomplish. When he has done so, his presence on earth in that form is no longer necessary, and Providence puts him to some other use. But since everything here below happens in a natural way, the daemons keep tripping him up until finally he succumbs. This is how it was with Napoleon and with many others. Mozart died in his thirty-sixth year, Raphael at about the same age, and Byron was only a little older. But they had all perfectly fulfilled their appointed tasks, and no doubt they were due to go, if there was to be anything else left for other people to do in this world; the world is after all designed to last for a long time."

234. *Eckermann*   *12.3.1828*

"It is hard to say whether it is a matter of ancestry, or of the soil, or of their liberal political institutions, or the healthy way they are educated—at all events, the English in general do seem to have certain advantages over many other people. Here in Weimar we only see a few of them, and they are probably far from being the best examples; but what fine good-looking men they are! And although they come here as young as seventeen, they never feel at all out of place or embarrassed in this foreign German land : on the contrary, their deportment and behaviour in society is as full of confidence and ease as if they were masters everywhere and the whole world belonged to them. And that indeed is what makes them attractive to our young women and enables them to wreak such havoc in those poor little female hearts. They are dangerous young men; but of course this very dangerousness is a virtue in them.

"It is not even a matter of rank and wealth. The essential thing is that they simply have the courage to be what nature intended them to be. They have grown entirely unstunted and unspoilt, there is nothing half-hearted or shilly-shallying about them : on the contrary, they are always absolutely complete men of their kind. And sometimes complete fools too, I willingly concede; but even that is something, even that has some weight on the scales of nature.

"Their good fortune in enjoying personal freedom, their consciousness of bearing an English name and of the importance attached to it by other nations—all this is an advantage to them even as children, for it means that both at home and at school they are treated with far greater respect, and develop far more freely and happily, than is the case here in Germany. I need only look out of my window in dear old Weimar to see how we manage things. Recently there was snow on the ground and the children who live near me wanted to try out their little sledges in the street, but at once a police officer came up and I saw the poor little things running for their lives. And now, when the spring sun tempts them out of doors and they want to play with their friends in front of their houses, I can see that they are always ill at ease, as if they felt unsafe and always dreaded the approach of some despotic policeman. No boy may ever crack a whip or sing or shout; the police are immediately at hand to forbid it. In our country everything is calculated to make youth prematurely tame and to extinguish all its naturalness and originality and wildness, so that in the end only philistinism is left."

235. Karl August of Saxe-Weimar (reported by F. von Müller)

I called on the Grand Duke one day in 1828 and he talked to me for about two hours in the most good-humoured fashion, telling me many things which he remembered about Goethe from earlier years. Goethe (he said) had always seen too much in women, loved his own ideals in them; he had never really felt great passion. The one he had loved longest, Frau von Stein, had been quite a good woman, but just not particularly bright. The Vulpius girl had spoilt everything, estranging him from society. The death of the Dowager Duchess had been another severe blow, she had been a centre of easy social intercourse; the Grand Duchess had been temperamentally unable to continue this role. It had been a great pity about Schiller—in him Goethe had lost a mainstay of his life for a long time. Goethe junior was by no means a fool, quite promising. A pity he had got into drinking habits and been brought up rather wildly.

236. J. Schwabe

Goethe was an unusually discriminating connoisseur of wine, and gave brilliant proof of this one evening at a small dinner-party given by the Grand Duke Karl August. During dessert, after various good wines had been tried, Hofmarschall von Spiegel asked the Grand Duke's permission to have one served which had no name. A red wine was handed round, tasted, and judged to be excellent. Several of the gentlemen round the table declared it to be burgundy, though they could not agree to which particular variety of that noble growth it belonged. Since burgundy, however, was the diagnosis of several well-tried palates, among them that of the Grand Duke, this classification found general acceptance. Only Goethe kept tasting and retasting, shook his head and thoughtfully set down the empty glass. "Your Excellency seems to be of a different opinion", said the Hofmarschall. "May I ask what name you would give to this wine?" "I don't know this wine at all", replied Goethe, "but I don't think it is a burgundy. I should be more inclined to guess that it is a well-picked Jena wine which has been stored for some time in a madeira vat." "And that", confirmed the Hofmarschall, "is exactly what it is."

237.   E. Schuchardt   5.9.1828

Luncheon was now served, and as the wine was placed before us (Goethe drank Würzburger, we were given red) Goethe began to talk about a book on the history of wines written by an Englishman, which had greatly interested him. Then he complained that they were forgetting in Weimar to keep him supplied with wine, and that last Saturday he had only been sent five bottles. He then set about preparing a salad himself, assuring us as he did so that he had invented a new salad made of pickled gherkins. Altogether he seemed to be rather an expert in these matters; he talked a lot about eating, and his own appetite was fairly hearty. When artichokes were served he seemed to notice that I found them difficult to handle, and instructed me on the correct method of eating them. He told us that these artichokes had been sent to him by his relatives in Frankfurt, to his great delight. We then discussed the Turkish wars, Gotha and other such matters. Towards the end of the meal he seemed to be overcome by drowsiness, for he clasped his hands as if he were praying, bowed his head and was silent for a while; but after this he continued the conversation. Coffee was handed round after lunch, but Goethe did not drink any. We then accompanied him into the garden and took our leave. This was at about five o'clock.

238.   Eckermann   1.10.1828

"Aristotle had a clearer view of nature than any modern thinker, but he was too hasty in his judgments. Nature will not yield us any of her secrets unless we treat her with patience and indulgence. When any scientific investigations led me to form some opinion, I did not expect her to confirm it at once; I simply followed it up with observations and experimental tests, and was satisfied if she occasionally obliged me by offering some evidence for my hypothesis. If she did not, she would usually suggest to me some other aperçu which I would follow up, and of which she was perhaps more willing to yield me the proof."

239.   Eckermann   9.10.1828

"Only in Rome did I ever feel what it really is to be human. I have never again achieved those heights, that sensation of joy; in fact, by comparison with my state of mind in Rome, I have never really been happy again."

240. *Eckermann* 11.10.1828

"My works can never be popular; anyone who thinks so and tries to make them so is mistaken. They are not written for the masses, but only for a few individuals who have similar aims and tendencies and are looking for the same sort of thing."

241. *Eckermann* 22.10.1828

Today at table we were discussing women, and Goethe made a delightful remark about them. "Women", he said, "are silver saucers into which we put golden apples. My idea of women was not formed by abstraction from reality and experience, but was inborn in me, or formed itself in me, God knows how. And the female characters in my works all benefited from this, they are all better women than can be found in reality."

242. *Eckermann* 23.10.1828

We then discussed the unity of Germany, and in what sense it is possible and desirable.

"I am confident", said Goethe, "that German unity will be achieved; our good roads and future railways will play their part in this. But above all let all Germans be united in affection for each other, and let them always unite against a foreign foe! I want Germany to be united in the sense that the German *thaler* and *groschen* currency will have one and the same value all over the empire; united in the sense that I shall be able to take my luggage across the frontiers of all the thirty-six states without having it opened; that the bearer of a Weimar passport will not be treated by the frontier officials of a large neighbouring state as if he were a foreigner with insufficient papers. There should be no more question of inland and foreign as between German states. Germany should also have a unified system of weights and measures, it should unite for purposes of trade and commerce and for a hundred other similar purposes which I cannot and need not mention.

"But if anyone imagines that the unity of Germany should consist in this very large empire having a single large capital, and that this one large capital would both favour the development of great individual talents and benefit the great mass of the people, then he is making a mistake.

"It has been said that a state is like a living body with many limbs, and similarly one might say that the capital of a state is like the heart, from which life and well-being flows into the different limbs, both near it and further from it. But if the limbs are a very long way from the heart, the life-stream flowing into them will be more and more weakly felt. A clever Frenchman recently sketched a map of the state of culture in France, indicating the greater or lesser enlightenment of the various départements by means of lighter or darker colours. Accordingly there are some, particularly in southern provinces remote from the capital, which he has coloured completely black, to symbolise their utterly benighted condition. But would this be the case if the fair land of France, instead of having one great centre, had ten centres all radiating light and vitality?

"What makes Germany great? An admirable national culture which has equally pervaded all parts of the empire. But where are its points of dissemination, and where else is it nurtured and fostered, if not in the individual principalities? Supposing Germany had for centuries had only two capital cities, Vienna and Berlin, or even only one: where would German culture be, I should like to know? And where indeed would be the all-pervading prosperity that goes hand in hand with culture?

"Germany has over twenty universities, distributed all over the empire, and over a hundred public libraries, equally widespread. It also has numerous collections of works of art and of every category of natural objects, because every prince has made it his business to surround himself with these beautiful and excellent things. There is an abundance of colleges for humane studies and of technical and industrial schools. Indeed there is scarcely a German village without its school. But how do such matters stand in France?

"And then there are the many German theatres, over seventy of them, all fostering and promoting higher national culture in an entirely praiseworthy manner. In no other country are music and song so widely appreciated and practised as in Germany, and that too is something!

"But think, now, of cities such as Dresden, Munich, Stuttgart, Kassel, Brunswick, Hanover and others like them. Think of their great intrinsic vitality; think of the influence of each of them on its surrounding province, and then ask yourself whether all this would be the case if they had not from time immemorial been the governmental seats of kings and princes? Frankfurt, Bremen, Hamburg and Lübeck are great and splendid, their effect on the prosperity of Germany is incalculable: but would they still remain what they are if they lost their own sovereignty and became incorporated into some large German empire as provincial towns? I have reason to doubt it."

243. *Eckermann* 16.12.1828

"The Germans", said Goethe, "will never cease to be philistines. At present they are fussing and quibbling about various epigrammatic couplets which have found their way into Schiller's printed works as well as into mine, and they regard it as important to decide for certain which of them belong to Schiller and which to me. As if it mattered, as if it were any use to know, and as if it were not enough that the lines exist!

"A pair of friends like Schiller and myself, with our long years of association, our similar interests, our daily contact and exchange of ideas, became so intimately identified with each other that it was impossible to say to which of us this or that particular thought belonged, and pointless to ask such a question. We composed many of those distichs together, often I had the idea and Schiller made the lines, often it was the other way round, and often Schiller wrote one line and I wrote the other. How can there be any question of proprietorship in such a case! One must really still be a hardened philistine if one attaches the slightest importance to the settling of that sort of scruple."

I remarked that something of the same sort often happens in the literary world when, for example, this or that famous man's originality is questioned and attempts are made to trace his culture to its sources.

"That is quite ridiculous", said Goethe. "One might as well ask a well-nourished man about the oxen and sheep and pigs he has eaten and which have given him his strength. We start with talent, to be sure, but we owe our development to countless influences which a whole world brings to bear on us, and from which we appropriate whatever we can and whatever is germane to our needs. I have much to thank the Greeks and the French for, I owe Shakespeare and Sterne and Goldsmith an infinite debt. But to say that is not to trace my cultural sources:

to do so would be an unending and quite unnecessary task. The essential thing is to have a mind that loves truth and is receptive of it wherever it finds it."

244. *Falk*

Goethe talked about professors and the way they stuff their treatises with quotations and notes, digressing hither and thither and obscuring the main point : he compared them to harnessed dogs which have no sooner given one a tug or two than they start lifting their hind legs again for this or that dubious purpose —"there is no budging an inch with such brutes," he said, "they make a day's journey out of a mile".

"Don't talk to me", he exclaimed on another occasion, "of the public or of posterity, or of the justice, as you call it, that will one day be done to my work. I say damn *Tasso*, precisely because they tell me it will go down to posterity; I say damn *Iphigenia*; in a word, I say damn every single thing of mine that this public likes. In fact I should be absolutely delighted if I ever succeeded—though I never could at my age—in writing a work that would cause the Germans to damn my name heartily and not have one good thing to say of me for fifty or a hundred years on end. A fine work it would be that could produce such an effect on the natural apathy of a public like ours. At least there is some character in hatred; and if we could only begin showing some real character again in some direction or other, I don't care what, then we should be on our way again to becoming a people. Most of us are fundamentally incapable of hating or loving. They don't 'like' me! Insipid word! Well, I don't like them! I've never really done anything to please them. If they happen after my death to read the passage in the continuation of *Faust* where even the Devil finds grace at the mercy-seat of God—I think they'll not forgive me that for many a day! They've been racking their brains for nearly thirty years now over things in Faust like the Blocksberg broomsticks and the apes' dialogue in the Witch's Kitchen, and they've made precious little headway with their interpretations and allegorisations of all that humorous dramatic nonsense. Why, even that clever Madame de Staël took it ill that in the scene with the angels' song I made God the Father treat the Devil with such good humour : she wanted him to be much fiercer. What will she say when she meets the Devil again, promoted to some still higher sphere, perhaps even right into heaven!"

245. *F. Förster* 1828

I would occasionally try to get him to tell me about the Second Part of *Faust* and how the whole work would end, but his answers were always evasive. I remember only that when I hazarded the guess that the closing scene would indeed be set in Heaven and that Mephistopheles would no doubt confess himself beaten and admit to the audience that "a good man, in the turmoil of his heart, well knows the way and how he ought to go", Goethe shook his head and said: "That would merely be in the spirit of the Enlightenment. Faust ends as a very old man, and in our old age we become mystics."

246. *Eckermann* 4.2.1829

"The Christian religion is a mighty force in itself, which again and again has helped sunken and suffering humanity to raise itself up; and if we grant that it has this power, then it becomes something superior to all philosophy and needs no philosophical support. So, too, philosophy has no need of the authority of religion to prove certain doctrines, such as that of eternal survival. A man should believe in immortality, he has a right to believe, it is his nature to do so, and he may well take his stand on the promises of religion; but a philosopher who tries to prove our soul immortal by appealing to a legend is on very weak and dubious ground. For myself, I base my conviction of our survival on the idea of activity: for if I work on incessantly until I die, nature is under an obligation to provide me with another form of existence when the present one is worn out and must release my spirit."

247. *Eckermann* 12.2.1829

I said that I had not abandoned hope of seeing some suitable music composed for *Faust*.

"It is quite out of the question", said Goethe. "It would have to contain grim, repellent, terrifying passages which are foreign to the spirit of this age. The music would have to be something like *Don Giovanni*; *Faust* would have to have been set to music by Mozart. Meyerbeer might perhaps be capable of it, but he will have no time for such an undertaking."

248. *Eckermann*   13.2.1829

"If it had not been for my work in natural science, I should never have got to know men as they really are. In no other activity can one approach so closely to pure contemplation and thought, or so closely observe the errors of the senses and of the intelligence and a character's weak and strong points. In everything else there is a greater or lesser degree of flexibility and uncertainty and one can come more or less to an accommodation. But Nature will stand no nonsense; she is always truthful, always serious, always rigorous; she is always right, and the mistakes and errors are always those of man. She scorns an inadequate student; only to one who is adequate and true and pure will she yield herself and reveal her secrets.

"Mere empirical intelligence (Verstand) cannot reach her; man must be capable of rising to the highest level of metaphysical reason (Vernunft) if he is to achieve contact with that divinity which manifests itself in primary phenomena, which dwells behind them and from which they proceed.

"The divinity, however, shows its power in living things but not in dead things; it dwells in that which grows and changes, not in that which is finished and fixed. And that is why metaphysical reason, aspiring as it does towards the divine, concerns itself only with growing and living things, whereas empirical intelligence studies finished and fixed things of which it may make use.

"It follows that mineralogy is a science for the intelligence, for practical life, for it studies dead phenomena which are no longer developing, and there is here no question of discovering a higher synthesis. The phenomena studied by meteorology are alive, to be sure; we witness their daily productive activity, and they presuppose a synthesis; but their subsidiary effects are so numerous and diverse that man is incapable of grasping this synthesis and his laborious observations and researches are therefore vain. In this field we navigate towards hypotheses as if towards imaginary islands, but the true synthesis will probably remain an undiscovered country. And this does not surprise me when I consider how difficult it was to achieve some sort of synthesis even in such simple matters as plants and colours."

249.   Eckermann   *18.2.1829*

We discussed Goethe's theory of colours, mentioning among other things those opaque figures engraved on glass goblets which look yellow when held against the light and blue against the dark, and which thus give one the opportunity to observe a primary phenomenon.

"The highest state man can achieve," remarked Goethe in this connection, "is that of astonishment; and when a primary phenomenon astonishes him, he should be satisfied. It cannot give him anything higher, and he must not look for anything more behind it : this is the frontier. And yet men are usually not content to be beholders of a primary phenomenon, they think there must be a way leading further, and they are like children who when they have looked into a mirror at once turn it round to see what is on the other side."

250.   Eckermann   *19.2.1829*

"For everything I have achieved as a poet," he would often say, "I take no credit at all. There have been excellent writers among my contemporaries, others even finer among my predecessors, and there will be others to come after me. But I do rather congratulate myself on the fact that in the difficult science of colours I am the only man in my century who knows the truth, and this gives me a sense of superiority over many."

251.   Eckermann   *March–April 1829*

(24th March): "The higher a man stands", said Goethe, "the more he is subject to the influence of the daemons, and he must always be on his guard, or his guiding will may go astray.

"Thus in the case of my association with Schiller there was undoubtedly some daemonic power at work; we might have been brought together earlier or later, but the fact that it happened just at that time, when I had been on my Italian journey and Schiller had begun to tire of his philosophical speculations, was highly significant and of great profit to us both."

(2nd April): "We must simply take note," I remarked, "of whether an influence is obstructive or beneficial, whether it harmonises favourably with our nature or runs counter to it."

"That", said Goethe, "is indeed the point; but here, too, is precisely the difficulty: to go on vigorously asserting our better nature and not to allow the daemonic forces to become more powerful than they should."

252. *Eckermann*   *2.4.1829*

We discussed recent French literature and the meaning of the terms "classical" and "romantic". Goethe said: "I have thought of quite a good new way of expressing this distinction. The classical I call the healthy and the romantic the sick. Thus the Nibelungenlied is as classical as Homer, for they are both healthy and vigorous. Most modern literature is not romantic because it is modern, but because it is weak, morbid and sickly; and ancient literature is not classical because it is ancient, but because it is strong and fresh and happy and healthy. If we distinguish 'classical' and 'romantic' by these criteria, we shall soon get this matter clear."

253. *Eckermann*   *5.4.1829*

We talked about his Italian journey, and he told me that in one of his letters from Italy he had found a poem which he would like to show me. He asked me to hand him a packet of papers that were lying in front of me on the desk; they were his letters from Italy, and he looked in them for the poem and read it out:

O master Cupid, wanton, obstinate playboy!
For some few hours you asked me to give you a lodging.
And look how many days and nights you have been here!
You have taken control and made yourself lord in my house
  now.

I once had a good wide bed, and you have usurped it;
I am forced to crouch on the ground, and my nights are made
  wretched.
You stoke great fires in my hearth and waste all my winter
Reserves of fuel and scorch poor me in your mischief.

My things are all shifted about and pushed from their places;
I search for them, thinking I must have gone blind or crazy.
You make such a noise and mess, that I fear my poor soul will
Be frightened away, and will move out of doors altogether.

I was delighted by this poem, which I did not think I had ever come across before. Goethe had read it very beautifully; I could not get it out of my head again, and it seemed to go on preoccupying him too. Several times he repeated the last lines to himself, as if in a dream:

> *You make such a noise and mess that I fear my poor soul will*
> *Be frightened away, and will move out of doors altogether.*

We spent some more time happily together, Goethe finally regaling me with a lot of honey, and with some dates which I took away with me.

254. *Eckermann*   *6.4.1829*

We sat for a little at table, drinking a few glasses of old Rhine wine, with some very good sponge cake. Goethe was humming something indistinctly to himself. I thought again of the poem we had discussed yesterday, and recited the lines:

> *My things are all shifted about and pushed from their places;*
> *I search for them, thinking I must have gone blind or crazy.*

"I still can't help thinking about that poem", I said. "It has a character quite of its own and expresses so well the havoc that love wreaks in our lives." "It conjures up a dark unhappy state of mind", said Goethe. "I find it hard to understand how you came to express such a mood", I remarked; "the poem is like something from another age and another world." "And it is something I shall not do again", said Goethe; "indeed, as is often the case, I could scarcely say how I came to write it at all."

"The poem has another peculiar feature", I said. "I always have the impression that it is rhymed, and yet it is not. Why is that?" "It is because of the rhythm", answered Goethe. "Each line begins with an unstressed syllable, then continues trochaically, with a dactyl near the end, which has a peculiar effect and gives the whole thing a sad, lamenting tone." Goethe took a pencil and divided a line as follows:

$$\breve{V}on \mid \overline{mei}n\breve{e}m \mid \overline{brei}t\breve{e}n \mid \overline{La}g\breve{e}r \mid b\breve{i}n \breve{i}ch \breve{v}er \mid \overline{trie}b\breve{e}n.$$

We discussed rhythm in general and agreed that such matters cannot really be thought about. Goethe said : "The measure seems to flow unconsciously from the poetic mood. If one were to try to think it out while writing the poem, one would go crazy and never produce anything decent."

255. *Eckermann*   *10.4.1829*

"While we are waiting for the soup I shall give you some refreshment for your eyes." With these obliging words Goethe put a volume of landscapes by Claude Lorrain in front of me.

"Here for once", he said, "you may see a complete man, who thought and felt beautifully and in whose mind there was a world the like of which you will not easily find anywhere in external reality. These pictures are supremely true, but not in the least realistic. Claude Lorrain knew the real world by heart down to its minutest details, and he used it as a means to express the world of his own exquisite sensibility. And that indeed is true ideality : so to use realistic means that the higher truth thus manifesting itself produces the illusion that it is real."

"I call that a good saying", I remarked, "and one that would apply just as well to literature as to the visual arts." "Precisely so", said Goethe.

256. *Eckermann*   *12.4.1829*

"The trouble is", continued Goethe, "that one has been so much hindered in one's life by mistaken ambitions, and that one never recognised them as such until one had already freed oneself from them."

"But how", I asked, "can one tell and know that an ambition is mistaken?"

"A mistaken ambition", replied Goethe, "is unproductive, or whatever it does produce is of no value. To perceive this in other people is not so very difficult, but with oneself it is quite another matter and requires great freedom of judgment. And even to perceive it does not always help; we are filled with hesitation and doubt and indecision, just as when one is finding it difficult to tear oneself away from a girl one loves, in spite of having long had repeated proofs of her infidelity. In saying this I have in mind how many years it took me to realise that my ambitions in the sphere of the visual arts were mistaken, and how many more it took me to rid myself of them after I had recognised this."

"But nevertheless", I said, "these ambitions have stood you in such good stead that one can scarcely call them mistaken."

"They increased my understanding", said Goethe, "and therefore I have no cause for regret. We can indeed profit from all our mistaken ambitions in this way. A man who works hard at music although he has insufficient talent for it will of course never become a master, but in the process he will learn to recognise and appreciate what a master has done. Despite all my efforts I of course never became a painter, but by trying my hand in every branch of the art I have learnt to account for every brush-stroke and to distinguish the meritorious from the inferior. This is no small gain; and indeed, a mistaken ambition seldom fails to be of some use to us."

257.   H. Crabb Robinson   2.8.1829

It was between ten and eleven when I left my card at Goethe's house for his daughter-in-law, and we proceeded then to the small house in the Park where we were at once admitted to the Great Man. "Well! you are come at last," he said. "We have waited years for you." I was oppressed by the cordial reception and as the cordiality increased during two most interesting conversations, the sense of unworthiness is but increased.—After an hour we took our leave, accepting an invitation to tea in the evening.—We then left our cards with the Chancellor von Müller—and being invited to dine we went again to Frau von Goethe: and I had a very pleasing chat with her.—Goethe calls her "a dear crazy creature" and I can already feel the force of the Epithet.—Her three children all resemble their great Ancestor, a girl of three years old is strikingly like him.

Returned to Goethe at six.—I feared to stay too long and we remained but an hour and a half.—He was friendly to a degree I cannot account for—most particular in enquiring when I would return.—Insisted on my staying several days in Weimar as he had much to enquire of me, and he kissed me three times at parting!—To note a few detached topics of our conversation.—Goethe made enquiries of the taste for German literature in England and I informed him of the several translations. He ardently enjoyed the prospect of his own extended reputation.— He spoke of Ossian with contempt and said: "No one remarked

*that while Werther is in his senses he talks about Homer and
only after he grows mad is in love with Ossian."—I reminded
him of Napoleon's love of Ossian—he said it was on account of
the contrast between Ossian and his own nature. "Napoleon
loved only melancholy and soft music. Werther was among his
books at St. Helena."—Goethe made enquiries about my own
studies and tastes. I knew not what to answer—but at the end
of our interview he renewed his invitation with a warmth that
was flattering.*

258.   A. E. Odyniec   *19.8.1829*

Yesterday at exactly noon an elegant carriage belonging to
Frau Ottilie stopped in front of our hotel, and a quarter of an
hour later we dismounted from it by the garden door of Goethe's
villa; here we were already awaited by an old servant of
Goethe's who conducted us through the garden, opened the
door of the drawing-room, admitted us and departed. We
waited, talking in undertones, for nearly a quarter of an hour.
Adam [Mickiewicz] asked me whether my heart was beating.
Indeed, our expectancy was as if some supernatural being were
about to appear. And without exaggeration, there is something
Jove-like about Goethe. A loftiness of stature, the figure of a
colossus, the impressive dignity of his countenance, and as for
his brow!—here is the very seat of his Jove-like quality. Though
wearing no diadem, it radiates majesty. He still has very little
white hair and only over the forehead is there some greyness.
The eyebrows are clear and lively, and the eyes have only one
distinguishing peculiarity, namely a light grey line, rather like
a line in enamelling, which surrounds both irises at their outer
edge. Adam compared it to the ring of Saturn. We have never
seen anything similar in anyone else. Like sunlight piercing the
clouds, a wonderfully charming, kindly smile transfigured this
stern physiognomy, as at his very entry he greeted us with a bow
and a handshake, saying: "Pardon, Messieurs, que je vous ai
fait attendre. Il m'est très agréable de voir les amis de Mme.
Szymanowska qui m'honore aussi de son amitié." Then, when
we were seated, he turned to Adam and assured him that he
knew him to be the chief representative of the new trend that
was beginning in our literature as in that of Europe generally.
"I know from my own experience", he added, "how hard it is
to swim against the current." "We too", answered Adam, "have

learnt from the experience of your Excellency that when great geniuses move against the current they make it reverse its course." Goethe nodded a little at this, as if to acknowledge the compliment, and went on to express his regret that he was very ill acquainted with Polish literature and could understand no Slavonic language. "Mais l'homme a tant à faire dans cette vie." But he added that he already knew Adam from reading about him in the papers. When Adam then, at his request, gave him a wonderfully concise and clear outline of the whole development of Polish literature from its earliest to its most modern period, at the same time relating and comparing the stages of this development to the various historical epochs, one could see in Goethe's eyes, which remained steadily fixed on him, not only a deep appreciation of Adam but also a lively interest in the subject of his narrative. The way he tapped his fingers on his knee seemed evidence of this. N.B. : I forgot to say that at the beginning of this conversation Goethe used German; but Adam told him, and in German too, that although he could indeed speak German, he dared not do so in Goethe's presence, and no sooner had the latter heard this than he reverted to French. Later on in the conversation Goethe remarked that the increasingly urgent quest for universal truth made it inevitable that poetry too, and literature generally, should become more and more universal in character; but he conceded to Adam that it would never cease to have specific national features. From this point the conversation turned to the subject of folksongs, and Adam, and to some extent I as well, described to him the varieties of character and melody in the songs of our provinces; Goethe asked questions and listened with keen interest, and later repeated it all himself during lunch for the benefit of the others. Thus ended our literary conversation.

When we rose to take our leave, he expressed great regret that as it was pouring with rain at the time he would be unable to show us his little garden ("son petit jardin"). "Mais j'aurai le plaisir de jouir encore de votre société à diner chez ma belle-fille." And turning to me with a smile, he added : "Et nous aurons quelques jolies dames et demoiselles; j'espère que ça vous fera plaisir". We both laughed, and he, laughing too, turned quickly to Adam and asked him with a confidential air : "N'est-ce pas ?" Thereupon he shook hands with us, and when we were already on the stairs he again opened the drawing-room door and repeated : "Au revoir !"

At table, when we returned, Adam sat between Goethe and Frau Ottilie; I was charmingly neighboured on one side by Frau Rosa Vogel and on the other by Fräulein Pappenheim. The conversation was lively, and needless to say I had willy-nilly to keep it up on either side, while at the same time straining my ears as much as possible to hear what Goethe was saying to Adam. But I could seldom catch anything except when Goethe raised his voice, either to speak to people sitting further off, or to address everyone, in which case everyone listened in silence. To Herr Eckermann, who was sitting opposite him, he repeated word for word what Adam had told him about the folksongs. This repeating of what other people say must be a habit with him, and I am sure he intends it as a courtesy. For after lunch, as we were taking coffee, he was standing by me with his cup in his hand and asked me good-humouredly in German : "Well, so how do you like our ladies?" And I, encouraged by this tone, replied with a bow and a smile : "A bird of paradise [paradiesischer Vogel], your Excellency !" At this Goethe laughed out loud and strode over to the ladies to repeat my answer to them. Frau Ottilie and the others looked across at me and smiled, and Frau Vogel blushed scarlet.

259. Eckermann   *1.9.1829*

I mentioned a visitor who had heard Hegel lecturing on the proofs for the existence of God. Goethe agreed with me that lectures of this sort were now out of date.

"The age of doubt is over", said Goethe; "no one now doubts the existence of God any more than he doubts his own. And yet the attributes of God, immortality, the nature of the soul and its relationship to the body, are eternal problems on which the philosophers cannot help us. Think how much philosophical speculation there has been about immortality ! and who is the wiser for it?—I have no doubt that we do survive, for our entelechy is necessary to nature. But we are not all equally immortal, and if one is to manifest oneself as a powerful entelechy hereafter, one must be one already."

260. K. L. von Knebel

Goethe was an extreme egoist : but he had to be, for he knew what a treasure had been given into his charge.

261. Baron von Löw und zu Steinfurt   *3.10.1829*

On arriving in Weimar I immediately despatched my letters of introduction to Goethe and his daughter-in-law. I was summoned for noon of the following day. It is hard to describe the condition of tension and constriction of spirit in which I passed the intervening time. During much of the night I was sleepless or dreaming uneasily, and next morning I rushed in great excitement through the streets and public gardens. At last the appointed hour struck. I entered the house at which I had already gazed several times in awe and reverence as I passed it. In front of the door through which I was admitted, the word SALVE is inlaid in wood. My solemn mood was heightened by so venerable and festive a setting.

I was led through one room into a second. Everywhere there were works of art of various kinds : paintings, engravings, busts, statues, and drawings in large folders laid out on stands. The furniture was not in keeping with this; it was tasteless, old, almost meagre. I waited a few minutes. Then, through the open door of the room in which I was standing, I saw Goethe come into the adjacent apartment, and walk across it towards me, fairly rapidly and in a very erect posture, moving his lips as he did so and now and then even talking softly to himself. As he entered, I found that his appearance on the whole did not live up to my expectations. After the many glowing descriptions I had heard and read, I had imagined that he would be taller and would have aged less. Only the liveliness and occasional fire of his glance, and the upright posture which during our whole interview he strove to retain, from time to time restoring it when the upper part of his body involuntarily sank forward, still bore visible witness to a powerful mind's mastery over this eighty-year-old body. But what was extremely remarkable and indeed astonishing was the way he talked. It was an absolutely pure and uninterrupted flow of speech, showing the utmost variety and dexterity of expression, no matter what the subject might be. When he turned to profounder matters on which even cultured talkers, even practised thinkers usually have to search for their words, he would move here too with no less facility than if he had been discussing the weather or some gossip of the town. It was evident all along that here was a man to whom ideas and ideals had been the concern of a lifetime and that these things, which to us are no more than sweetmeats, had become his daily bread.

In short, here was our German language spoken as one might imagine it being spoken by supernatural beings.

Among other things we discussed the most recent theological controversies, and Goethe said: "No doubt, as long as the human race exists, there will continue to be heated disputes about the nature of the Trinity, about whether man is naturally good or evil, whether he was redeemed and delivered from his sins by Christ, and whether he can attain to blessedness and be saved from damnation by his own efforts or only by the grace of God—or whether indeed", he added with a laugh, "he ought to count himself blessed to be damned. In these matters men have strayed far too far from the path of simplicity; children could well be our instructors in things of this sort."

I turned the conversation to his literary works, especially *Faust* and the *Italian Journey*. He spoke of them with the most charming modesty and unpretentiousness. The *Italian Journey*, he said, consisted of letters he had written to his friends and which he had had returned to him and printed because he thought there might be a number of people who would find them interesting. In the new edition of his works which is now just about to appear, he would make a few additions to them. In his *Faust* he had simply tried to depict the restless surging and stirring in human nature. I told him I had been much amused to find the words "To be continued" at the end of the first published fragment of the second part of *Faust*; for as he knew, there had always been so much controversy about whether or not the poem could be continued at all, and whether the Devil had taken Faust or not, and now these poor readers had after all been left in doubt and uncertainty. "Indeed", he replied with a charmingly roguish air, "that may still be the case for a long time to come. Well, I suppose an old man must be forgiven for indulging from time to time in a little joke of this kind."

A considerable time had elapsed during our conversation; I noticed that he wanted it to end, and stood up. He concluded by advising me to visit the Dowager Grand Duchess, whose high qualities he praised, and so dismissed me. I went upstairs to his daughter-in-law, in whose company, being wholly absorbed in what I had just experienced, I spoke scarcely a word, and no doubt cut a poor figure.

262. *Ottilie von Goethe (reported)*

Once when we were discussing the haughty ministerial attitude which Goethe adopted towards strangers who called to pay him inquisitive homage, Ottilie von Goethe asserted most positively that—incredible as it might seem in a man so urbane and accustomed to ceremony—Goethe only did so because he was really ill at ease and trying to conceal his embarrassment behind a seemingly arrogant bearing. Goethe was, she assured us in conclusion, a truly modest and deeply humble man.

263. *W. Zahn*   *1829*

He found the throng of inquisitive people wanting to see him increasingly burdensome, and many of them were refused admission. He remarked to me: "What am I to do with people who only want to gape at me and from whom I can learn nothing?" I must here mention two German professors who visited him at that time and made themselves irksome to him by their much too pressing enquiries into the intentions underlying his works. A crossfire of interrogation was let loose at the aged poet's head: "What did your Excellency have in mind there?" and "What did your Excellency mean to convey by that?"— Goethe nudged me meaningfully under the table, gnawed his lips, growled out a few unintelligible words and changed the subject. After the learned brain-pickers had left he exclaimed impatiently: "Wanting to know things I don't know myself. How this work or that work came into being—after all only God knows that."

264. *Count Alexander Grigorevitch Stroganoff*   *1825/30*

I must say that I was in no mood for paying my homage to a great man when, a few hours after arriving in Weimar, I had our cards handed in at the house of Geheimrat von Goethe. Being of a serious nature and having—I confess it frankly—a certain inborn pride, I have always considered it rather humiliating that men who are neither our masters nor our benefactors should receive reverence from us merely on account of their talents or general merits. I should myself just as little relish this sort of homage if I possessed any other distinction than that of my outward station in life, which is the gift of chance fortune

exactly as all great talents and natural endowments are. In
addition, Goethe's works have never inspired in me any feeling
resembling admiration. His pithy sayings, his good humour, his
deep insight into human nature, have often evoked in my mind
a strong impulse of assent; but this assent had little in it that
was flattering to humanity, and I took pleasure in only a few of
his works. Most of the others, especially the much discussed
Wilhelm Meister, have always been quite repugnant to me.
Goethe is admirable when he achieves concentration in his
language and in his treatment of a subject, as he does in *Faust*;
it is true that the latter strongly recalls the inimitable example
of Shakespeare, nevertheless there is still a great originality in it,
which makes him a phenomenon of world importance. But it is
when he expands and begins to analyse and elaborate and cir-
cumscribe that I have come to find him quite repulsive, with his
cold complacent circumstantial way of listening to himself, his
disingenuous intertwining of trivial threads of thought, his imitative reconstructions, as crafty as any goldsmith, of feelings he
has never felt. It is true that I have often heard these very
qualities which I so dislike extolled by the Germans in hyperbolic phrases; but I have come to know the national German
vice of sentimentality too well to let myself be misled by their
disagreement with me. There is no other nation in the world
that could take such pleasure in the whimsical sentimental bab-
blings of its writers, and the most conclusive proof of this is that
they have in fact not been translated into any foreign language.
This being my view of Goethe's work I naturally, despite my
respect for his great intellect, felt none at all of the enthusiasm
and admiration which were displayed, as I often had occasion to
observe, by the special sect of hysterical devotees of this national
deity. I had the honour of being pressingly recommended to
him by the chief members of this literary clique. They appeared
to have made it their serious purpose to proselytise an unbeliever
like myself, but in this they had hitherto so signally failed that I
should not have been much put out if Goethe had found some
polite pretext for declining my visit. What increased my ill
humour still further was the fact that German notabilities of
every kind expect even foreigners, and indeed foreigners above
all, to conform to a ceremonious etiquette which to me was
very irksome, for I disliked changing out of my comfortable
travelling clothes. My lighthearted brother took this more easily
in his stride, and when we finally received the invitation to visit

Goethe, he scented himself and did his hair as carefully as if he were about to pay a morning call on some beautiful woman. Feeling a little apprehensive that Alexei's high spirits might get us into trouble, but to some extent reassured by my knowledge of his well-tried social adroitness, I drove with him to Goethe's villa. Our first visit was received in a very stiff and formal manner; the pomposity of the Saxon servants and the measured gravity of our host himself greatly appealed to my brother's sense of humour. Goethe's personality is well known; for his admirers have described it so fully that there is nothing left for any foreigner to say about it. He was rightly reputed to be a very well-built man with expressive features, but so far as his manners were concerned, I found them more German than ever and far removed from the more subtle and charming court etiquette which prevails in the highest circles in my own country.

Alexei thought Goethe's pride deeply grounded in his whole nature, though I, with my more thorough knowledge of his work, questioned this. I found his outward haughtiness no less of a contradiction than the degree of deference with which he received us, in consideration of our rank as Russian noblemen. This man, I reflected, cannot possibly have either so high an opinion of himself as would justify his pride, or so great a respect for us, whose rank betokens no merit. The sequel showed that I had judged Goethe's character correctly.

The conversation I had with him at my farewell visit was as remarkable and unforgettable as our first exchanges had been trivial and insignificant. On the previous evening he entertained a large company, obviously for the sole purpose of letting his native admirers see such rare birds as a pair of Russians from the Crimea, who had read and understood his works. We, and especially my high-spirited brother Alexei, had been casting him in the role of a remarkable tourist curiosity, but in the meantime he very skilfully contrived to make us objects of curiosity ourselves: we were besieged on all sides by the strangest enquiries about the manners and usages of our country and could scarcely draw breath to answer them. Allusions were made, with all due delicacy, to Russian despotism, and there was a full display of the usual assortment of confused notions about our system of serfdom and similar matters. In this cultivated circle I of course encountered some people who were very well informed—and Goethe's own knowledge was indeed considerable —but they viewed the whole thing from a mistaken standpoint;

and in consequence there developed between myself and the other guests a polite dispute, in the course of which my patriotic ardour was quite misunderstood by these strangers and I came to appear as a champion of the detested serfdom in my attempts to explain to them the patriarchal way of life of the Russian people.

Goethe remained more or less neutral during all this, but was visibly amused by our discussion and seemed to be gloating over our embarrassment. To take my revenge on him for this trick, I managed to force the conversation round to the subject of his works. I deliberately questioned him on the most delicate points with a boldness which at once gave me an advantage over everyone else present. I raised problems which had often been stoutly debated by the learned gentlemen of Germany, whom the lofty master had never condescended to assist out of their perplexity. I was seconded in this by my brother, who no sooner gave offence by his lively roguish manner than he made amends by his good nature. How was the *Westöstlicher Divan* to be interpreted? What did *Faust* mean? What philosophical idea underlay his work?—All this was discussed as openly and unabashedly as if Goethe had been a hundred miles away. He, however, remained quite unperturbed by this indiscretion; for it was, as I later heard, by no means a new experience for him. He was content to answer with a smile and a few equivocal phrases, and to leave the talking to a professor from Leipzig or Jena who was present and whose name I have forgotten. This man had made it the chief business of his life to interpret Goethe's works, and he now set himself to answer our enquiries in the most circumstantial manner. He did so with such profusion of unintelligible hocus-pocus, philosophical jargon and scholarly platitudes as would have reduced any other foreigner to consternation. It struck me as not unlikely that Goethe, who kept encouraging this insufferable windbag with smiles of approval, made use of him as a means of warding off importunate questioners without committing himself. And indeed, as a tool for this purpose he was remarkably well chosen; for it was as hard to get in a word through the continuous drone of this walking philosophical machine as it was to make it a suitable answer if one had not read the vast pile of books and periodicals whose contents the doctor carried in his head. As I understood not a word of his mumbo-jumbo, I requested him, with an air of edification, to translate the gist of his long discourse into

French for my benefit, since I had not the good fortune to be very familiar with the recent enrichment of the German language by thousands of debased Greek, Latin and French words and especially by the technical terms of Berlin philosophy. But the learned professional glossmonger and panegyricist informed me roundly that it was impossible to discuss this great master in any language but German. While I was treating this assertion with duly polite irreverence, Goethe had left the room; but I am convinced that he listened through a side door to the end of my discussion with the professor. I concluded the dispute by declaring that it was impossible for the opposing parties to reach any mutual understanding when they set out from points of view so totally divergent; for whereas the learned doctor was convinced that other nations were quite incapable of judging Goethe's genius and his philosophical and moral influence on his age, I was equally inclined to agree with Lord Byron and his fellow-countrymen in their opinion that no nation in the world has so completely misunderstood Goethe as the Germans.

No sooner had I humbly uttered this bold proposition than Goethe came in, looking unembarrassed but serious, and invited the guests to move to another room for supper. His behaviour towards me seemed to express a certain annoyance at the poor compliment I had paid the German people; but he occasionally glanced across at me, as if surreptitiously, in a manner that betokened no resentment. Despite this, the conversation remained strained, and I left with the feeling that I had offended the company, and particularly my host, and wounded the national pride of both. But I was soon disabused of this; and having the occasion later on to speak individually to a number of those who had been present, I found to my great astonishment that my words, which in Russia or France or England would have been counted against me as little short of a deadly insult, had perhaps displeased no one except the pretentious professor himself. All the others assured me that unfortunately there was much truth in what I had said, though each regarded himself as an exception to it. I must confess however that I would have preferred to hear them defend their national errors against a foreigner.

Next morning I received a note addressed to me in Goethe's own hand, with my Christian and family names, in which he invited me in very polite terms to come for a drive with him. Although surprised by this unexpected courtesy, I nevertheless accepted, and an hour later I was alone with the great man in a carriage. It was a beautiful morning, and the vigorous old man seemed to take a fresh lease of life and youth in the spring air. His face was radiant with unusual good humour and his eyes shone with an inner vitality moderated, aged as he was, only by his manly composure. After greeting me, he said with an air of flattering familiarity: "Yesterday, Count, you were so negligent as to let fall a number of valuables such as we Germans usually take better care not to waste, and they have made me very much desire the closer acquaintance of so rich a man". "And to what riches of mine", I asked, "can your Excellency's interest refer?" "To that of your ideas", he replied. I bowed my thanks for this compliment, for which there seemed to me to be insufficient reason. "Sans compliments, my dear Count!" he continued, anticipating the utterance of my thought. "I often have occasion to distinguish between the applause of commonplace persons and that recognition by men of judgment which is the only truly honouring tribute. So you need not hesitate to credit me with the ability to see beyond the most unpromising appearances in speech and behaviour, and to discern the man who has a mind of his own. I find myself in the same position as Voltaire, who longed for nothing more ardently than to be recognised by those who refused him their praise. You will tell me that you are not one who refuses to praise me, but by even appearing to hold a view that runs counter to public opinion— the correctness of which you questioned yesterday—you show me that you are a man of independent mind and character; for only such a man dares to contradict where everyone else is in agreement. I leave it to you to decide whether I have judged you rightly." I replied that his judgment was too flattering for me to be able simply to confirm it, but that I was inclined in all modesty to doubt that to a man so great and who enjoyed world fame the opinion of a travelling cavalier and commonplace sightseer could possibly be of the very slightest importance. This opening led to a highly interesting discussion of the reputation, significance and fortunes of Goethe's works, and the poet spoke his mind with a most engaging frankness which allowed me to see into the innermost recesses of his character. Immediately after our excursion I made the following summary of his most important remarks, intending to publish them at a later date, when after the death of the speaker I should no longer be bound in any way by obligations of discretion.

Here are his words : disconnected, rhapsodical, abbreviated, and set down as faithfully as memory can record them.

"Fame, my dear Count, is a fine spiritual food : it strengthens and elevates the mind and revives the soul; no wonder the weak heart of man relishes this refreshment. But the path of renown soon leads us to despise it. Public opinion deifies men and blasphemes gods; it often commends the faults we blush for and scorns the virtues that are our pride. Believe me : fame is almost as insulting as ill-repute. For the last thirty years I have been fighting a vexation of spirit which you would understand if you could be with me for even a few weeks to see how every day a number of foreigners demand to be allowed to admire me, many of whom have not read my works—nearly all the French and English, for example—and most of whom do not understand me. The meaning and the significance of my works and of my life is the vindication of essential humanity. That is why I never turn my back on man, and always enjoy such fame as good fortune has granted me, but I taste a sweeter reward in my understanding of wholesome human qualities. That is why I value even the adverse criticism of those who have grasped the true human meaning of art more highly than the sickly enthusiasm of our hysterical German poets under whose phrases I am smothered; and that is why I am most willing to concede the truth, in a certain sense, of your remark that Germany has misunderstood me. There prevails among the Germans a spirit of sensuous hysteria which to me has an alien flavour : art and philosophy have been detached from life and have become something abstract, remote from the fountainheads of nature which should nourish them. I like German ideas, they are a real part of the national life, and I enjoy wandering in their labyrinths, but only if I am constantly accompanied by living, natural things. I rank life higher than art, for art is only the embellishment of life.

"You are right : Byron understood me perfectly, and I think I understand him. I value his judgment as highly as he honoured mine; but I never had the good fortune to hear his opinion of me in its entirety." This remark, spoken with a particular emphasis, revealed to me quite clearly the main reason for the interest which Goethe appeared to be taking in my conversation. On the previous evening I had let fall a few words about Byron which not only disclosed my fairly intimate acquaintanceship with that remarkable man, but also suggested that I had perhaps

had the opportunity of enquiring quite closely into his opinion
of Goethe. I had in fact, in Venice, on repeated occasions had
the good fortune to enjoy an intimate association with Byron,
after succeeding with some difficulty in dispelling, at least so far
as I myself was concerned, his prejudice against all Russians,
which was intensified at that time by the Greek troubles.
Strangely enough, it was not exactly my good qualities that
reconciled him to my nationality, but my wild youthful character, for in those days I was one who exploited life and art with
the hottest appetite, intent only on pleasure and caring little for
the enlargement of my talents and knowledge. Our association
was not one of like-minded connoisseurs of art, but a partnership
of exuberant and insatiable bons viveurs. In this way, however,
I learnt a number of particular details of Byron's private life,
and Goethe listened with the keenest interest to my recital of
these, which served to interrupt my host's self-analytical discourse
only to furnish it with fresh materials. It had, moreover, been
Byron's habit to interlard our constant discussions of beautiful
women, whom we both zealously pursued, with interesting
aesthetic digressions: in this way he had confided his literary
views to me and qualified me to satisfy Goethe's curiosity. I
therefore told the latter that I had, indeed, the good fortune to
be able to give him some information about Byron's views on
him, and I delivered a résumé of my conversations with Byron
about art and literature, such that Goethe was in fact its main
topic, and the discussion of this necessarily led him further in
his interesting description of himself. The account I gave was
not entirely frank and disinterested, since I was debarred by
considerations of propriety and good taste from doing more
than conveying Byron's views as distinct from his actual remarks;
for most of the latter were of a kind that might easily have
displeased Goethe, despite Byron's considerable good will towards him. He had, for example, often spoken with more
humour than reverence of Goethe's hypocrisy, and once said
of him: "He's an old fox who won't leave his hole, and preaches
a fine sermon from inside it". His *Elective Affinities* and *Sorrows
of Werther* he described as a mockery of marriage, such as his
familiar spirit Mephistopheles himself could scarcely have written
better; the endings of both these novels, said Byron, were the
non plus ultra of irony. However, my memories of what Byron
had said about Goethe furnished me with so much flattering
material that I could, without fearing to offend him, also drop

some hints as to the points on which Byron's opinions had differed from his. Goethe was so gratified by this that he continued the conversation with unwonted cordiality, and its one topic preoccupied his thoughts all that day.

Since I had many opportunities of making clear to him my interpretation of his philosophy, I did so quite candidly, and it appeared to give him particular pleasure, as he found that it was confirmed by Byron's judgment by which he set great store. Matters were mentioned which I am sure Goethe has never dared to repeat. I made a remark to this effect, and he confessed with a smile that he had no wish to contradict my forecast. "But now that we are talking frankly", he said, "I will confess to you that I have put the gist of all we have talked about into the Second Part of my *Faust*, and I am therefore quite certain that after my death this conclusion of the poem will be declared by my fellow-countrymen to be the most tedious thing I ever wrote."

And lo and behold! a few years after this conversation there fell into my hands, together with the second volume of *Faust*, a well-known German newspaper in which I read the following words: "Just as this book has physically appeared after the end of Goethe's bodily life, so also its intellectual content has survived his genius".

265. *Eckermann*

Most of the Second Part of Goethe's *Faust* was written in the period during which I was myself present in Weimar and in daily contact with the poet, so that I can rightfully describe myself as an eyewitness of its composition. Much of this took place in 1823, the year of my arrival in Weimar, and it continued until March 1832, when *Faust* lay finished and Goethe could look upon his work as complete. It was the last thing he wrote, and it bears the stamp of the lofty wisdom of his old age. Its beginnings go right back to Schiller's life-time, and Goethe could still boast in his last years of having had the good fortune to hear a long passage from the Helena episode read aloud by Schiller.

If Goethe could acknowledge himself fortunate to have heard Schiller reading his work, then the converse must have been still more true for Schiller or anyone else; for Goethe was capable of arousing admiration by his reading aloud, especially from

works such as *Faust* which is truly part of his own soul. The
very sound of his voice was extremely remarkable. Sometimes a
whisper, sometimes like a roll of thunder, it spanned the whole
gamut of natural sounds, and could make sudden transitions to
quite different effects, such as the grunting of the griffins in the
Classical Walpurgisnacht, which he tried to imitate exactly : the
resulting sounds were usually quite horrible, squeezed out of his
throat with visible effort. And his vocal power was also great
when he declaimed majestic and moving lines in the style of
Greek tragedy. But we enjoyed hearing him most of all when
his voice rose to no passionate heights but rolled quietly along
in a calm flow of speech—as for example in the passage from the
Helena episode about the cry of the cranes, which from high in
the air makes the listening traveller look up at the sound.

266. *Eckermann*   6.12.1829

Today Goethe read me the first scene of Act 2 of the Second
Part of *Faust*, remarking afterwards :
"As this work was conceived so long ago and I have been
thinking about it for fifty years, there has been such an accumu-
lation of material in my mind that the difficult task now is that
of eliminating and rejecting. The invention of the whole Second
Part really does date from as long ago as I say, but the fact that
I have not written it until now is probably to its advantage,
since my understanding of the world has now become so much
clearer. I am rather in the position of a man who in his youth
has a great many silver and copper coins which in the course of
his life he changes for larger and larger denominations, until
at last his youthful wealth lies before him in pieces of pure gold."
We continued to discuss *Faust* and its composition, and related
topics. Goethe was absorbed in silent meditation for a while,
then spoke as follows :
"In old age, one's view of the world is not what it was when
one was young. Thus I cannot help thinking that the daemons,
to tease and make fun of mankind, occasionally set up isolated
figures who are so alluring that everyone emulates them and so
great that no one can equal them. For instance, they set up
Raphael, who was perfect both in conception and in execution;
some of his distinguished successors have approached him but no
one has ever equalled him. Or they set up Mozart as an unattainable perfection in music. Or Shakespeare in poetry. I know

what your objections to Shakespeare may be, but I am referring only to the natural endowment, the great innate qualities. And Napoleon is a similar unattainable figure."

This fruitful theme led to much discussion; but I privately reflected that perhaps the daemons had intended something of the kind of Goethe, by making him, too, a figure too alluring not to be emulated but too great ever to be equalled.

267. *Eckermann*   *3.1.1830*

"*Faust* is really a quite incommensurable quantity, and all attempts to make it rationally intelligible are vain. It must also be remembered that the First Part is the product of a rather obscure individual state of mind. But it is this very obscurity that people find stimulating, and they keep working away at it, as at all insoluble problems."

268. *F. von Müller*

I have often heard him assert that if a work, especially a poem, leaves nothing to conjecture, it is not a true work of art fully worthy of the name. "Its highest function must always be to stimulate reflection, and it can only really commend itself to the beholder or reader by compelling him to interpret it in his own way and to complete it, so to speak, by creative re-enactment."

269. *F. von Müller*   *11.1.1830*

When I met Goethe towards the end of the day he was rather dull and monosyllabic, but after many unsuccessful efforts I at last managed to wake him up and raise his spirits and set him talking.

I was very glad to have been able to do so, for nothing is more embarrassing than being with him at times when he drops or breaks off the thread of every topic one raises, and answers every question one puts to him by exclaiming "Dear good people! but there's nothing at all one can do about them", or "You young folk had better see to it, I'm too old for that kind of thing", and when there are long pauses during which he says nothing but "Hm! hm!" and even lets his head droop as if he were half asleep.

270. Eckermann 3.2.1830

We discussed Mozart. "I saw him when he was a boy of seven", said Goethe, "giving a concert on his way through. I was about fourteen myself, and still quite clearly remember the little man with his powdered hair and his sword." I stared, thinking it almost miraculous that Goethe was old enough to have seen Mozart as a child.

271. Soret (as adapted by Eckermann)* 15.2.1830

On the day after the death of the Dowager Grand Duchess Luise, which for Goethe severed a friendship of fifty years' standing, he remarked: "Death is so strange a thing that despite all experiences to the contrary we do not believe it could possibly happen to someone we love, and when it does it is always something incredible and unforeseen. It is, so to speak, an impossibility which suddenly becomes reality. And this transition from a familiar existence to another of which we know nothing is so violent that the survivors cannot fail to be profoundly affected."

272. Soret 8.3.1830

"In the old days", Goethe told me, "I never worried about my poems in advance; they satisfied me then at the first impulse. An idea would come to me spontaneously: I had no time to do more than seize my pencil, and occasionally I did not even notice that the sheet of paper was lying crooked on the desk, but began writing diagonally until I came at the bottom of the page to a corner where there was no room for the whole line. I am sorry I have not kept some samples as evidence of these poetic frenzies."

From several remarks I have heard him make it is evident that Goethe now has death very much in his thoughts; for he clings hard to anything that can strengthen his hold on life! He has often alluded to this, for example this evening when some books arrived for him: "These gentlemen have sent me something to nourish my life with", he said.

* See Introduction, pp. 19f.

273. *Soret*   *14.3.1830*

Goethe disapproves no less of the over-exclusiveness of present-day romanticism than of the narrow-minded pedantry of certain classicists. He has no wish at all to see any literary form ruled out; dramas in the grand regular style are indispensable to the theatre for certain subjects eminently favourable to classicism. "I set an example of this myself", he said, "by treating in rigorously classical form those subjects which had to be treated in the Greek manner if they were to remain true to themselves. Whereas on the one hand it would have been folly for me to observe the three unities in *Götz*, I should on the other hand have offended against all feeling for beauty if I had given my *Iphigenia* romantic trappings." In short, Goethe is completely impartial in this otiose and foolish dispute; others would do well to imitate him.

274. *Eckermann*   *14.3.1830*

"I know very well that I am a thorn in the flesh to many people, who would all be glad to be rid of me; and since they can't touch my talent, they attack my character. First I am said to be proud, then selfish, then envious of younger talents; I am accused of being a sensualist, of not being a Christian, and now, finally, of having no love for my native country and the Germans, bless their hearts. You have known me for years now well enough to judge all that talk for what it is worth.

"As a poet I have never been guilty of affectation. I have never expressed anything in poetry unless it was something I was living through, something that personally and urgently concerned me. I never wrote love poems unless I was in love. So how could I have written hate poems without feeling any hatred? And, between you and me, I did not hate the French, although I thanked God when we were rid of them. How could I, after all, who attach no importance to anything except culture and barbarism, hate one of the most cultivated nations on earth, a nation to which I owed so large a part of my own education!

"In any case, national hatred is an odd thing. It will always be found to be strongest and most vehement at the lowest cultural levels. But at a certain level it disappears altogether, one stands as it were above the nations and feels the weal or the woe of a neighbouring people as if it were that of one's own. It was this level of culture that was natural to me, and I had settled down on it long before reaching my sixtieth year."

275.   *Soret (as adapted by Eckermann)**   *17.3.1830*

"So Sömmering is dead", said Goethe, "and scarcely seventy-five miserable years old. What wretched creatures men are, not to have the spirit to hold out longer than that! All honour to my friend Bentham, that ultra-radical idiot; he's lasting well, and yet he's even a few weeks older than I am."

"One might add", I replied, "that there is another point of resemblance between you, in that he is still working as actively as any young man."

"That may be", replied Goethe. "But he and I are at opposite ends of the chain: he wants to pull down, and I should like to conserve and construct. To be such a radical at his age is the height of folly."

"I suppose", I answered, "that one must distinguish between two kinds of radicalism. One kind seeks to pull down everything first and make a clean sweep, in order to rebuild later; whereas the other is content to point out the weaknesses and defects in a system of government, in the hope of achieving good results without recourse to violent methods. If you had been born in England I am sure you could not have failed to adhere to this latter kind."

"What do you take me for?" retorted Goethe, now wholly assuming the tone and expression of his Mephistopheles.† "Do you suppose I should have spent my time nosing out abuses, and exposing and publicising them into the bargain—I whose liveli-hood, in England, would have depended on abuses? If I had been born in England I should have been a rich duke, or rather a bishop with an income of thirty thousand pounds a year."‡

"Excellent!" I replied, "but supposing you had chanced to

* Eckermann's version of this discussion between Goethe and Soret is a fairly close translation of the latter's original report. The divergences, where of interest, are indicated in the following footnotes.

† Soret: "Assuming the paradoxical and ironical tone of his Mephisto-pheles, and thus giving a fresh turn to the conversation, no doubt in order to avoid political discussion, which he dislikes".

‡ Soret: "If I had been born an Englishman—which thank God I was not!—I should have been a millionaire duke or rather a bishop with a salary of sixty thousand pounds sterling."

draw an unlucky number instead of the winning one? There are a great many unlucky numbers."

"My dear fellow", replied Goethe, "not all of us are born for the winning draw. Do you really think I should have committed the sottise of drawing unlucky?—I should have made it my business, first and foremost, to defend the Thirty-nine Articles; I should have championed them against all comers, especially Article Nine,* to which I should have given most particular attention and tender devotion. I should have lied and dissembled so hard and so long, both in verse and in prose, that my thirty thousand a year would have been a certainty. And having once reached that eminence, I should have kept myself there by hook or by crook. Above all I should have done everything in my power to make the night of ignorance, if possible, even darker still. Ah, how I should have cajoled the poor simple mob! With what a rod of iron I should have ruled the youth of the land, bless their hearts, in their schools and universities, to make quite sure that no one would realise, that no one would so much as have the temerity to notice on what a mass of administrative turpitude my wealth and glory were founded!"†

"In your case at least", I remarked, "we should have taken consolation in the thought that you had achieved your eminence by outstanding talent. But in fact, in England, the largest share of this world's goods is often enjoyed by those who are stupidest and most incompetent, and who owe it to no personal merit whatever but to patronage, chance, and above all to noble birth."

"In the last resort", replied Goethe, "it is a matter of indifference whether earthly riches fall to one by personal achievement or by inheritance. Those who first took possession of them were in any case men of genius who profited from the ignorance and feebleness of others.—The world is so full of fools and imbeciles that there is no need to look for them in the madhouse. That

* "Of original or birth-sin." In Soret's version, less probably, Goethe refers to "Article Thirteen" ("Of works before justification").

† The last half of this paragraph is a substitution by Eckermann. Soret (after ". . . my sixty thousand a year would have been a certainty") wrote: "One must get right to the top if one is not to be crushed, and at the height of one's greatness one must bear well in mind that the mob is a collection of fools and imbeciles. One would only be increasing their number if one could not turn to one's own advantage the abuses which have been established thanks to their folly, and from which others would profit if we ourselves did not."

reminds me of an occasion on which the late Grand Duke, who knew of my distaste for lunatic asylums, tried to take me by surprise and inveigle me into one. But I smelt a rat in time and told him that I felt absolutely no need to see the fools who are locked up as well as those who are left at large; on the contrary, the latter were quite enough for me. 'I am prepared', I said, 'to follow your Highness into hell if need be, but not into a madhouse.'"

Goethe later reverted, in the same malicious ironic vein, to the subject of the colossal salaries enjoyed by the higher English clergy, and he then told the anecdote of his encounter [in 1797] with Lord Bristol, Bishop of Derry.

"Lord Bristol", said Goethe, "was passing through Jena; he wanted to make my acquaintance, and induced me to visit him one evening. It was sometimes his whim to be offensive, but if one treated him equally offensively he would become perfectly amenable. In the course of our conversation he tried to preach to me about *Werther* and lay it to my conscience that by writing it I had tempted people to suicide. '*Werther*', he said, 'is a completely immoral, damnable book.' 'Stop!' I cried. 'If that is how you talk about the wretched *Werther*, what tone do you propose to take against the great of this world who with a single stroke of the pen send a hundred thousand men to war, eighty thousand of whom will kill each other and excite each other to fire and slaughter and pillage? And you, after these horrors, thank God and sing a *Te Deum*!—And what about your sermons on the terrors of hell, which so frighten the feebler spirits in your congregations that they lose their wits and end their miserable little lives in a madhouse? Or your orthodox dogmas, many of them untenable by any rational man, which sow the fatal seeds of doubt in the minds of your Christian listeners, so that these poor souls, who are neither weak nor strong, lose themselves in a labyrinth from which death is the only way out!* How do all those things lie on your consciences, and what sermons do you preach to yourselves about them?—And yet you try to call a writer to account and condemn a book which, owing to the misinterpretations put upon it by a few shallow minds, has at most rid the world of a dozen fools and idlers who had nothing better to do than blow the feeble remnants of their confused little

---

* Soret's version of this sentence was: "—not counting all those who commit suicide to get to Paradise sooner, or to escape from their religious terrors".

brains out altogether! I thought I had done a real service to mankind and earned their gratitude, and now you come along and try to turn my good little feat of arms into a crime, and yet all this while you priests and princes are permitting yourselves such almighty liberties!'

"This outburst worked on my bishop like a charm. He turned meek as a lamb and treated me from then on, during the rest of our conversation, with the utmost courtesy and subtlest tact. Thus I passed an extremely pleasant evening with him. For Lord Bristol, for all his occasional rudeness, was a man of some intellect and cultivation, and fully qualified to discuss a wide variety of subjects. When I left he accompanied me to the door and then sent his chaplain to do the further honours. The latter, when we reached the street, exclaimed to me: 'Oh, Herr von Goethe, what a fine speech that was you made! You have quite won his Lordship's heart—how clever it was of you to hit upon the secret of pleasing him! If you had been a little less rough and forthright with him I am sure you would not be going home feeling so satisfied with your visit as you do now.' "

276. *Eckermann*   *21.3.1830*

"The distinction between 'classical' and 'romantic' literature, which is now becoming universally fashionable and causing so much strife and dissension, can be traced back originally to Schiller and myself. I wrote according to the principle of objectivity, and would acknowledge no other. But Schiller, whose work had a quite subjective character, felt that his method was the right one, and to defend himself against me he wrote his essay on *Naïve and Sentimental Literature*. He proved to me that I myself was willy-nilly a romantic and that my *Iphigenia* was so full of sensibility that it was by no means so classical and ancient in spirit as one might suppose. The Schlegel brothers took up the idea and developed it further, with the result that it is now universally diffused and everyone is talking about classicism and romanticism, whereas it would never have occurred to anyone to do so fifty years ago."

277. *J. Burton Harrison*   *25.3.1830*

Next day at eleven drove to his Excellency von Goethe's. House rather extensive and of pretty fair exterior. Conducted up. Passed two bronzes from antiques, besides a bronze grey-hound. At threshold of his receiving-rooms Salve written. He dressed in brown surtout, wrapped around his body. Noble presence. Rich, rather voluptuous cheerful expression of the eye and in a supreme degree of the mouth, though somewhat col-lapsed. The room was crowded with bits of relief, medals and so on. His actual study *no foreigner is allowed to see, from a just dread of indecent exposure to the travel reading public. He saluted me unexpectedly in French, asked pertinent and shrewd questions about Virginia, evidently determined to make me the talker. Asked where I was educated—Harvard. If young men from America any longer went to England for their educa-tion. Made a hasty adieu, exceedingly soft hand. Wished me success in life. I agree with other strangers that his manner is not free from a slight embarrassment; he is evidently not quite easy in his French.*

278.   F. von Müller   23.11.1830

"My studies of nature and art have always really been entirely egocentric, namely for my own enlightenment. And I only wrote about them for the sake of my further education. What people make of my writings is a matter of indifference to me."

279.   F. von Müller   5.4.1830

"There is really no longer anyone with whom I can discuss the matters which most deeply concern me, for no one knows and understands my premisses."

280.   Eckermann   5.4.1830

It is well known that Goethe has an aversion to spectacles.

"It may be a fad of mine", he told me on several occasions, "but I simply cannot overcome it. The moment a stranger steps into my room with spectacles on his nose, I am filled with a feel-ing of distaste which I am unable to master. It embarrasses me so acutely that a large part of my good will towards the visitor vanishes while he is still on the threshold, and my thoughts are so disrupted that it becomes impossible for me to express myself with any degree of naturalness or ease. It always gives me an impression of discourtesy, rather as if a stranger

were to say something insulting to me at the very first greeting.
I have had this feeling even more strongly since stating in print
some years ago that I cannot bear spectacles. Thus if a visitor
arrives wearing them, I at once think: 'He hasn't read my most
recent poems, and that is already rather in his disfavour; or else
he has read them, and knows this foible of mine, and is choosing
to ignore it, and that is even worse'. The only man whose
spectacles do not irritate me is Zelter; I cannot bear them on
anyone else. I always feel that strangers who wear them are
treating me as an object to be carefully inspected, that their
armed gaze is piercing the most secret recesses of my mind and
searching my old face for its tiniest wrinkle. But in trying to get
to know me in this way they are destroying all just equality between us by preventing me from getting to know them in return.
For what good do I get of a man if I cannot look him in the eye
as his mouth talks to me, and if he masks the mirror of his soul
with two flashing pieces of glass!"

281. F. von Müller   7.4.1830

The conversation then turned to the subject of Greek love
and Johannes Müller.

He argued that the root of this aberration is really the fact
that by purely aesthetic standards men are after all much more
beautiful, excellent and perfect than women; and that once
such a feeling arises it can very easily take a crudely material
and animal direction. "Paederasty", he said, "is as old as
humanity, and can thus be said to be within nature, although
it is against nature.

"Civilisation has gained certain ascendancies over nature
which must not be lost again or sacrificed at any price. Thus the
idea of the sanctity of marriage is another such triumph of
Christian civilisation and is of inestimable value, although marriage is really an unnatural state.

"You know how highly I respect Christianity; or perhaps
that is something you do not know. Which of us nowadays is a
Christian the way Christ wanted them? I am perhaps the only
one, although you all consider me a pagan. Anyway, civilising
ideas of the sort to which I refer have been ingrafted into the
minds of nations once and for all and can be traced throughout
the centuries; certain ineradicable qualms are everywhere felt
about irregular, extramarital sexual relationships, and it is a very

good thing that this should be so. Divorces ought not to be proceeded with so lightly.

"What does it matter if a few couples beat each other and make each other's lives a misery, provided the general principle of the sanctity of marriage is upheld? After all, such individuals would have other sufferings to bear, if they were relieved of their present troubles."

282.   *Jenny von Pappenheim*   *22.4.1830*

The decision to flee to Italy gradually took shape in August von Goethe's mind. He resembled his father in this, who had always liberated himself from suffering by tearing himself suddenly away from his usual surroundings. Only a few people knew of August's plan. I was told of it by Ottilie, and I could not refrain from giving him my warmest good wishes for his journey. I was convinced I should see him again as a man reborn. Apparently his parting from his father was a deeply upsetting scene. I was told that August had suddenly fallen at his feet weeping and then rushed away, while Goethe collapsed on his chair, overwhelmed by evil forebodings.

283.   *E. Genast*   *24.4.1830*

He received Madame Schröder-Devrient with great kindness and affection. Among other things she sang him Schubert's setting of the *Erlking*, and although he did not approve of poems in separate stanzas being composed right through from beginning to end, preferring the strophic style, the incomparable Wilhelmine's highly dramatic performance nevertheless moved him so deeply that he took her head between his hands and kissed her on the forehead, saying: "Thank you a thousand times for that magnificent piece of artistry". Then he added: "I once heard that setting before and it did not appeal to me at all; but performed like this, the whole thing shapes itself into a visible image".

284.   *F. von Müller*   *24.4.1830*

When I remarked that his opinions on various matters used to be quite different, he exclaimed: "What! do you suppose I've reached the age of eighty just to keep on thinking the same thing? On the contrary, I try every day to think something different, something new, to avoid turning into a bore. One must continually change and renew and rejuvenate oneself, if one is not to stagnate."

Later he said: "As to answering letters, one simply has willy-nilly to declare oneself bankrupt, and just pay one or two of one's debts surreptitiously. My rule is: if I see that someone is merely writing to me for his own sake, with some personal aim in mind, then that is no concern of mine; but if they are writing for my sake, if they send me something that benefits me and concerns me, then I must reply."

In general he was very lively today, animated and witty, but ironic and bizarre rather than kindly, negative rather than positive, humorous rather than good-humoured. I think I have hardly ever seen him give a more graceful exhibition of the Protean nature which impels him to transform himself endlessly, to play with everything, to accommodate and endorse the most antithetical views.

285.   F. Mendelssohn-Bartholdy   21–24.5.1830

I had Zelter's letter sent straight in to Goethe. He sent back word inviting me to lunch. So there I found him, outwardly unchanged, but at first rather silent and withdrawn; I think he just wanted to see how I might behave; this annoyed me, and I thought: perhaps he is always like that now. Then, fortunately, we began to talk about the women's societies in Weimar and about *Chaos*, a crazy periodical which Ottilie and the other ladies edit and distribute among themselves, and to which I have achieved the distinction of being a contributor. Suddenly the old man's spirits rose, and he began to tease Ottilie and her sister about their good works and their intellectuality and their subscriptions and their nursing activities, which he seems to abhor particularly. He called on me to join in the attack; and as I needed no second bidding to do so, he at last became his old self again completely and showed even more kindness and familiarity than I had yet known in him. So nothing was spared. Of Ries's opera *The Robber's Bride* he said that it contained everything that an artist needs nowadays to make his fortune: a robber and a bride. Then he denounced the widespread discontent and melancholy of the younger generation; then he told anecdotes about a young lady whom he had once courted and

who had also shown some interest in him; then it was the turn of
the exhibitions and sales of work for distressed persons, at which
the Weimar ladies acted as saleswomen and at which, he
declared, it was impossible to buy anything, because the young
people arranged it all in advance about who should have what,
and then hid the goods until the right purchasers came; and so
forth.

Then after lunch he suddenly began : "Dear creatures—pretty
creatures—must always keep one's spirits up—delightful
people!" And as he spoke he made eyes like an old lion who
wants to go to sleep. Then I had to play to him, and he remarked how strange it was that he had heard no music for so
long; and now we had gone on developing the art further behind
his back; he must ask me a lot of questions about it, "for we
must have a proper talk about this some time".—Then he said
to Ottilie: "I dare say you have already made very clever
arrangements of your own, but they will not excuse you from
obeying my orders, which are that you are to take your tea here
today, so that we can be together again". And when she asked
if it would not be too late, because Riemer was going to come
and work with him, he said: "You let your children off their
Latin this morning so that they could hear Felix play, so surely
for once you could let me off my work too". Then he invited me
for a second time that day, and I played a lot to him in the
evening.

I had asked Goethe to call me *du*, and the following day he
sent Ottilie to tell me that in that case I must stay longer than
two days, as I had planned, because otherwise he would not be
able to get into the habit of doing so again. And then he told
me this himself, and said that he did not think I would miss anything by staying a little longer, and invited me to have meals
with him every day if I had no other engagements. So I have
visited him every day until now. In fact, you will agree that I
should have been mad not to spare the time. Today I am to play
him things by Bach, Haydn, and Mozart, and then (as he put
it) lead him on further till we reach the present day.

286.   F. Mendelssohn-Bartholdy

Yesterday evening, 24th May, I was at a party at Goethe's
house and played solo all evening: Weber's *Konzertstück*, *Invitation*, and Polonaise in C, and the three Italian pieces and the

Scottish sonata. It was over at ten, but of course I stayed on till twelve fooling around, dancing, singing and so forth, in fact I am living a high life altogether. The old man always goes to his room at nine, and as soon as he has gone we dance on the benches, and have never yet parted company before midnight.

Tomorrow my portrait will be finished; it is going to be a big black crayon drawing, a very good likeness, but I look very cross. Goethe is so kind and affectionate to me that I don't know how to thank him or deserve it. Every morning I have to play the piano to him for about an hour, pieces by all the various great composers in chronological order, and I have to explain to him what advances they all made, and there he sits in a dark corner like Jove the Thunderer, with his old eyes flashing. He did not want to listen to any Beethoven, but I told him he would just have to, and played him the first movement of the C minor Symphony. This made an extraordinary impression on him. At first he said : "But it isn't at all moving, merely astounding; very grandiose!" Then he went on muttering away, and after some time he began again : "It's very great indeed, quite fantastic! Enough to make one afraid the house will fall down. And to think of all those people playing that simultaneously!"— And during lunch, in the middle of another conversation, he began talking about it again.

I now have meals with him every day, as you know already. So he questions me very searchingly, and after the meal he is always so happy and communicative that we usually sit on alone in the room for another hour or more during which he talks without a moment's pause. It's absolutely delightful the way he suddenly fetches some engravings for me and explains them, or pronounces judgment on Victor Hugo's *Hernani* and Lamartine's *Elegies* or something to do with the theatre or pretty girls. He has already several times invited people for the evening, which nowadays is a very rare thing for him to do, so that most of the guests have not seen him for a long time. Then I have to play a lot, and he pays me compliments in front of everyone, his favourite expression being "quite stupendous!" Tonight he has invited a number of Weimar beauties all together to meet me, because, as he says, after all I must live with young people too. And if I approach him during a party of this kind, he says : "Good gracious! you must go to the ladies, and behave very nicely to them."

I do, however, know how to be tactful, and yesterday I got

Ottilie to ask him whether I was not in fact perhaps coming to see him too often. But he growled at her when she brought him the message and declared that he had not even properly begun to talk to me yet. I knew my subject so well, he said, that he clearly had many things to learn from me. I grew to twice my height when Ottilie repeated this to me, and yesterday he even reiterated it himself and told me that he still had many things in mind which he must ask me to explain to him; to which I replied: "Oh, with pleasure!" and thought: It will be an unforgettable honour.

287. *Jenny von Pappenheim*   *21.5–3.6.1830*

Goethe's own nature was so extraordinary that he found any kind of one-sidedness incomprehensible, and he often tried to teach Felix things. It was all in vain; on one occasion it even appears that Goethe—just like King Saul!—angrily turned his back on his favourite because the latter failed to understand him. Mendelssohn, startled out of his wits, sat at the piano as if petrified, until almost unconsciously his fingers touched the keys, and as if to console himself he began to play. Suddenly Goethe was standing beside him again and saying in his tenderest voice: "You have got enough; hold on to it!"

288. *F. Mendelssohn-Bartholdy*   *31.5–3.6.1830*

A few days after my last letter from Weimar I was about to leave and come here to Munich; and at table I duly announced my departure to Goethe, who fell very silent at the news. But afterwards he drew Ottilie aside to a window and told her: "You are to get him to stay!" And so she tried to persuade me, walking up and down in the garden with me, but I was determined to be a man of my word and stuck to my decision. Then the old gentleman came himself and said there was no need for me to be in such a hurry, he still had a lot to tell me, I still had a lot to play to him, and as for what I had told him about the reasons for my journey, that was all nonsense. Weimar had now turned out to be the real goal of my journey, and he failed to see that I lacked anything here that I should find at my restaurant tables; after all, in my lifetime I should see plenty of hotels—and so it went on. I was touched by this, and then Ottilie and Ulrike joined in too, pointing out to me that the old gentleman never forced people to stay, and all the oftener forced them to go; that the number of man's happy days was not so surely predestined that he could afford to throw away a few which he was certain to enjoy; and that afterwards they would come with me as far as Jena. So in the end I changed my mind about being a man of my word, and stayed. I have seldom in my life so little regretted a decision as this one; for the next day was the most perfect I ever spent in that house. After a drive in the morning I found old Goethe in the best of spirits; he launched into narrative, passed from Auber's *Masaniello* to Walter Scott and from him to the pretty girls in Weimar, from girls to students, hence to the *Robbers* and thus to Schiller. And from this point he went on talking happily and uninterruptedly for rather more than an hour, about Schiller's life, his work, and his position in Weimar. This soon led him to the subject of the late Grand Duke and of the year 1775, of which he said that it had been an intellectual springtime for Germany and that no one would ever be so well qualified to describe it as himself; and this he intended to do in the next volume of his autobiography, but of course one could never get round to writing it on account of one's botany and meteorology and all the rest of that nonsense for which one got no thanks from anyone. Then he told stories about the period when he had been director of the Court Theatre. When I tried to thank him, he declared: "Oh, just random talk; it all just comes out, evoked by your delightful presence". These words were wonderfully sweet to hear. In short, it was one of those conversations which one remembers for the rest of one's life.

Next day he gave me a sheet of his *Faust* manuscript, and had written at the foot of it :

"To my dear young friend Felix Mendelssohn-Bartholdy, a powerful and delicate master of the piano, in affectionate memory of happy days in May 1830.
                                        J. W. von Goethe."

And then he gave me three letters of introduction for Munich as well.

At the very beginning of my stay in Weimar I had mentioned a picture by Adriaen van Ostade called *Peasant Family at Prayer* which I said had made a great impression on me nine years ago. So when I came in in the morning to take my leave, there he was sitting in front of a large folder, and he said:

"Well, well! So off they go! Must try to carry on till you come back. But let's not part here without a little piety; we must take another look together at this *Prayer*." Then he asked me to write to him occasionally; and then he kissed me, and so we drove off.

289. *Soret*   *20.10.1830*

When I pointed out to him that the true utilitarian does not preach egoism, but the co-operation of every man in the happiness of all, as an indispensable condition of individual happiness, Goethe replied approximately as follows: "I do not understand this desire to sacrifice the advantage of individuals to that of the masses. I maintain that every man should remain what he is, and work creatively in accordance with his own inner conviction. As a writer I have never considered the interest of the masses, but I have tried to say things which were true and to write nothing but what I thought and believed to be good in itself. The good of others resulted from this without having been my primary aim. Thus, to say that each man should sacrifice himself to the good of all is in my view a false principle. Each man should sacrifice himself to his own conviction."

"But you will agree", I said, "that this individual conviction must, of course, be just and proper and useful to the individual who feels it, before he gives it outward expression."

"That goes without saying", replied Goethe. "If this were not so it would be fruitless for others and harmful to myself."

"In that case," I went on, "we are not far from agreement; for personal interest, rightly understood, is nothing other than the interest of the greatest number."

"Yes, but where we do not agree is that for you the interest of the greatest number is the principle; for me it is the consequence."

"Pardon me, I make it the principle in so far as it is surely the best basis for general applications. When I say: the principle of utility, or of the greatest good of all men, I am saying: such is the basis which should guide me as a legislator."

"Oh! if you are talking about legislation I have no more to say, that is none of my business, it lies outside my normal competence and activities. I leave it to others to make laws and to devise the best way of improving the state of society, and I will merely remark to you that in my opinion laws ought to diminish the sum-total of evils without aspiring to increase the sum-total of good. Do what you like in your legislation, that is no longer any concern of mine. But don't compel me, as an individual, to regulate my private conduct according to the greatest good of all men. For if I had regard to the masses and not to my own personality, I should tell them fairy-tales and make fools of them, like the late-lamented Kotzebue."

"I nevertheless believe that I differ from your Excellency only in that we define the same words in different ways."

I think, morever, that this conversation left us nearer together rather than further apart.*

290. F. von Müller   10.11.1830

His son has been suddenly carried off by a stroke in Rome, on October 27th.

You can well imagine how bitter a task it was for me to break this terrible news to the venerable father! But he took it very calmly, with great submission. "Non ignoravi me mortalem genuisse!" he exclaimed, his eyes filling with tears.

291. Johanna Schopenhauer   10.11.1830

That eternal Pasquale, Chancellor Müller, had undertaken to break the tragic news to the father, accompanied by Dr. Vogel. The old man stopped them in mid-sentence. "The day he left here, I gave him up for lost", he said, and dismissed them; the two gentlemen could not agree whether he had really understood what they had come to tell him. To Ottilie he said : "August is not coming back; you and I must stick together all the more closely now".

* Eckermann's version of this discussion attributes the following statements to Goethe: "I think everyone should begin with himself and work in the first instance for his own happiness, and from this, in the end, the general happiness will infallibly follow. If only every individual does his duty, if only every man acquits himself honestly and well in his immediate calling, the general weal will look after itself ... I have always merely tried to make myself wiser and better, to broaden and enrich my personality and then simply to express what I perceived to be good and true. I will of course not deny that what I wrote did exert a wide and useful influence; but this was not my purpose, it was an entirely necessary consequence such as follows from the operation of any natural force."

292. *G. F. A. von Conta*   *November 1830*

When his only son had died in Rome, he spoke of this grievous blow to no one; even the widow was not allowed to mention it, and he told his weeping grandsons amusing stories to distract them. Nevertheless it is known that as a result of this loss he fell ill, and that he suffered a relapse after speaking to the young painter Friedrich Preller in whose arms his son died, although he had said not a word to him about his son but talked about art with the greatest composure.

293. *Soret*   *22.12.1830*

Returned the day before yesterday from Geneva. Yesterday I wrote a letter to Goethe in which I alluded to our double loss.* Today he received me in a very friendly manner, said not a word about his son or about my father, but behaved affectionately towards me, calling me "my son" as he talked. It was his only reply to my letter, and the only reply I wanted.

294. *V. Cousin*   *(ca. 1830)*

We saw him again in Weimar only two years ago; he was already very bowed down with age. Both in body and mind he showed signs of the burden of the years; his brow was still high and noble, but his eyes were dim and his mouth had caved in quite a lot. In his conversation there were still occasional flashes of greatness; he was especially interesting when he talked about himself, about his works, but above all about his plans (for at eighty and over he still had plans). He told me: "First I shall finish my *Faust* episodes, and then I shall set to work on this and that", naming two or three works which he intended to write. It is moving to hear so aged a man constantly talking of the future, as if there were still life and genius at his disposal!

295. *Eckermann*   *(ca. 1830)*

"These critics all hate me, the whole lot of them", said Goethe, "and I am in the way of them all; but I propose to go on living and writing for a little while yet just to spite them. I

* Soret's father had also died recently.

have hopes that I may still produce one or two good things, the existence of which they will at least have to tolerate."

296. Th. Voigt   (ca. 1830)

I still remember clearly how a hussar rode into Jena one afternoon and delivered a letter to my father, asking for a verbal reply; the carriage, he said, would follow in an hour. The letter contained an invitation from Goethe for the evening. My father at once put on his best things and was driven to Weimar. When he entered the drawing-room he found Riemer, Eckermann and the rest of them sitting round the table, and the old gentleman was wearing his green eyeshade. No one said a word, and everyone had a bottle of red wine in front of him. When my father began introducing himself and asking how he could be of service to his Excellency, Riemer stopped him with a whisper : "His Excellency is thinking !" Eventually, at ten o'clock, their host retired with his well-known formula : "I wish you goodnight, my friends !" Next morning his Excellency had completely forgotten about the invitation. Presumably it had just been some idea passing through his head, in connection with which he had felt he needed to speak to my father.

297. L. A. Frankl

Goethe was exceedingly attached to his two grandsons. He observed them most tenderly, took an interest in their lessons, and in order to have them with him even while they were doing their tasks, he set up a little desk for each of them by the windows in his study, at which they wrote their homework. As he walked to and fro thinking or dictating Goethe liked, especially in his later years, to empty a bottle of hock; and with his grandsons there busy learning he took particular pleasure in making them drink out of his glass, chuckling with delight when they became quite merry and forgot all about their work.

298. Jenny von Pappenheim   (ca. 1830)

Goethe's grandson Wolff was describing how his grandpapa had had another quarrel with Aunt Ulrike von Pogwisch. He stooped forward the way the old man does, and stumped to and fro in the room, with his hands on his back, his head raised, glaring at us with wide-open eyes and muttering angrily: "Young woman, young woman! You'll make me lose my patience!" I could not help laughing, but told my young friend that he really must not make fun of his grandfather.

299. *Eckermann*   *13.2.1831*

I remarked that each of the various episodes of Parts I and II of *Faust* (Auerbach's Tavern, the Witch's kitchen, the Blocksberg, the Reichstag, the masquerade, the paper money, the laboratory, the Classical Walpurgisnacht, the Helena) is really a quite independent small self-contained cosmos, and that although they perhaps influence each other, they in fact have little to do with each other. The poet's purpose is to express a world full of variety, and he uses the story of a famous hero merely as a sort of central thread on which hang whatever items he pleases; rather as in the *Odyssey* or Lesage's *Gil Blas*.

"You are absolutely right", said Goethe. "And in a work of this kind all that matters is that the individual component masses should be meaningful and clear, although it will always be incommensurable as a whole—while nevertheless for that very reason remaining, like an unsolved problem, a constant stimulus to repeated study."

300. *Eckermann*   *13.2.1831*

I told Goethe about a letter I had had from a young officer whom I and other friends had advised to get himself posted abroad, but who now found that living in a foreign country did not appeal to him, and was cursing all his advisers.

"Giving advice is a tricky thing", said Goethe, "and when one has had enough experience of the world to know how unsuccessful the most sensible undertakings can be and how the craziest things can produce fortunate results, one may well conceive a disinclination to give any advice to anyone. In the last resort, too, asking for advice is a weakness and giving it is a presumption. One should only advise people on matters in which one is willing to take an active part oneself. If someone asks me for good advice I tell him that I am prepared to give it, but only on condition that he will promise me not to take it."

301. *Eckermann* *14.2.1831*

I remarked that it was strange that musical talent should declare itself at an earlier age than any of the others, so that Mozart when he was only five, Beethoven when he was only eight and Hummel when he was only nine astonished their immediate entourage by their playing and compositions.

"Musical talent", said Goethe, "may well be the first to show itself, because music is something altogether innate and internal which does not need much nourishment from outside or any experience of life. And yet it is true that a phenomenon such as Mozart remains an inexplicable miracle. But how would the divinity find any occasion to work miracles if it did not sometimes show its power in extraordinary individuals at whom we gaze in amazement, unable to understand whence they came."

302. *Eckermann* *17.2.1831*

"It is generally supposed that one has to grow old in order to be wise; but in reality one finds it difficult with advancing years to remain as sensible as one was. It is true that as a man passes through the various stages of his life he changes, but he cannot claim to be improving, and on certain matters he is just as likely to be right when he is twenty as when he is sixty.

"To be sure, one has one view of the world from down in the plains, another from up in the foothills and yet another from among the glaciers of ancient peaks. From one of these standpoints one sees rather more of the world than from the other; but that is all, and it cannot be said that one sees more of the truth from any of them than from the rest."

303. *Eckermann* *2.3.1831*

When I dined with Goethe today we again talked about daemonic forces, and to make his conception of them clearer he added the following observations.

"The daemonic", he said, "is that which intelligence and reason cannot account for. It is something external to my nature, but to which I am subject."

I remarked that there seemed to have been something daemonic about Napoleon. "He certainly was daemonic", said Goethe, "in the highest degree, which puts him almost beyond comparison. The late Grand Duke was a daemonic nature too, full of boundless energy and restlessness, so that his own dominions were too small for him and indeed the greatest would have been too small. Daemonic figures of this kind were regarded as demigods by the Greeks."

"Does not the daemonic also manifest itself in events?" I asked. "Most particularly", said Goethe. "It lies behind every event that is empirically and rationally inexplicable. In fact it shows itself in all sorts of ways throughout visible and invisible nature. Many creatures are completely daemonic in character, and in many there are daemonic elements at work."

I asked if there were not also some daemonic features in Mephistopheles. "No", said Goethe, "Mephistopheles is a much too negative figure. The daemonic manifests itself in absolutely positive energy.

"Among artists", he continued, "it is chiefly to be found in musicians, and not so much in painters. There is a high degree of it in Paganini, which is why his playing has such a powerful effect."

304. *Eckermann*   *8.3.1831*

"There is definitely something daemonic about poetry, and most especially about the unconscious kind which baffles all understanding and reason and consequently has such extraordinarily compelling effects.

"Such is also the case with music, in the very highest degree, for it occupies a place far above all understanding, and its influence has an absolute power which no one can explain. That is why religious worship finds it indispensable; it is one of the chief means of exercising a miraculous influence upon men."

305. *Eckermann*   *18.3.1831*

Goethe then told me that he was making good progress with his new edition of the *Metamorphosis of Plants* and Soret's increasingly felicitous translation. "And yet the book is giving me more trouble than I expected; indeed I was involved in the enterprise rather against my will at first, but some daemonic power was at work in this matter and there was no resisting it."

"You did well", I said, "to yield to such influences, for the daemonic seems to be so powerful a force that it will always get its way in the end."

"Nevertheless", replied Goethe, "man must also try to get his way against the daemonic, and in the present case I must go on making every possible effort to produce as good a piece of work as lies in my power and as circumstances will allow. These things are rather like the game the French call *codille*, in which a great deal depends on the throw of the dice, but it is still left to the skill of the player to place his men well on the board."

306. Eckermann   25.3.1831

Goethe showed me an elegant green easy-chair which he had recently had bought for him at an auction.

"But I shall use it very little or not at all", he said, "because comfort of all kinds is really quite uncongenial to me. As you see, there is no sofa in my room; I always sit in my old wooden chair and it was not until a few weeks ago that I had a sort of headrest fitted to it. To be surrounded by comfortable tasteful furniture paralyses my thinking process and reduces me to a complacent passive condition. Unless one has been accustomed to them all one's life, luxurious rooms and elegant furniture are for people who can't think and don't want to."

307. Eckermann   28.3.1831

We discussed the fourth volume of his autobiography, and the remarkable passage (in Book 18) in which Goethe describes his sister. "This chapter", he said, "will be read with interest by educated women, for there will be many of them who resemble my sister in possessing outstanding intellectual and moral qualities while at the same time not being blessed with physical beauty."

I remarked that the fact that she was habitually afflicted with a facial rash just before parties and dances was something so strange that one was tempted to ascribe it to some daemonic influence.

"She was a remarkable person", said Goethe. "She had very high moral standards and there was not a trace of sensuality about her. The thought of surrendering herself to a man was repellent to her, and it may be imagined that there must have been many unpleasant moments in her marriage as a result of this peculiarity. Women who have the same aversion or who do not love their husbands will understand what I mean. And this was why I could never think of my sister as married; on the contrary, she would really have been in her proper place as the abbess in a nunnery.

"Although her husband was a thoroughly worthy man she was not happy with him, and it was for this reason that she advised so passionately against my intended marriage to Lili [Schönemann]."

308. *Eckermann*   *30.3.1831*

We again discussed the daemonic.

"It likes to attach itself to outstanding personalities", said Goethe, "and also prefers rather murky epochs. In a clear prosaic city like Berlin it would have little occasion to manifest itself."

309. *J. J. Schmied*   *17.4.1831*

From Gotha we continued next day to Weimar. And here I cannot help laughing at my temerity, verging as it did on impudence. I was bound by my declared principle to send and inquire if Goethe were at home. I did so merely on principle, and would have wagered a thousand to one that I should not be received. As a result I was absolutely taken aback when the servant brought back word: "His Excellency the Minister, Herr von Goethe, presents his compliments, and would you please come to see him at once". All over Germany Goethe's inaccessibility is proverbial, and here was I, a theology student, a mere boy, not worthy to unloose the latchet of his poetical shoe, and I was to be granted so great a favour! Fortunately I had, as you know, already paid several important visits to distinguished persons; otherwise I should scarcely have dared to accept this unexpected invitation. It is true that it was always my plan to visit Goethe, but the nearer I got to Weimar the harder my heart beat at the thought of so bold an undertaking. Finally my embarrassed surprise resolved itself into exultation. I put on my full student's regalia, a clean shirt, shoes, silk stockings (with all of which, to be sure, my travelling-cap made an unsuitable combination); and thus accoutred, I betook myself to his house. On entering it I was confronted with several life-size statues, all in the ancient

Greek taste. A first footman announced me to a second, and when I had waited a few moments in an anteroom decorated in ancient classical style and was beginning to reflect with irritation that the footmen were out of keeping with the rest of the setting, I was requested to enter. Gone were all my well-prepared phrases—gone my carefully rehearsed salutation—gone were my wits! There I stood, just as God made me—but in a condition of exaltation, combined with a certain presence of mind of which I should never have supposed myself capable. At first (just after everything had been swept out of my head) I was tongue-tied, and there may have been a pause of about four pulse-beats before my open mouth could find words. But then they came fresh and lively! I know for certain that I said nothing foolish and no longer even seemed ill at ease; Goethe himself no doubt noticed my whole condition, and he answered me with Attic urbanity. For me the great hour had now struck in which I was privileged to stand before the greatest figure of two centuries and to see face to face this man who goes before humanity like a star of first magnitude, this fountainhead at which thousands of noble spirits have drunk the satisfaction of their highest needs—to see him, to talk to him on subjects of eternal interest, and to have him to myself for more than half an hour—to express to him in person my own modest but spontaneous opinion of him, and to be treated by him with affection! I shall acquaint you with one further fact, which since my visit to Goethe I have mentioned to no one. I was speaking in the warmest terms of the impression that his *Faust* had made and still makes upon me; and at that moment, as I watched him, the aged Goethe, bright tears came to his wide-open beautiful eyes, and his voice betrayed his emotion. I too was overwhelmed by my feelings, and when he began again to speak, my soul rejoiced. When I took my leave, he grasped my hand, pressed it with both of his, and said : "Goodbye, and may God and your genius of goodness go with you. If it should happen that you come again to Weimar during my life-time, please call on me, without having yourself announced in advance." To be singled out in this way, in addition to all else, was a crowning honour; I left with mixed feelings of pride and humility, and rejoined my travelling companions, who were mere ordinary human beings. Oh would to God I might once more behold him, and feast my mind's eye once more on his splendid mind!

9—G

310. *Jenny von Pappenheim*   *May 1831*

It was Goethe himself, when I visited him one day in his
garden-house, who gave me the following account of how it
came to be haunted : "I have invisible servants who always keep
the landing swept clean. Very early one morning I had what I
suppose was a dream, but it was exactly like reality : upstairs
in my bedroom the door leading to the stairs was open, and I
saw an old woman with a young girl leaning against her. She
turned to me and said : 'We have been living here for twenty-
five years on condition that we must be gone by daybreak; now
she has fainted and I can't go!' When I looked more closely
she had vanished."

311. *F. Förster*   *4.8.1831*

"Schiller and myself had very different natures, in that he
would never write or compose anything without first discussing
it at length; he gave me detailed verbal accounts of whole scenes
of *Wallenstein, Tell* and so forth before writing them down; I
could have written the continuation of his *Demetrius*, so precisely had he informed me of his intentions. It was quite otherwise with me; if I betrayed any of the secrets of my Muse before
she had actually conferred her gifts on me, nothing ever came
of them!" He praised Schiller's incredible industry despite his
very poor health. "He was such a sick man when I first knew
him that I did not expect him to live another year; and yet we
lived together for another twelve. How rapid his development
was! He worked so hard and read so much that he had increased in stature every time I met him.

"Please do greet the dear Körners from me; she* and her
sister were two lively, lovely girls—they often got very high-
spirited and used to tangle my hair for me, and then their
mother would have a lot of trouble combing it straight again.
But she enjoyed doing that, even when my hair was tidy. Their
father was a hard-working skilful artist, and I always enjoyed
visiting him."

* Schiller's friend Körner had married one of J. M. Stock's daughters
(see No. 6) to whom Goethe here refers.

312. F. Förster   *25.8.1831*

Goethe was in a particularly jocular and teasing mood today, and his daughter-in-law was once again made the chief victim of his wit on account of her predilection for Englishmen. "Now let me tell you", he said, "what curious protégés my Ottilie has. Yesterday she begged me most urgently to accept a visit from a young Englishman; he was a brilliant, charming, very entertaining, lively young man, she told me. So of course I had to give way, unwilling though I was. 'Well', I said to myself, 'for once you had better make the most of this brilliant, charming, lively conversationalist and not utter a word.' The young man was announced; I went out to meet him, and performed a polite gesture which invited him to be seated; he sat down, I sat down opposite him; he said nothing, I said nothing; we both said nothing; after a full quarter of an hour, or perhaps a little less, I stood up, and he stood up; I took my leave with the same sort of dumbshow, he did the same, and I accompanied him to the door. But now I had a slight pang of conscience on my poor dear Ottilie's account, and I thought to myself: 'You really mustn't let him go without saying at least something'. So I pointed to Byron's bust and said: 'That is the bust of Lord Byron'. 'Yes', he replied, 'he is dead'; and so we parted; and that was all I learnt from that brilliant, charming, lively, talkative Englishman."

313. F. Förster   *25.8.1831*

When I visited him for the last time, two thick folio volumes of manuscript were lying on his desk, and he pointed at them and said: "Here is the Second Part of *Faust*, sealed with seven seals; but no one else is to touch it until I am no longer in a position to do so". I tried to get him to talk again about the question of adapting *Faust* for the stage, and Goethe agreed with my view that it was only after they had been presented on the stage that the great dramas and tragedies of ancient and modern and most recent times had come to be generally understood and their greatness generally recognised. "But as to adaptation", Goethe remarked, "that is precisely where the difficulty lies, especially with a drama like *Faust*, which the author from the start never envisaged as being acted at all. After all, even Shakespeare's most concentrated plays are hard enough to

stage effectively in our theatre, and he wrote everything expressly
for acting. You yourself found that, didn't you, when you were
adapting Richard III."

314.   J. Ch. Mahr   27.8.1831

Towards evening on the 26th August 1831, Goethe arrived
here in Ilmenau* at the "Lion", with his two grandsons and his
servant. He had immediately sent to inform me of his arrival, so
I called on him on the morning of the 27th; he had already been
busy at his desk since four o'clock. He declared that he was
delighted to be back in this district, where in former times he
had been so often and for so long, but which he had not re-
visited for thirty years; his two grandsons, he said, had already
gone off into the hills, accompanied by the servant, and would
not be back until midday. After enquiring if there had been any
further interesting geological developments he asked whether
it was not possible to drive conveniently to the top of the Gickelhahn. He would like, he said, to see the little hunting-lodge on the
Gickelhahn, for he had very distinct memories of it from past
days; and he asked me to accompany him on this excursion. So we
drove along the forest road through Gabelbach; the weather
was excellent. We reached the highest point of the Gickelhahn
without difficulty, and having alighted, he first praised the magnificent panorama from the view-point, then expressed his
pleasure at the splendid afforestation, exclaiming: "Oh, if only
my dear Grand Duke Karl August could have seen this beautiful
sight once more!" Then he said: "The little forest hut must be
near here. I can walk there; tell the chaise to wait here till we
get back." And in fact he strode off through the bilberry shrubs,
which grew quite high on the top of the hill, towards the familiar
hunting-lodge, a small two-storey building of timber and boards.
There is a steep stair to the upper floor; I offered to help him
up, but he declined with youthful high spirits, though the next
day was to be his eighty-second birthday, and said: "Don't you
take it into your head that I can't climb these steps. I am still
perfectly well able to do so." As he entered the upper room he
said: "I once stayed in this room for a week with my servant,
one summer long ago, and wrote a little piece of verse here on
the wall. I should rather like to see that piece of verse again, and

* A small town in the Thuringian hills, about thirty miles from
Weimar. This is Goethe's last recorded journey.

if the date of its composition is noted under it, would you be so kind as to make a note of it for me." I at once took him to the south window of the room, to the left of which is written in pencil:

> *Now stillness covers*
> *All the hill-tops;*
> *In all the tree-tops*
> *Hardly a breath stirs.*
> *The birds in the forest*
> *Have finished their song.*
> *Wait: you too shall rest*
> *Before long.**

6th September 1780   *Goethe*

Goethe read these few lines, and tears ran down his cheeks. Very slowly he drew his snow-white handkerchief from the pocket of his dark brown coat, dried his eyes and said in a sad and gentle voice: "Yes: wait, you too shall rest before long!" He was silent for half a minute, gazed once more through the window into the dark pine-wood and then turned to me and said: "Let us go now".

I offered him my help on the steep stair, but he replied: "So you think I can't manage these steps? They're still quite easy! But go ahead of me, to stop me looking down." In this nostalgic mood he again mentioned the loss of his dear Grand Duke Karl August.

When we got back to the carriage he again praised the magnificent view and the splendid surroundings, which were looking their best on so fine a day; then he stepped into the carriage again and made me sit beside him. Thus I accompanied him back to the "Lion", and on the way he told me many excellent things in his forceful and expressive language.

When he arrived, his two grandsons had already returned from their excursion in the hills. Goethe asked them about what they had seen, and was greatly pleased by their answers and observations, which at times were really quite acute.

315.   F. Preller (reported)   Autumn 1831

When Preller told Goethe that he had drawn portraits in his

* For the original of this famous poem see *Selected Verse* (Penguin Books) p. 50. Goethe's autograph on the wall of the hut read "die Vögel"; the version with the diminutive "Vögelein" was adopted later.

sketch-books of all the people he had known in Rome, Goethe asked if he might borrow the books to look through them himself. Preller realised that what he wanted was to look for the sketch of his son's features, which was indeed there among the rest, and he brought him the books. When he returned a few days later Goethe handed them back to him with a serious expression and without saying a word. But when he got home and opened one of them at the familiar place, Preller found that he had been right, for August's portrait was no longer there.

316.   C. A. Schwerdgeburth   21.1.1832

There was another remarkable thing about the last occasion on which he sat to me for my drawing of him, namely that during a pause in the conversation, as he sat there in front of me, he suddenly began to murmur softly some words which I could not understand, and as he did so he drew a roman W with his right index finger in the air. Then he woke as if out of a dream and asked me if he were sitting correctly. He repeated this drawing of a W in the air once more, with an appearance of profound thought, and an inexpressible feeling came over me as I watched him.

317.   Soret (as adapted by Eckermann)   17.2.1832

"Basically, whatever our pretensions may be, we are all composite beings. For how little we have and are that we can in the strictest sense call our own! We all must be receptive, we can none of us help learning, both from those who preceded us and those who are our contemporaries. Even the greatest genius could achieve little if he owed nothing to any influence outside his own mind. But there are many excellent men who do not understand this, and who spend half their lives groping in the darkness dreaming of originality. Poor fools! As if it were even possible! As if the world were not thrusting itself upon them at every step and educating them in spite of their stupidity! I will even assert that if any such artist were so much as to walk past the walls of this room and glance fleetingly at the drawings by a few great masters which I have hung there, it would be impossible, if he had any genius in him at all, for him not to leave this house a changed and nobler man.

"And what special gift do we possess in any case, if it is not a power and a desire to attract useful impressions from the world outside us and to make them serve our own higher purposes? Perhaps I may speak of myself and say with due modesty what I feel about this. It is true that in the course of my long life I have done and accomplished a number of things of which I might well be proud. But if we consider the matter honestly, what have I really had that was my own apart from a capacity and a desire to see and to hear, to distinguish and to choose, to impart some life and sense to what I saw and heard and to reproduce it with a certain amount of skill? I owe my works by no means only to my own wisdom, but to thousands of things and persons outside me, for these were the materials I used. Fools and wise men came to me, lucid minds and narrow minds, children and young people and those of ripe old age; they all told me their views and their outlooks, their ways of life, their activities, and what experiences they had collected, and all I had to do was to reach out my hand and reap what others had sown.

"It is in the last resort folly to enquire whether someone has thought of something on his own or taken it from someone else, or whether he is acting through himself or through others. The essential thing is that one should have a great intention, and the skill and patience to carry it out; everything else is a matter of indifference."

318.   Soret   *27.2.1832*

We talked about modern French novels, particularly those of Balzac. Of his *Peau de Chagrin* Goethe remarked that every detail of it is open to criticism, that one can find technical faults and extravagances on every page; in short, that there are more than enough imperfections in it to spoil a good book, and that nevertheless it is impossible not to recognise it as the work of an unusual talent, or to fail to be interested by it.

From this we passed to Goethe's own compositions, to their characteristic total effect, to the variety and keenness of the poet's taste for things which at first seem incompatible with each other and for studies of which very few men would be capable of keeping abreast simultaneously. Goethe admitted very frankly that he had been infinitely indebted to the favourable circumstances in which he had found himself and of which he had been able to take advantage. This is the last conversation with Goethe that I have noted down; I paid several further calls

on him during March, he died on the twenty-second of that
month.

319. Eckermann   March 1832

"If a writer wants his work to be politically effective he must
become a partisan, and as soon as that happens he is finished as
a poet : he has to say goodbye to his freedom of judgment and
his impartial view of things, and pull the cap of bigotry and
blind hatred over his ears.

"As a man and a citizen, the poet may love his native land;
but the native land of his poetic talent and of his work as a poet
is the good, the noble and the beautiful, and these qualities are
not confined to any one province or any one country : he seizes
upon them and shapes them wherever he finds them. In this he
is like the eagle, hovering free-eyed over many lands, and caring
little whether the hare he dives down on is running through
Prussia or through Saxony.

"And what does 'love of one's native land' mean anyway?
What does 'patriotic endeavour' mean? If a writer has fought
all his life against pernicious prejudices, against mean and narrow views, if he has striven to enlighten the minds of his fellow-
countrymen, to refine their taste and ennoble their outlook, what
better task can he set himself than that? What more patriotic
duty can he perform?—To make such inappropriate and un-
grateful demands on a writer is just like telling the officer in
command of a regiment that he is no true patriot if he does not
become involved in political agitation, thus neglecting his proper
calling. But an officer's country is his military command, and he
will be an excellent patriot if he does not meddle at all with
political matters except in so far as they concern him, but con-
centrates his whole attention and care on the units in his charge
and on keeping them so well trained and disciplined that when
the nation is in danger they will be men and do their duty.

"I hate and detest all bungling amateurs, but amateur poli-
ticians most of all; they do nothing but harm to thousands and
millions of people.

"As you know, I generally take very little interest in the things
that are written about me, but I do hear of them, and I know
very well that hard as I have laboured all my life, my whole
work counts as nothing in the eyes of certain persons, simply
because I have disdained to engage in party politics. To please

such people I should have had to join a Jacobin club and preach murder and bloodshed!—But let us drop this miserable subject, or I shall say something foolish myself in protesting against folly."

320. *Eckermann*   *11.3.1832*

"So far as the Bible is concerned it is really quite inappropriate to ask about authenticity or otherwise. Nothing is authentic except true excellence, that which harmonises with pure nature and reason, and is of supreme value to our development even to this day. And nothing is spurious but what is absurd and hollow and foolish, and bears no fruit, or at least no good fruit! If one were to decide the authenticity of a book in the Bible by asking whether nothing but strict truth has been handed down to us in it, then one might well doubt the authenticity even of the gospels on certain points. And nevertheless I consider all four gospels to be absolutely genuine, for they transmit the radiance of a nobility which emanated from the person of Christ and was as divine as ever any manifestation of the divine on earth. If I am asked whether it is natural to me to worship and venerate Christ, I answer: certainly! I bow before him as the divine revelation of the supreme moral principle. If I am asked whether it is natural to me to venerate the sun, I again say: certainly! For the sun too is a revelation of the supreme glory, and mightier than any other revelation vouchsafed to our mortal eyes. In it I worship God's light and procreative power, by which alone we and all the plants and animals live and move and have our being. But if I am invited to bow down before the thumb-bone of St. Peter or St. Paul, I say: keep that rubbish to yourself and leave me out of it!

"We do not realise what an incalculable debt we owe to Luther and the Reformation. We have been liberated from the chains of bigoted narrow-mindedness, and our advancing culture has enabled us to return to the source and apprehend Christianity in its original purity. We have regained the courage to stand firm on God's earth and feel proudly aware of our God-gifted human nature. But however much our culture may progress, however much the sciences may increase in scope and depth and however far the human intellect may develop—the lofty radiance of Christianity, the civilised moral nobility that shines through the Gospels, will never be excelled.

"We Protestants, however, must give the lead in this noble process of advancement, for the further we go, the faster the Catholics will follow us. As soon as they feel themselves caught up in the great ever-spreading enlightenment of the age, they are bound to fall into line with it, and in the end unity of religion will be achieved.

"The tiresome sectarian divisions of Protestantism will also cease, and with them the hatred and hostility that they sow between fathers and sons and brothers and sisters. For as soon as men have grasped the pure teaching and love of Christ, just as it is, and grown used to practising it in their lives, they will feel free and great as men, and will no longer attach particular importance to trifling differences in the outward forms of worship.

"And little by little we shall all increasingly adopt a Christianity of deeds and attitudes instead of a Christianity of words and creeds."

Our conversation turned to great men who had lived before Christ, in China, India, Persia and Greece, and in whom the power of God had been just as active as in certain great Jews of the Old Testament. We also discussed the question of how God's power is manifested in great figures of our own modern world.

"To hear people talk", said Goethe, "one might almost suppose they think that since those old days God has retired into complete silence, and that man has been set entirely on his own feet and left to get on as best he may without God and without his daily unseen inspiration. At most, a divine influence is still admitted to operate in the religious and moral sphere, but the achievements of science and art are believed to be entirely terrestrial and the products of nothing more than purely human powers.

"But let any man just try, by human will and human strength, to create one work worthy to be set beside those that bear the names of Mozart or Raphael or Shakespeare! I well know that these three noble figures by no means stand alone, and that in every branch of art there are numberless outstanding minds whose work has reached no lesser heights than theirs. But in so far as they equalled them in greatness, then they excelled common human nature in equal measure and were as divinely gifted as those three.

"And what, indeed, is the nature and purpose of it all? God

certainly did not go into retirement after his famous fictitious six days of creation: on the contrary, he is still continuing his work as actively as on the first of them. I am sure it would not have been very rewarding for him to put together the simple elements that make up this gross world, and roll it round in the sun's rays year in and year out, if it had not been his plan to found a seminary for a world of spirits on this material basis. Thus in higher natures he is now continuing his work, using them to draw lesser natures to himself."

Goethe fell silent. But I stored up his great and good words in my heart.

321. K. Vogel   1826/32

Goethe regarded illness as the greatest of earthly evils. Sick people could count with especial confidence on his active sympathy. He was not really afraid of death, though he did have a dread of dying painfully. Pain was to him the most intolerable of physical ills, and anything causing disfigurement upset him nearly as much. He rivalled Epicurus in his praises of the painless state, and often boasted, as of a piece of good fortune which must surely be envied by many, that he had never suffered from toothache or headache. His teeth had remained in sound condition until he was a very old man.

Light and warmth were his most indispensable vital stimuli; he felt best when the barometer stood highest. He detested winter and would often jokingly declare that people would hang themselves in late summer if it were possible then to imagine the horrors of winter with full vividness.

Goethe did not like discussing the state of his health with anyone but his doctor. Merely courteous specific inquiries about how he was, especially if he was in fact not feeling very well at the time, tended to irritate him. He would often ill-humouredly declare it to be a positive piece of impertinence to ask a man how he is, when one has neither the power nor the wish to help him. He found the usual expressions of condolence even more intolerable, especially if they were lengthy and plaintive. "One has quite enough trouble and anxiety of one's own at such times, but on top of it all to have to listen to someone else's lamentation is more than I at least can bear", he would exclaim, as soon as the importunate visitor had left.

Goethe had an uncommonly high esteem for the healing art

and its true disciples. He enjoyed medical themes as subjects of
conversation. His diaries quite often contain records of medical
discussions with me which had particularly interested him.

He was a very grateful and docile patient. When he was ill
he liked to have the physiology of his symptoms and the thera-
peutic programme explained to him; and this, given his remarkable insight into the laws of organic systems, neither presented any great difficulty nor acted as an obstacle to his cure.
He did not ask for prognoses in his own illnesses, for he realised
that candour on this point was something which a doctor could
not always find possible or permissible. If there was a consulta-
tion between several doctors he would look on sceptically and
take much the same view of it as Molière.

There must be few patients who had a greater gift than
Goethe for describing their sensations to the doctor. In his case
there was only one condition that was an exception to this : if
one had prescribed him slightly too high a dose of some so-called
stimulant—and this occasionally happened in the early days of
our acquaintance, before I had become convinced of his quite
unusual sensitivity—he would define the resulting sensation as
follows: "My functions have come to a stop". He was never
able to give any clearer description of this condition.

322. *K. Vogel*   *16–20.3.1832*

On March 16th Goethe sent for me at an unusually early
hour; it was only eight o'clock. As a rule I did not pay him my
regular morning visit on medical and official business until nine,
and on the previous day, after a long conversation, I had left
him at that time in the best of health and spirits. I found him
dozing in bed. He soon woke, but still seemed half asleep at
first, and complained that he had begun feeling unwell yesterday, while returning from a drive between one and two o'clock
on a very cold windy afternoon; he had gone to bed early and
spent a largely sleepless night, disagreeably troubled by a re-
current short dry cough, flushes of heat alternating with shiver-
ing fits, and pains about the chest. The cause of his present
symptoms, he thought, was probably a chill which he might very
well have caught just before going out for the drive, by crossing
the cold lobby between his very well heated study and the
reception rooms overlooking the street.

(*19th*): In the morning I found the patient sitting beside his bed, in very lively spirits though still rather weak physically. He had been reading a French book, enquired as usual about a number of recent events, and expressed a strong desire for the glass of madeira which for the last few years had become the traditional accompaniment of his breakfast. I saw no reason to oppose his wish; he drank and ate with great satisfaction, and stayed up nearly all day. In the early evening I found him examining some engravings, and discussed with him what had occurred during his illness in the Department for which he was responsible. He spoke jestingly, and above all expressed great pleasure that he would be fit to take up his usual occupations on the following morning.

During the night of March 19th the patient at first slept peacefully for a few hours and his perspiration increased. At about midnight he woke up feeling cold: the chill increased minute by minute, beginning at his hands, which had lain exposed, and then spreading from them to the rest of his body. This was soon accompanied by a stabbing pain, variably located, which affected the limbs at first and in a short while the thoracic area as well, inhibiting his breathing and causing him great anxiety and agitation. The symptoms became more and more acute; but the patient, who usually sent such urgent calls for medical attention at the slightest ailment, would not allow his anxious servant to bring me word: because, as he said, he was in pain but not in danger.

(*20th*): I was not fetched until the next morning at half past eight. A pitiful spectacle awaited me! This aged man had for years never moved except with measured dignity, and now the most terrible fear and agitation were driving him frantically to and fro between his bed and the armchair beside it; when in bed he vainly sought relief by lying in a different position from moment to moment, and the agonising pain, now increasingly located on his chest, forced him to moan and sometimes cry out loudly. His features were convulsed, his countenance ashy pale, his eyes dimmed and dull, deep-sunk in their livid sockets and filled with the horror of death. His whole ice-cold body dripped with sweat; his abnormally rapid, dry knocking pulse was scarcely perceptible; there was pronounced abdominal swelling and a racking thirst. A few isolated words which he managed to utter suggested the fear of another pulmonary haemorrhage.

323. *K. W. Müller*   *21.3.1832*

At about eleven o'clock at night he begged his daughter-in-law to go to bed, and to make the children sleep too. He insisted that it was quite unnecessary for anyone to stay up with him except his manservant and his secretary, John. At the same time he asked to see the list of those who had called that day to enquire after his health, and read it through, pausing at certain names and remarking that he must on no account be allowed to forget to acknowledge their sympathy when he was well again. He then again urged the members of his family to retire for the night, saying that they would waste their strength pointlessly by staying up.

324. *Luise Seidler*   *21–22.3.1832*

During the night he had light brought to him and tried to read; but finding it impossible, he lifted the book on high and said jokingly: "Well, let us at least venerate it, as mandarins do". His daughter-in-law had remained surreptitiously in the next room, and he greeted and caressed her with renewed affection whenever she came to him, but always soon sent her away again. At seven o'clock, on the morning of his death, he even asked her to bring a portfolio and tried to make optical experiments with her to demonstrate colour phenomena; he explained a number of them to her, and spoke about the approaching spring, saying how he hoped it would soon make him well again. He also made another attempt to write, and had sheets of paper handed to him from the desk so that he could number them. At ten he stopped speaking almost entirely, except for occasional words such as: "Sit by me, Ottilie darling, close by me", or "Give me your nice little paw".

325. *Amelie von Stein*   *22.3.1832*

He behaved very tenderly to Ottilie, saying: "My dearest girl, sit down by me, close to me, close, close". To his youngest grandson, of whom he was fond, he said: "How are you, my little boy?" and with his mind half wandering he asked his servant: "Have you sold my dictionary, then, or given it away, maybe?" Then he gradually fell asleep, but did not think he was dying; for on the previous day he said to Hofrat Vogel:

"Just see to it that I have a good night, then I'll be able to carry on all right by myself". And he ordered some crabs to be bought, so that he might eat them with Vogel, who liked crabs.

326.   C. F. A. von Conta   22.3.1832

He certainly realised that he was going to die; but until his last hour he talked happily and even jestingly to his daughter-in-law (whom he now kept constantly by him) and to his doctor. "April is coming now", he said, "so I shall be taking the sun in my garden."

327.   K. W. Müller   22.3.1832

Towards sunrise—as the doctor had predicted—he got considerably worse, and his strength continued to ebb. The room had been left quite dark, to keep the patient quieter, but he said : "Give me light; it's unpleasant in the dark". Soon, however, his eyes seemed to be hurting him, for he kept shading them with his hand as if to protect them or to look at some distant object; so they gave him the green eye-shade which he always wore when reading in the evening. Then he asked his daughter-in-law to sit beside him, took her hand and held it in his for a long time.

At about nine o'clock he requested a drink of water mixed with wine, and when it was brought he sat up in his armchair, seized the glass firmly and drained it, though before doing so he asked : "I hope there is not too much wine in it?" Then he called for his secretary, John, and with the assistance of the latter and of his manservant he got right up from his chair. Standing before it, he asked what day of the month it was, and on being told it was the twenty-second he replied : "So spring has begun, and we shall get well all the sooner". Then he sat down again in the armchair and dozed gently off into pleasant dreams, to judge by his murmured remarks such as : "Look, a fine head of a woman—black hair—splendid colouring—on a dark background". Indeed his mind seemed to be entirely occupied with art, for a moment or two later he said : "Friedrich, give me that folder there with drawings in it !" As there was no folder in the place he pointed to but only a book, his servant gave him this, but the patient insisted: "No, not the book, the portfolio!" His servant assured him that there was nothing but a book and no portfolio there, whereupon Goethe woke right out of his doze and said with a smile: "Well, then I suppose it was a ghost".

Shortly after this he asked for some cold chicken for breakfast. This was brought; he took a little of it and wanted something to drink. Friedrich handed him a glass of water and wine, but he only sipped it, saying: "You haven't put any sugar in the wine, have you? it's bad for me". Then he gave instructions about what he would like for lunch, and also ordered one of Hofrat Vogel's favourite dishes for the Saturday (March 24th), as Vogel was coming to lunch with him on that day. Such was his affectionate thoughtfulness towards his friends until the very last moment of his life.

Once more Goethe got Friedrich and his secretary to help him up, and tried to go to his study; but he only reached the door, swayed, and soon sat down again in the armchair. After sitting for a little he asked them to give him a certain manuscript by Kotzebue. No such manuscript could be found. Then his thoughts turned to his friend Schiller who had preceded him in death. For when he noticed a sheet of paper lying on the floor he asked: "Why has Schiller's correspondence been left lying about here? Please pick it up at once." And a moment later he called to Friedrich: "Will someone please open the other shutter in this room as well, to let in more light!" These are said to have been his last words.

Since he was now finding it more and more difficult to speak, but still felt the impulse to convey and communicate, he raised his hand and at first moved it in the air as if he were drawing, as indeed had been his habit when he was well; then, with the index finger of his right hand, he wrote a few lines in the air. As his strength ebbed and his arm sank lower, he went on writing lower down, and finally seemed to be writing the same thing over and over again on the featherbed which covered his knees. It was noticed that he inserted precise punctuation-marks, and the initial letter was clearly recognisable as a capital W; but the rest of the script could not be deciphered.

As his fingers were beginning to turn blue, they removed the green shade from his eyes and found that the light had already gone out of them. His breathing became increasingly impeded, though without actually turning into a death-rattle; without the least sign of pain the dying man leaned comfortably over into the left side of his chair, and his heart, that heart which had brought forth and carried and cherished a whole world within itself, had ceased to beat.

328. Pauline Hase   22.3.1832

He died in Ottilie's arms, and his breathing ceased so quietly and gently that she cannot say exactly when he died, and still believed him to be asleep when he was already dead.

He seems to have been in good spirits to the last; an hour before the end he said to her for instance: "Well, young lady, give me your dear little paw!" And indeed he went on clinging to her, until at last she had to let go of his lifeless hand.

329. F. von Müller   22.3.1832

He died the happiest of deaths, conscious and serene, with no pain at all, and no suspicion that he was dying until he had breathed his last. The vital flame in him sank lower and lower and went out without a struggle. His last request was for light—half an hour before the end he ordered: "Open the shutters, to let more light come in".

330. Eckermann   23.3.1832

On the morning after Goethe's death I was seized by a deep longing to see his earthly remains once more. His faithful servant Friedrich let me into the room where they had laid him. He was lying on his back like a man asleep; deep peace and strength reigned in the features of his sublime and noble face. Behind his powerful forehead he still seemed to be thinking. I wanted to have a lock of his hair, but reverence prevented me from cutting one off. The body lay naked, wrapped in a white sheet; large blocks of ice had been placed round it quite close by, to keep it fresh as long as possible. Friedrich drew the sheet back, and I wondered at the god-like magnificence of these limbs. The chest was very powerful, broad and vaulted; the muscles of the arms and thighs were full and soft; the feet small and faultlessly shaped; and nowhere on the whole body was there any trace of obesity or emaciation and collapse. A perfect man lay in great beauty before me, and the joy of this sight made me forget for some moments that the immortal spirit had left so splendid a tenement. I laid my hand on his heart—there was deep silence everywhere—and I turned away to let my pent-up tears flow freely.

Index

INDEX

(Reference to the translated texts is by *number*. The Introduction is not Indexed)

I. PERSONS

ABEKEN, B. R., 1780–1866 (philologist, tutor to Schiller's children from 1808 to 1810): *26, 86*

ADAMS, J. Q., 1767–1848 (sixth President of the United States of America, from 1825 to 1829): *180*

AESCHYLUS, 525–456 B.C.: *221*

ALEXANDER I, 1777–1825 (Tsar of Russia from 1801 to 1825): *75, 76, 103*

ALTHOF, L. C., 1758–1832 (physician): *30*

AMPÈRE, J. J. A., 1800–64 (French critic, professor of literature at Marseille, contributor to *Le Globe*): *211, 212, 213, 214*

ANDRÉ family (music publishers in Offenbach-am-Main): *19*

ARIOSTO, Ludovico, 1474–1533: *73*

ARISTOTLE, 384–322 B.C.: *233, 238*

ARNIM, Bettina von (née Brentano), 1788–1859 (wife of the poet Achim von Arnim, sister of the poet Clemens Brentano, author of a memoir on Goethe based on reminiscences by his mother): *1, 2, 3, 16, 97*

AUBER, D. F. E., 1782–1871 (French operatic composer): *288*

AUSTRIA: Emperor Francis I, 1768–1835, and Empress Maria Ludovica, 1787–1816: *197*

Austrian general (unidentified): *54*

BACH, J. S., 1685–1750: *141, 142, 285*

BALZAC, Honoré de, 1799–1850: *318*

BANCROFT, G., 1800–91 (American historian and statesman): *134*

BAVARIA: King Ludwig I, 1786–1868: *190*

BEETHOVEN, Ludwig van, 1770–1827: *98, 142, 286, 301*

BENTHAM, Jeremy, 1748–1832: *275*

BIEDENFELD, Baron F. von, 1788–1862 (writer and translator): *119*

BLUMENBACH, J. F., 1752–1840 (physician and scientist): *25*

BOISSÉREE, J. S., 1783–1854 (art historian): *115, 117, 118, 188, 189*

BOOTHBY, Sir Brooke, 1743–1824 (English writer): *136*

BÖTTIGER, K. A., 1760–1835 (classical archaeologist in Weimar): *37, 47*

II. Works by Goethe

III. List of Sources

(Except where otherwise stated, reference is to the Artemis edition by volume and page, using "I", "II", and "E" to represent vols. 22, 23 and 24 respectively.)

1 I 9. *2* I 9f. *3* I 11. *4* I 12–14. *5* I 14f. *6* I 16–19. *7* I 27f. *8* I 28. *9* I 29. *10* I 32. *11* I 34–6. *12* I 39f. *13* I 59f. *14* I 61f. *15* I 63–5. *16* I 70. *17* I 71f. *18* I 76f. *19* I 78. *20* I 87. *21* I 99f. *22* I 108. *23* I 108f. *24* I 110f. *25* I 140f. *26* I 156. *27* I 166. *28* I 172–4. *29* I 182. *30* I 183–5. *31* I 187f. *32* I 188. *33* I 189. *34* I 199–201. *35* I 211f. *36* I 221. *37* I 227. *38* I 246f. *39* I 248. *40* I 250f. *41* I 278. *42* I 284. *43* I 319. *44* I 321f. *45* I 323f. *46* I 327. *47* I 336. *48* I 330f. *49* I 331. *50* I 346f. *51* I 349f. *52* I 369f. *53* I 387. *54* I 397–9. *55* I 400. *56* I 417. *57* I 416. *58* I 417. *59* I 419. *60* I 423. *61* I 424f. *62* I 518f. *63* I 431. *64* I 435. *65* I 519f. *66* I 437. *67* I 440f. *68* I 444. *69* I 454. *70* I 457f. *71* I 462–4. *72* I 461. *73* I 500f. *74* I 504–6. *75* I 507–9. *76* I 514f. *77* I 516f. *78* I 526f. *79* I 530f. *80* I 537f. *81* I 538f. *82* I 546f. *83* I 554f. *84* I 560. *85* I 563. *86* I 567. *87* I 579. *88* I 580. *89* I 616f; note refers to I 876. *90* I 596. *91* I 598. *92* I 612. *93* Biedermann (2nd edn.) vol. 5, p. 92. *94* I 638. *95* I 640. *96* I 642. *97* I 646. *98* I 656. *99* I 664. *100* I 670f. *101* I 672–80. *102* I 681. *103* I 684–6. *104* I 691. *105* I 702. *106* I 713f. *107* I 719f. *108* I 722. *109* I 725. *110* I 733–40. *111* I 741f. *112* I 743. *113* I 741. *114* I 749. *115* I 812f. *116* I 822f. *117* I 830. *118* I 833. *119* I 847. *120* I 879. *121* II 14, 16. *122* II 876. *123* II 28–30. *124* II 33f. *125* II 35. *126* II 39f. *127* II 58f. *128* II 79–81. *129* II 87. *130* II 91. *131* II 102f. *132* II 114. *133* II 144f. *134* II 122f. *135* II 125. *136* II 129–33. *137* II 133–6. *138* II 137. *139* II 154–7. *140* II 160. *141* II 180. *142* II 181–6. *143* II 191f. *144* II 214. *145* II 215. *146* II 238. *147* II 245. *148* II 247–51. *149* E 37, 39. *150* E 45. *151* E 48f. *152* II 299. *153* II 301. *154* II 312. *155* E 66f. *156* II 314f. *157* E 74f. *158* II 876. *159* E 540f. *160* E 542f, 545.

ERRATUM: *No. 244*: This undated conversation with Falk must
have taken place not later than 1826.